ASSET-BASED WORKING CAPITAL FINANCE

Richard Hawkins,
Robin Peers and
Edward Wilde

institute of financial services

UMIST

Financial World Publishing
c/o The Chartered Institute of Bankers
Emmanuel House
4-9 Burgate Lane
Canterbury
Kent
CT1 2XJ
United Kingdom
Telephone: 01227 762600
e-mail: editorial@cib.org.uk

Financial World Publishing publications are published by The Chartered Institute of Bankers, a non-profit making registered educational charity.

The Chartered Institute of Bankers believes that the sources of information upon which the book is based are reliable and has made every effort to ensure the complete accuracy of the text. However, neither the authors nor any contributor can accept any legal responsibility whatsoever for consequences that may arise from errors or omissions or any opinion or advice given.

Typeset by Kevin O'Connor

Printed by CPD, Harmonsworth, Middlesex

ISBN 0-85297-516-3

FINANCIAL
WORLD
Publishing
THE CHARTERED INSTITUTE OF BANKERS

Disclaimer

These course notes so far as they deal with legal issues are designed to give a broad understanding of legal issues which might be encountered under English law. They do not cover any special provisions or changes needed under the laws of Scotland, Northern Ireland or any other jurisdiction in the British Isles. Nor do they cover every situation or all the law on a particular topic. If you come across legal problems, you should seek professional advice using your company's established procedures.

Asset-Based Working Capital Finance

This textbook has been written for both students and practitioners of the subject. It has been written to a syllabus drawn up by subject experts, including current senior practitioners, which forms part of the Diploma in Financial Services Management (DFSM). The DFSM qualification is administered by the Institute of Financial Services, a wholly-owned subsidiary of The Chartered Institute of Bankers (CIB) and is awarded jointly by The CIB and the University of Manchester Institute of Science and Technology (UMIST). The role of UMIST in this partnership is to benchmark all aspects of the delivery of the DFSM, including this text, to first year undergraduate standard.

Though written to a syllabus specific to the DFSM it is intended that this text will serve a useful purpose for anybody studying for a business or finance-related qualification. Furthermore, this book will serve as an excellent reference tool for practitioners already working in this or related fields. All books in the DFSM series reflect the very latest regulations, legislation and reporting requirements.

Students of the DFSM will also receive a separate Study Guide to be used in conjunction with this text. This Study Guide refers the reader to further reading on the topic and helps to enhance learning through exercises based upon the contents of this book.

The Factors & Discounters Association

Although our industry is only thirty years old, the foundations of the FDA were laid in 1976, when the Association of British Factors was formed. All major members of the industry joined this association, which was much strengthened in 1996 when they amalgamated with the Association of Invoice Factors and the European Chapter of the Commercial Finance Association.

For 25 years the FDA and its predecessors have been providing education and training to those working in the industry. Courses have evolved with the passage of time, ensuring that the subject matter remains relevant to today's employees.

Although much of the course content is generated and delivered from within the industry, we have also been ready to embrace external skills, particularly in specialized areas. The contribution of specialists from both this country and the USA continues to be immense.

The FDA Educational Foundation is just one activity for which the FDA is responsible. We also promote members' services to businesses, trade associations, professional bodies and the Government. We seek to influence legislation by providing industry input.

All FDA members agree to abide by the FDA Code of Conduct in order to maintain high standards in the industry.

The FDA has a number of chaired committees, which reflect and combine the interests of all members.

The Authors

Richard Hawkins

Richard has eighteen years experience working with and for the industry. He was at the forefront of developing asset-based finance techniques in the UK during the 1980s. Richard's career history spans many roles, including credit management, auditing, account management, underwriting and recoveries.

Richard launched Atlantic Asset Based Finance Consultancy in 1997, which provides specialist risk management services to the industry both in the UK and Europe, including loan reviews, portfolio management, crisis management, recoveries and training.

Robin Peers

Since starting in factoring in 1972 Robin Peers has worked in most industry roles. He spent his last four years with Alex Lawrie Factors as Training Manager. Then, in 1988, he formed FaCTS International. As Managing Partner, he delivers specialist training and consultancy to the asset-based working capital industry across the world with clients in some 27 countries – from Sydney to Istanbul and from Dublin to New York. FaCTS International also acts for almost all the factoring and discounting companies in the UK. Robin has also written the FDA Certificate Course and the Foundation Course for the International Factors Group.

Edward Wilde

Edward Wilde is a Solicitor of the Supreme Court and has a post-graduate degree in law from the University of Cambridge.

He has over 30 years of commercial law experience in advising UK and overseas asset-based financiers on all aspects of their businesses, including documentation, collections, contested litigation and mergers. For 22 years he was the senior partner of the specialist London law firm of attorneys specializing in the worldwide enforcement of creditors' rights. He continues as a full-time consultant at Wilde and Partners and is also the Secretary and Hon. Legal Adviser to the Factors and Discounters Association. He is governor of the FDA Educational Foundation and has taken a leading role in developing this diploma course. He also sits on the international legal committee of Europafactoring, the international grouping of National Factoring Associations.

CONTENTS

Contents

1

ASSET-BASED WORKING CAPITAL FINANCE

1.1   History

In order to consider better the present activities of the asset-based finance industry in the UK, the following section looks at how the industry was initially established in the USA and its subsequent development.

To find the origins of asset-based working capital finance, as we know it today, we have to look back to the USA in the early 1900s when the traditional lending criteria of the American commercial banks restricted the advancing of funds to growing businesses. This left businessmen with the choice of either:

● passing up sales growth until their own capital base had grown sufficiently; or

● finding alternative sources of working capital finance.

Arthur R Jones of Chicago, who provided finance to John L Little, who sold *Encyclopedia Americana* on an instalment basis, probably conceived the first alternative to a traditional bank loan. Jones agreed to provide finance to Little against the security of the debts due to Little from his sales. Little provided the outstanding sales invoices as evidence of such security.

This arrangement worked well. In 1904 Jones and Little formed the Mercantile Credit Company to provide similar funding arrangements to other businesses. Their initial arrangement was that when funds were advanced to a client, the debtor was notified of Mercantile's interest in the debt. However, Mercantile Credit soon found that some of their clients disliked the fact that their customers were aware of their borrowings against the debts. Clients were concerned their customers might consider them as financially unsound.

To overcome this, Jones and Little started making advances against the debts without any notification to the debtor. This confidential facility was done on a 'with recourse' basis. This meant that if, at the end of the agreed period, the debtor did not pay the debt then Mercantile Credit could recover, from its client, the funds previously advanced. However, Jones and Little then became concerned at the risk of not being paid by either their debtor or the client.

Accordingly, they consulted Alexander E Duncan, an insurer. He saw the opportunity of providing financing against debts not only without giving notice to the customers but also 'without recourse' to the clients. In 1912 the Manufacturers Finance Company was formed.

Debt financing continued to grow and develop over several decades. There are now many companies worldwide that solely provide financing against specific assets to meet the same business needs that were identified in Chicago in 1904.

Since 1904 financiers have developed products that also enable stock to be financed either as a stand-alone facility or in conjunction with debt financing. In this way, companies have been assisted that cannot meet their working capital needs through their own resources, from commercial banks or purely from financing of debtors.

Entrepreneurial financiers who, in the main, were independent of the commercial banks pioneered the development of debt financing and stock financing.

As competition grew between the independent financiers, other assets were looked at to provide security for funding. These included plant, machinery and buildings. Many US finance houses were able to provide a whole range of financial products based upon a client's assets. The term 'asset-based finance' evolved to define this activity, where the funding is primarily related to the value of the assets providing 'security' in its widest sense, e.g. by way of purchase, subject to a formal charge or merely forming part of the client's general assets, generating profits from which to repay the financier. As the value of the assets increase or decrease the funding correspondingly changes.

Typical examples of such asset-based financing include:

- disclosed factoring of debts
- confidential invoice discounting of debts
- plant and machinery finance
- stock finance
- import and export finance
- leasing and the hire purchase of assets

In the 1970s the commercial banks, in the USA, entered into asset-based finance. Many banks saw asset-based finance as a way of offering creative financial solutions to their customers. Its profitability and the relatively low level of losses, even while funding businesses with low credit ratings, impressed them. Some banks entered the market as a defensive measure in order to avoid losing their existing banking customers, to maintain their income streams and to protect existing loans following the 1974/75 economic downturns. In due course asset-based working capital finance became a mainstream commercial bank product.

Modern style factoring started in the UK in the early 1960s. The service offered has changed little since then. It is based upon the assignment of a business's debts to its factor in exchange for a prepayment of typically up to 80% of its value. The factor takes over responsibility for the sales ledger management, credit control and collections. Notice of assignment is detailed on the invoices and statements of account. Collections are made by and in the name of the factor. Some of the larger factors developed non-recourse services. We shall look at the difference between the two products later.

While most factors were interested only in financing a client's entire turnover, some were prepared to offer a facility so that the client could choose which debts to sell to the factor. This selected debtor facility remains available today on both a recourse and non-recourse basis.

Currently the most common form of factoring is on a 'whole turnover basis'. Under the master factoring agreement all debts generated by the client automatically belong to the factor upon their creation. The factor makes a prepayment against all debts generated by the client subject to the debts being approved by the factor.

During the late 1960s and early 1970s some factoring companies started to provide invoice-discounting facilities. This enabled the client to continue to administer its sales ledger and credit control functions while still having the ability to take prepayments. This service is now provided both with and without a notice of assignment being given to the debtor. During the late 1970s and the 1980s, as computer systems became accessible to small and medium-sized companies, the burden on them of credit control and ledger management was reduced. Accordingly, the demand for invoice discounting increased as the original benefits from factoring, of transferring the sales ledger management and credit control functions to the financier, reduced in significance.

The widespread use of invoice discounting and its obvious benefits meant that debt financing has lost much of the stigma associated with factoring in the 1960s and 1970s, when a factor was considered as a lender of last resort. Since then debt financing has made great strides. It has become recognized as an important method of providing working capital to small and medium-sized businesses in the UK and beyond.

Most major UK factors and invoice discounters are members of the Factors and Discounters Association (FDA). At 31 December 1999 the Association had 35 member companies. Membership continues to grow as new financiers come into the market. A list of members as at January 2000 and their services appears in Appendix 9.

The FDA was launched in September 1996 as a result of the merger of the following associations:

- Association of British Factors and Discounters
- Association of Invoice Factors
- European Chapter of the Commercial Finance Association

As at 30 September 1999 member companies of the FDA had total funds in use of £4.7 billion with 25,178 clients. This represented a 14% increase in funds in use and a 6% increase in client numbers compared with the same date in 1998. The vast majority of the funds provided by FDA members to their clients are by way of factoring and invoice discounting.

The value of debts dealt with under these facilities for the 1999 calendar year are:

	£million
● Domestic factoring	14,766
● Invoice discounting	46,133
● International debts	3,226
	64,125

The Commercial Finance Association (CFA), which is the US association for the providers of asset-based finance, was founded in 1944. During 1998 the total level of advances made by CFA members grew to $254 billion in respect of their clients' turnover of $2.3 trillion.

In respect of the previous year (1997) the CFA calculated that its members were responsible for funding 27% of US GDP

We shall now consider the reasons why a client uses the services of an asset-based financier.

1.2 Reasons for Using Asset-Based Working Capital

In this section we shall consider the traditional use of the bank overdraft for a business start-up in order to understand the concept of gearing. We shall then look at the three main reasons that cause a company to utilize an asset-based working capital facility. These are:

1. Business expansion
2. Transactional finance
3. Seasonal sales patterns

Business Start-ups

Historically new business start-ups in the UK have turned to the High Street banks to provide working capital finance by means of a commercial overdraft. Banks are happy to provide initial overdraft facilities to new companies provided that the bank is given sufficient security for the loan and that the company has a good chance of success. Such security usually comprises a charge, which gives the financier security over all the assets of an incorporated business. This is often called an 'all assets debenture'. In addition, personal security is usually required from the principals. This personal security may include the guarantees of the principals and sometimes charges over their personal assets, including their family homes.

Although overdraft levels are usually set for a period of 12 months, the loan remains instantly repayable on demand, at the absolute discretion of the bank. If the overdraft is unlikely to be recovered from the business the bank will exercise its rights over any guarantees or security over the principals' personal assets.

The overdraft level is usually limited to the recoverable value of the secured assets. Banks may often limit the funding available to the net worth of the business. In effect this is the capital invested and the earnings retained by the business.

For example, a business starts up with £10,000 invested by its shareholders or proprietors. After one year's trading it makes a profit net of all costs and taxes of £10,000. Its net worth is then £20,000.

Based upon the above example, a bank providing funds may then determine its lending criteria by reference to its net worth of £20,000. This is the basis for stating the gearing. If the bank lends £40,000 to the business, this is in the ratio of 2 to 1 or a 200% gearing.

Business Expansion

Commercial bank overdrafts have, for many years, been provided at gearings of 100% to 200%. Although there are many exceptions to this, including the exercise of discretion by a local manager, it is important to understand the concept of gearing when comparing an asset-based financier's attitude to providing funding with that of a bank.

Should a company's working capital requirements increase beyond the usual bank limit on gearing of 200%, there may be an opportunity for an asset-based financier, such as a factor, discounter or specialized lender, to provide greater working capital finance.

Subject to the quality of the assets of the business, a financier may be able to provide a higher level of funding to a business with a net worth of only £20,000.

This is demonstrated in the following example:

Company A

Assets	£000s	£000s
Debtors	140	
Stock	50	
Plant and machinery	10	
Total		200

Liabilities	£000s	£000s
Creditors	(110)	
Bank	(40)	
Other liabilities	(30)	
Total liabilities		(180)
Net worth		20

A factor or invoice discounter can potentially make a prepayment of 80% against the £140,000 value of the debtors. The resulting £112,000 can be used both to repay the bank's overdraft of £40,000 and provide the company with an additional £72,000 of extra working capital.

This simple example shows the key benefit of debtor-based finance. However it is based on the debts being entirely 'clean'. In practice, the proposed prepayment level of 80% would not be fully achieved. Disputed debts, debts disapproved for ageing etc. would restrict the availability of funding. However extra working capital far in excess of a bank overdraft would still be available. Factoring, invoice discounting and other forms of debt financing can provide a business that has a low capital base with the necessary working capital to finance its growth.

Having seen how Company A can obtain a higher level of funding against its debtors than from a traditional bank overdraft, we need to appreciate how such funding increases as the volume of sales grows.

This is illustrated below:

Company A	Month	Month	Month	Month
	1	2	3	4
	£000s	£000s	£000s	£000s
Opening outstanding debts	140	160	190	220
Sales	100	120	130	140
(Less debts paid)	(80)	(90)	(100)	(120)
Closing outstanding debts	160	190	220	240
Funds available at 80% of outstanding debts	128	152	176	192

The funding available to Company A will grow from £128,000 to £192,000 in line with the increased sales levels. As a business grows so does its need for working capital to purchase finished goods and raw materials, to pay wages and to meet its operating costs, while at the same time continuing to offer credit to its debtors.

Transactional Finance

Asset-based finance is increasingly used to facilitate transactions such as mergers, acquisitions, management buy-outs and management buy-ins.

Those involved in or advising on such transactions appreciate the advantages of using an asset-based financier both to facilitate the transactions and to finance the future capital requirements of the business.

There are four principal ways for a company to raise additional finance for such purposes:

1. Issue of shares (sometimes called an 'equity investment')

2. Profit generation

3. Borrowings

4. Disposal of assets

The attraction of using debt financing, such as an invoice discounting or factoring facility, to facilitate such transactions is the substantial reduction in external equity investment or borrowings that can be achieved. This can be very attractive to the shareholders or principals. The proportion of money that is raised through their own resources usually determines the level of control that they will retain over the equity of the business and their personal returns. The relationship between borrowing and equity investment fundamentally affects their position, as the following examples show.

First Approach

A purchaser is looking to raise £10m to acquire a target company and to finance the target's needs for ongoing working capital. The proposed financial structure is:

● £2m from the purchaser's own resources (as an equity investment)

● £4m from external borrowings

● £4m from external investors. (e.g. venture capitalists taking shares)

In these circumstances the external investors will require a substantial level of control over the company and seek returns based upon £4m of their funds invested.

Second Approach

If, as an alternative, the existing assets of the business can be used to raise £6m, by financing the debtors and stock, the financial structure for raising the necessary £10m will change to:

● £2m from the purchaser's own resources (as an equity investment)

● £6m from asset-based finance

● Only £2m from external investors (venture capitalists taking shares)

The degree of risk for the external investors should be less. Accordingly, their requirements for control and earnings will be correspondingly reduced. In turn, the purchaser can then retain higher levels of ownership, control and remuneration.

Season Sales Patterns

Traditional providers of working capital such as High Street banks are often unhappy with wide fluctuations in the demand for funding. An asset-based financier will feel more secure with the fluctuations because the value of the funding provided will relate to actual debts assigned and can be adjusted through changes to the prepayment percentage.

An asset-based financier is often asked to fund a business whose sales and consequent working capital needs have a pattern of fluctuation, over a twelve-month period. An example of this is given below. You will note the seasonal sales peak in September.

Figure 1.1: Sales Graph

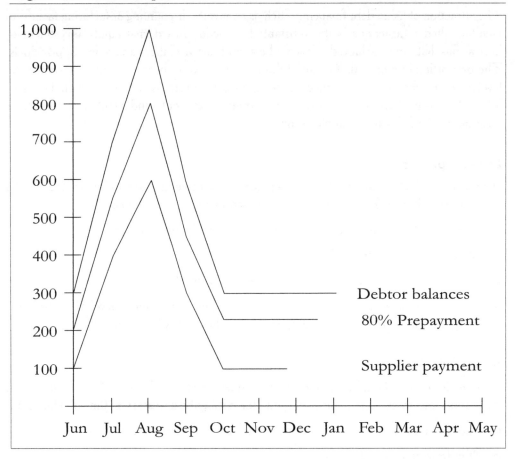

The graph shows a peak requirement of £600,000 in August which is easily met by a debtor-funding facility, whereas if ABC Ltd sourced working capital from a bank providing a static £300,000 overdraft there would be insufficient funding to meet the seasonal flow peak.

	June	July	Aug	Sep	Oct	Nov
Opening debtors	300	300	700	1,000	600	300
Sales	200	600	900	500	200	200
	500	900	1,600	1,500	800	500
Cash receipts	(200)	(200)	(600)	(900)	(500)	(200)
Closing debtors	300	700	1,000	600	300	300
80% Pre-payment	240	560	800	480	240	240
Payments to Creditors	100	400	600	300	100	100

A debt-financing facility can provide sufficient working capital for the needs of a highly seasonal business. However, the financier needs to actively monitor the debts and manage the funding.

Let us now consider the various types of asset-based finance products that are available.

1.3   Asset-Based Finance Products

The principal products are:

● Factoring – recourse and non-recourse

● Invoice discounting – confidential and disclosed

● Stock finance and floor planning

● Plant and machinery finance

Insurance, while strictly not an asset-based product, is often used as security to support other products. Hire purchase, leasing and conditional sales are means of financing specific business assets. Although these are recognized products they are not covered in this course.

We shall now consider further the four main product types listed above.

Factoring

Factoring was the first and, for many years, the foremost method of asset-based finance.

There are a number of descriptions of the product. Some people still use factoring as the generic term to describe all types of debt financing. The following definition has been taken from *Factoring in the UK*:

> *A continuous arrangement between a factoring concern and the seller of business goods or services on credit, whereby the factor purchases accounts receivables for immediate cash, and may, depending upon the exact nature of the arrangement*

- *Maintain the sales ledger and perform other administrative tasks relating to accounts receivables*
- *Collect the accounts receivables*
- *Provide bad debt protection by absorbing losses that may arise as a result of the debtors' insolvency*
- *Disclose this arrangement to the debtors*

Figures 1.2, 1.3 and 1.4 explain the factoring process and the relationships between the client, the factor and the debtor.

Figure 1.2

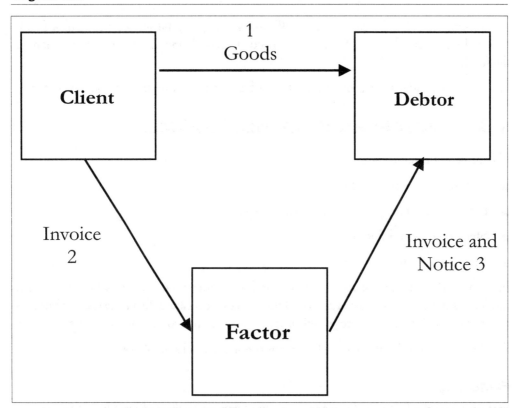

1. Client sells goods to debtor. A debt arises.
2. Client sends invoice to factor.
3. Factor sends invoice to debtor - giving notice of assignment.

Figure 1.3

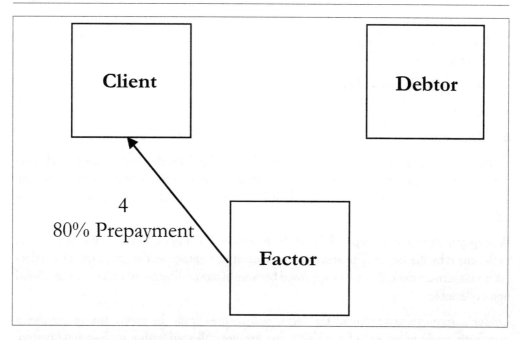

4. Factor makes 80% prepayment to the client against the value of the invoice, less any service charges.

Figure 1.4

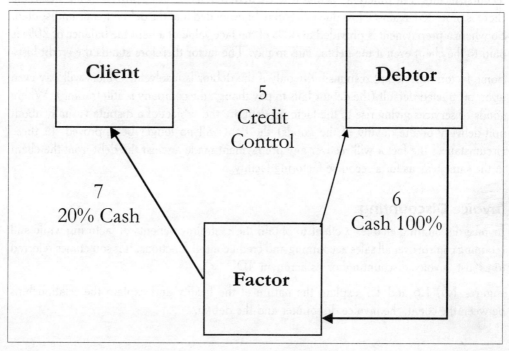

5. Factor provides sales ledger management and credit control.

6. Factor collects payment from the debtor (100%).

7. Factor remits the balance of the purchase price (20% of the debt) to the client less any charges.

There are two main types of factoring:

- Recourse

- Non-recourse

Recourse factoring – This involves the purchase of the debts due to a business, including their assignment to the factor. Notice of assignment is given to the debtors. The factor then takes responsibility for the sales ledger administration, credit control and management of the debts.

A prepayment of typically up to 80% of the total value (including VAT) of the debt is paid to the client by the factor. The average prepayment percentage across an entire sales ledger takes into account debts that are unapproved because of age or disputes or which are considered non-collectable.

Under a recourse arrangement the factor will recover from the client any prepayments previously made in respect of any debts that are not collected within a given time period. This is usually between 90 and 120 days following the month of invoice, and is often referred to as the 'recourse period'.

Non-recourse factoring – The purchase of the debts operates in the same way as the recourse facility. The difference is that where a debt that has been approved by the factor, the client is protected against a loss due to a bad debt, provided that the debt remains undisputed. So where a prepayment is provided at 80% of the face value of a debt the balance of 20% is paid to the client even if the debtor fails to pay. The factor therefore stands the credit loss.

Some factors will accept responsibility only if the debtor is insolvent. Others will pay even upon protracted default (the debtor fails to pay though the company is still trading). Where goods or services giving rise to the factored debt are the subject of a dispute (usually about non-delivery or the quality of the goods) the debt will no longer be approved. In these circumstances the factor will recover any prepayment made against the debt from the client in the same way as for a recourse factoring facility.

Invoice Discounting

Invoice discounting enables a client to obtain the cash flow benefits of factoring while still retaining control over all sales accounting and credit control functions. It is sometimes referred to as just 'invoice discounting' or its acronym 'ID'.

Figures 1.5, 1.6 and 1.7 explain the nature of the facility and explain the relationships between the client, the invoice discounter and the debtor.

Most invoice discounting is undertaken on a confidential basis. This means that no notice of the discounter's interest in the debts is given to the debtor. However, it is possible to provide this product on a disclosed basis. With a disclosed facility notification is given to the debtor of the assignment of debts to the invoice discounter by the client and/or the discounter. However the client still undertakes the accounting and collection procedures. This is usually called a 'disclosed invoice discounting' facility.

The following diagrams show the process and relationships in a confidential facility.

Figure 1.5

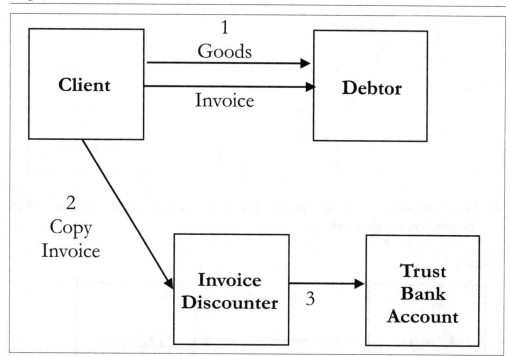

1. Client sells goods and invoices debtor in the normal way
2. Copy invoices sent to invoice discounter
3. Invoice discounter opens trust bank account

Figure 1.6

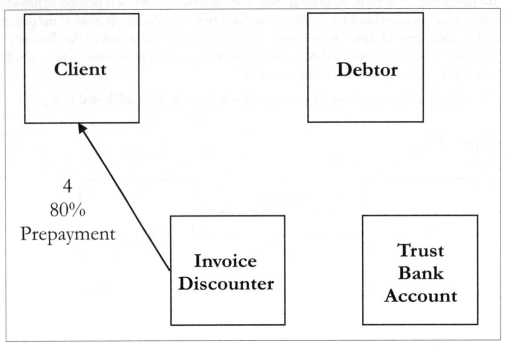

4. Invoice discounter makes 80% pre-payment to the client against the total value of the invoices, less any service charges.

Figure 1.7

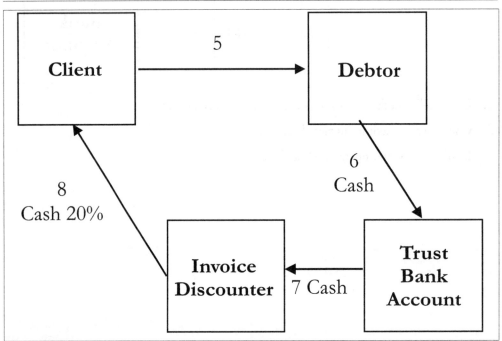

5. Client maintains sales ledger and chases debtor for payment.

6. Debtor instructed to remit payment to trust account. If debtor pays the client direct then client will deposit payment into trust account each day.

7. Trust account receipts automatically transferred to invoice discounter daily.

8. Invoice discounter pays the balance of the purchase price (20% of the debt) to the client less any discounting charges.

Stock Finance

Stock finance is provided to meet two specific working capital needs:

● Those of a seasonal business

● To exploit a hard core collateral base.

Before finance can be provided against stock its nature as security and its method of valuation needs to be understood. A financier will categorize stock into one of three main categories:

● Finished goods

● Raw materials

● Work in progress (i.e. unfinished goods)

Appropriate advance rates are then calculated against the expected forced sale value of the raw material and finished goods. Work in progress is normally not suitable for financing.

Stock finance can be provided as a stand-alone facility or can be provided as part of a package including the financing of debts or other assets. In the UK there are two major problems with providing finance against the security of stock.

Firstly, the financier's security is usually by way of a floating charge over the stock. Upon the client's insolvency, the government's claims as a preferential creditor for unpaid tax including PAYE, National Insurance and VAT will be paid from the recovered value of stock in priority to the financier's claim.

Secondly, a creditor of the client who has delivered goods, under a contract containing a retention of title clause (whereby such goods become the property of the client only once they are paid for) can demand their return in priority to the financier's claim on them. However, the original supplier must be able to identify the goods, which is usually done through the same serial numbers appearing on both the unpaid invoices and the goods.

These two problems have a major effect on the level of finance that can be provided against stock.

To avoid these problems some financiers prefer to become the owner of the stock. If the borrower becomes insolvent it is then a relatively straightforward process to sell the stock in order to recoup the client's indebtedness. There are a small number of finance houses that specialize in this service. They are sometimes described as providers of 'merchant finance' or 'trade finance'.

However, direct stock purchase is usually possible only if:

- There are a limited number of suppliers of the stock

- The stock requires no modification by the client before its onward sale

- The client has obtained the goods in order to satisfy specific orders, which can be confirmed by the financier.

Floor-Plan Financing

Floor-plan financing is a specialized form of stock financing designed to meet the needs of businesses selling high-value products such as cars, motorcycles, computers and boats, who need substantial stock for display purposes. Variations of this process are now developing into many other sectors.

This situation is best illustrated by considering a private car dealership selling to the general public. The dealer needs to have on display a full range of cars to fill the showroom. However, the cash flow demands on the dealer of directly purchasing stock from the manufacturer would be prohibitive.

By entering into a floor-plan facility the financier purchases the cars in its own name from the manufacturer and sells them on to the dealer on credit terms maturing in say, 60 days from delivery. The financier protects its position by selling with 'reservation of title'. This means that should the dealer become insolvent before paying the financier, the financier can repossess the vehicles as the unpaid owner. The dealer is often appointed as the financier's disclosed agent to arrange purchases from the manufacturer. He is also the undisclosed agent of the financier to sell cars to the public.

On the maturity date the financier can either:

- Receive the sale price from the dealer

- Give the dealer more time to sell the car

- Sell the car back to the manufacturer

It is very common for floor-plan deals to be instigated by the manufacturer, in order to get its products into dealers' showrooms without any credit risk. To encourage a financier to become involved the manufacturer enters into guaranteed buy-back arrangements with the financier to cover the possibility that the financier has to repossess the stock upon the client becoming insolvent or committing a breach of the facility.

This arrangement can be shown diagrammatically:

Figure 1.8: Stage 1

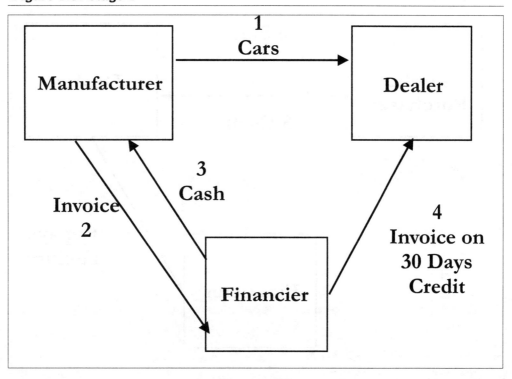

1. Manufacturer delivers cars to dealer.
2. Manufacturer invoices financier.
3. Financier pays on delivery or pre-delivery.
4. Financier invoices dealer on 30-day credit terms plus interest and service fees, and reserves title to the cars.

Figure 1.9: Stage 2

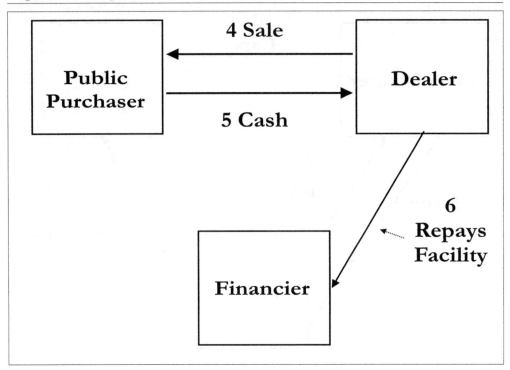

4. Dealer sells car 14 days later to public purchaser.

5. Purchaser pays cash to dealer.

6. Dealer pays financier invoiced price of the car, plus interest and fees.

Floor-plan facilities are normally provided on a revolving basis against an agreed credit line so that the dealer (as agent of the financier) can keep ordering new cars from the manufacturer within the value of the facility. Its continued right to do so is conditional upon the dealer complying with the terms of the facility, the most important of which is to repay the financier promptly upon a sale.

The financier normally monitors the dealer's compliance with such terms by way of regular audits. These involve visiting the dealership and checking that each unit purchased and outstanding on the financier's ledger physically exists and is in good order.

Floor-plan finance, although very common in the USA, is relatively new in the UK. Recent developments include major manufacturers setting up captive finance companies to facilitate dealers' floor planning plus consumer finance for the purchaser of the car. Under these arrangements the manufacturer derives profits both from financing the initial sale to the dealership and the retail credit sale by the dealer to its debtors.

Plant and Machinery Finance

Plant and machinery finance can be made available either:

- As part of a larger working capital finance facility; or

- To finance the purchase of new plant and machinery.

Under both arrangements the financier is concerned with both the initial value of the assets and their ongoing depreciation.

For example:

- Company A is looking to purchase a printing machine for £1m.

- A financier will lend 80% of its purchase price on the basis that the machine will depreciate immediately by 20% upon delivery.

- The expected life of the machine before becoming exhausted or obsolete is 3 years.

- Therefore in this case the loan must not exceed 3 years (the expected useful life of the asset).

- Repayments of the advance and interest will normally be taken at monthly or quarterly intervals.

Insurance as a Source of Collateral

Credit insurance is widely used where debts are financed to protect both the client and financier against credit losses.

Insurance can also be used as collateral to support financing made available to a client against assets, which are or may be insufficient to repay the funds in use. Under these circumstances a financier is effectively taking out insurance against the failure of the client to repay the advance. Such circumstances are likely where a static financing line is being provided for a fixed period but where the underlying assets acting as security fluctuate in value during that same period.

For example:

- A £10million credit line is provided for three months against specific collateral.

- Analysis of the collateral movements shows that the predicted realizable value will fluctuate between £6 and £12million over this period.

A financier may take credit insurance against the transaction to secure the potential exposure. In practice cover would be taken for 110% to 120% of the exposure to allow for any slippage.

'Key-man' insurance is taken as security when the future viability of the client is dependent on one person or a small number of key personnel. This protects both the client and the financier from losses caused by the death or incapacity of such people.

Checking that there is sufficient insurance cover is an important part of both the survey of prospective new clients and the routine audit process of established clients.

In the next section we shall look more specifically at how the UK has developed the asset-based working capital finance.

1.4 Asset-Based Financiers in the UK

The UK has been perceived by a number of US banks as lacking the sophistication and diversity of asset-based financing facilities being offered in North America, particularly in relation to assets other than debts. Accordingly, over the last few years a number of US banks have entered the UK asset-based financing market. Their reasons for doing so include:

- The maturing of the asset-based finance market in the USA forcing a search for new markets;
- Their perception that UK lenders have been slow to embrace the techniques of asset-based finance.
- The UK being seen as an entrance to the EU.
- The globalization of national economies, business and finance.

The development in the UK of financing techniques in relation to assets other than debts began in the early 1990s. Based upon the US experience it is widely believed that the provision of asset-based finance will grow significantly in the UK over the next few years. This may be particularly so in relation to assets other than debts.

Although the majority of factors and discounters, most of whom are FDA members, offer only debt-financing facilities, there are several companies offering other facilities such as stock finance in conjunction with debt finance. A few members now offer full asset-based facilities, which may not necessarily involve the financing of debts. A full list of FDA members and their products appears in Appendix 9.

The UK's commercial banking scene has changed dramatically over the last 10 years. Many more institutions now promote the full banking services that were traditionally the domain of 'The Big Four Banks'. Scottish, Irish, European and American banking groups have now become more active in the commercial and corporate finance market. Asset-based financing services are now provided by a wide range of non-UK banks either directly or through specialist subsidiaries.

Historically the most common providers of working capital and financial services in the UK have been the clearing banks, dominated by:

- Lloyds TSB
- HSBC (formerly Midland Bank)
- National Westminster Bank
- Barclays Bank

All of these banks have subsidiaries, which provide asset-based finance. Some of these subsidiaries are primarily concerned with providing debtor finance through factoring and invoice discounting. Others are recognized as able to provide working capital solutions through the financing of other assets.

Those bank subsidiaries that concentrate only on debtor finance often do so in order not to offer services that would compete directly with their parent company's products. While such parents realize the benefits and opportunities from providing debtor finance, they see factoring and invoice discounting either as stand-alone products or subsidiaries to the bank's traditional methods of commercial lending, by means of a bank overdraft secured by an all-assets debenture. This still remains at the forefront of many bank's product offerings to small and medium-sized growing businesses.

In the past UK banks were enthusiastic in their provision of finance against the security of properties. However the recession of the late 1980s/early 1990s followed by the collapse in commercial property and values has somewhat curbed their enthusiasm for property-based lending.

1.5   Other Types of Funding

In this section we shall look at the ways in which factors and invoice discounters can co-operate with:

● Banks
● Venture capitalists

Banks

Much of the growth of factoring and invoice discounting has been due to the unwillingness and/or inability of many banks directly to meet the increased working capital needs of their existing customers. Under these circumstances banks introduce their customers to their own factoring subsidiary with a view to converting all or part of the bank's loan to a debtor-based financing facility.

The following case study involves a bank wanting to reduce its exposure at the same time as the client is demanding greater facilities.

ABC Ltd is looking to raise additional working capital. Its bank is uncomfortable with its exposure and is unwilling to continue its support. The bank prefers its factoring subsidiary to become involved.

Current Position	Assets £ 000s	Bank Loan £ 000s
Building	600	
Debtors	1,000	
Plant and machinery	400	
Stock	400	
Total	2,400	800

This client is currently borrowing £800,000 from the bank. The bank's exposure is covered 3 to 1.

If the bank introduces its factoring subsidiary it should be able to provide a prepayment facility of 75% against the debtors. After taking account of debts that are unapproved due to age or disputes etc. and making reserves for costs, the actual prepayment calculation is:

	£000s
Total debtors	1,000
Less aged and disputed debts	(100)
Less disputed debts	(75)
Less costs reserve	(25)
Approved debts	800

At a prepayment rate of 75% the funding available will be £600,000. If the bank commits to a reduced loan of £600,000 the future will look like this:

Future Position of ABC Ltd

	Assets	Bank loan	Factoring prepayments
	£000s	£ 000s	£ 000s
Building	600		
Debtors	400		
Plant and machinery	400		
Stock	400		
Total	1800	600	600

This shows that the bank can reduce its exposure to £600,000 while retaining the cover of £1.8m of assets. The bank's exposure remains covered at the same ratio of 3 to 1. ABC Ltd has increased its working capital facilities by 50% from £800,000 to £1.2m.

This solution enables the bank to retain its client and its income stream without significantly increasing its risk. If the factor had not been introduced and the bank had increased its facilities to £1.2m against assets of £2.4m, the bank's cover would have reduced from 3:1 to 2:1.

In the restructuring scenario shown above the financier will purchase all the debts. The bank will need to give a waiver to the financier of its interest in the debts under any charge created by the bank's debenture. These arrangements will give the financier clean title to the debts.

However the bank's charge remains effective upon any monies due from the financier to the client and upon any unpaid debts transferred back (re-assigned) to the client.

Venture Capitalists

Although venture capital is not a primary source of working capital finance, asset-based financiers find themselves increasingly involved with businesses that have some form of venture capital. It is not our intention to explore in detail the many facets and types of venture capital. However you should appreciate the nature and relationship of venture capital to asset-based finance.

We have already considered the advantages of using an asset-based financier in connection with transaction finance such as management buy-outs, buy-ins, mergers and acquisitions. These transactions are usually supervised by the corporate finance departments of merchant banks and major firms of accountants.

It is the prime responsibility of the corporate finance team to enable the transaction to be completed successfully. In doing so they will be involved with:

- Equity providers – principals and venture capitalists
- Loan providers – banks
- Asset-based financiers
- Solicitors
- Tax advisers
- Pension advisers

An asset-based financier will typically become involved if:

- The banks and venture capitalists cannot provide sufficient equity or loans on acceptable terms: and /or
- A higher level of financing is required against the debtors than the banks are prepared to provide.

The ability to provide finance against assets such as stock, plant and machinery as well as the debtors may give an asset-based financier a competitive advantage even if only asked to provide finance against debtors.

If the final package involves funding from an asset-based financier and loans being provided by either a venture capitalist or a bank (or a combination of such providers), this will involve complex priority arrangements regarding the rights of competing charges taken by way of security. A factor or invoice discounter must always ensure that it obtains unencumbered priority over the debts that it is asked to finance.

Hire Purchase and Leasing

Apart from the methods of finance we have already mentioned, businesses can use hire purchase and/or leasing to finance their assets. This type of finance is normally provided to enable a business to obtain specific types of assets such as plant and machinery, vehicles and computers. Businesses in the UK looking to invest heavily in such assets often seek a specialist hire purchase or leasing company to meet their needs. Because of the specific and specialist financing nature of this type of activity it is generally seen as complementary, rather than in direct competition, to stock and debtor-based finance. The need for this type of funding rarely coincides with a prospective client's decision to seek asset-based financing through factoring or stock finance.

1.6   Factoring in an International Context

Having considered the types of products available and their applications for businesses, it is important that we consider the ways in which the factoring and discounting industries have looked to develop their markets through the inclusion of international trade. The following section looks at the problems involved in financing international debts and the ways in which this aspect of the market has grown.

Factoring is a very rapidly developing product internationally, with overall volumes growing at around 15% pa and over 125,000 businesses using factoring worldwide. The latest figures (end 1997) show a worldwide factoring volume of around £280 billion. The UK's volume of £50 billion turnover makes it the largest market, closely followed by Italy (£46 billion) and the USA (£ 44 billion).

Within this overall factoring figure is a rapidly growing market for international factoring transactions (export and import sales), with this international trade accounting for around £8 billion (6%) of the total market. In the UK our international trade is 5% of our overall volume: some £3billion.

International factoring is seen as a very effective and efficient method of assisting an exporter in protecting against the difficulties of dealing outside its own domestic marketplace.

Before looking at the structure of international factoring we shall look at some of the problems that the exporter faces and then the solution provided by the international factoring services.

Distance   It is not so easy to visit a client/debtor; telephone calls need proper planning because of time difference and possible call delays to the more remote areas. Correspondence takes longer. Disputes are so much more difficult to resolve over long distances. Long delivery times can add to the risk of damaged or lost goods and the subsequent dispute over payments.

Language   Obviously it is a great advantage if we speak at least one other language, preferably that of the customer to whom we sell our product/service. It could be accepted that English is the commercial language of the world, but this is of little use when a problem crops up and the debtor, a previous fluent speaker of your language and/or of English, 'suddenly(!)' can only speak a remote dialect of his/her own language. Collections are difficult enough without a basic ability to communicate.

National Customs/ Culture

These will certainly differ from those of your own country. Accounts must therefore be judged against the character of the account by local standards and not entirely by your own national cultural and behaviour standards.

Trying to understand the courtesies needed when dealing in different markets is also extremely difficult. For example correspondence tends to err on the over-polite, rather than the blunt. And be aware of the 'mañana' complex (tomorrow will do) in parts of the world. It is important to understand the effect of the local culture – for example in parts of the world the British way of proceeding may be considered slow.

The exporter must also be aware of social and religious attitudes and trading customs. For instance, the refusal of certain Arab countries to deal with any goods that originate from or have even passed through Israel, and the observance of religious festivals in some countries, can delay any attempt to communicate.

Local Legislation

The Law will be different in many ways from your own law and in most cases – certainly in the less developed countries – it can be very protracted and costly. The message is: always avoid going to law if at all possible, but how can the exporter avoid it when your overseas debtor is refusing to pay the debt or even discuss it with you? Local customs controls may insist on special documentation such as Certificates of Origin, Insurance Certificates and Inspection Certificates. Although there are reference books, which provide much valuable information covering this area, they may not be up to date with the latest rules.

Foreign Currency

Debtors normally prefer invoices to be raised in their currency. This builds in a further problem, with its attendant risk of exchange loss. From the financier's viewpoint, it may be preferable to encourage the clients to invoice in their own currency, but the response is often that this would lose the sale. The main risk is one of currency fluctuation during the period between order and payment. If invoicing in a foreign currency, then the forward market can be used to protect the financier and client against exchange rate loss. The financier will also need to arrange special statements to cope with the different currencies.

Local Economic and Political Conditions

All countries largely pay for their imports from the proceeds of their exports and invisible earnings. Thus the payment risk for exports is always tied in some way to the local economic/balance of payments position. Political ideology may make a government deliberately delay settlement or refuse to trade with a country with which it is not in political sympathy. A coup d'état can change market/credit conditions overnight.

It is therefore vital to look at the risk to payment prospects on a 'country' basis before assessing them on a debtor basis. It is not uncommon to find a very sound debtor risk in a thoroughly unsound overseas market. This places extra responsibility on the credit and collections departments because all these factors have a direct bearing on the ultimate success of the collection performance in each market.

Overview of International Factoring Operations

Against the background of all these difficulties have grown the factoring 'chains'. International factoring can be seen as two main activities, which form the basic structure of all international factoring operations:

Export Factoring   the factor provides a factoring service to a client company in its own country to assist with the client's export business, e.g. factor and client are both UK-based with client selling to other countries worldwide.

Import Factoring   the factor provides directly or indirectly a factoring service to a client company in a foreign country in respect of the client's exports to the factor's own country. E.g. factor based in the UK has a client in Italy and arranges factoring services for the client's exports to the UK.

There are two major factoring chains:

> International Factors Group SC

> Factors Chain International

Both have members based around the world and use sophisticated computer communication networks to pass and track transactions between member companies on behalf of their clients.

The chain can best be seen as a correspondent system of sub-contracted services. The aim of this sub-contracting is to make arrangements for foreign debts to be handled by a factor based in the debtor's own country. This assists in overcoming many of the problems of the export markets that we have already seen, because the factor understands the market and all the economic complications of that market. The 'chain' effectively turns an export debt into a domestic debt, and the relationship between client and debtor is also altered.

Figure 1.10: Normal Domestic Factoring Cycle

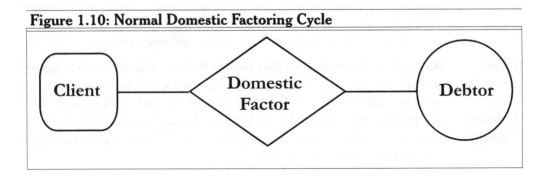

Figure 1.11: International Factoring Cycle

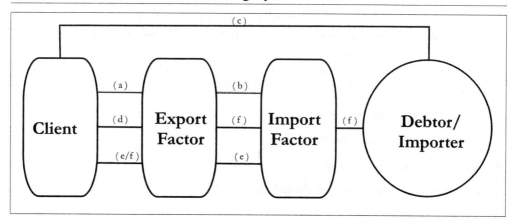

Export Factor

There is a factoring agreement between factor and client, in this case covering the assignment of export debts as well as domestic ones. Any pre-payments due under the agreement are made against export debts by the export factor. The flow of the transactions is as follows (refer to diagram):

a. The client requests credit cover on the overseas buyer.

b. The export factor asks the import factor to assess the creditworthiness of the importer.

c. Given satisfactory credit approval the client delivers the goods, and

d. Raises an invoice, which is assigned to the export factor.

e. The export factor prepays against the invoice and then assigns the debt to the import factor.

f. The import factor collects payment when it is due and repays the export factor, passing the balance of the prepayment to the client.

The export factor is also responsible for:

● Monitoring the export sales ledger.

● Maintaining communication with the import factor.

● Assisting the import factor by resolving disputes and queries with the client.

● Receiving and passing credit notes.

● Accounting to the client for currency transactions.

The Import Factor

The import factor needs a good assignment of the debt and a clear precise invoice.

Ideally the invoice sets out all the terms of trade and carries the assignment notice in the debtor's own language, indicating that payment is to be made to the import factor.

The import factor then takes over all the normal factoring procedures and attempts to obtain payment of the debt. As part of the service it is normal for the import factor to offer credit protection to the client. Because the debt is effectively being dealt with as a domestic debt, the exporter can offer open account terms and compete with local suppliers on an almost level footing.

The import factor is responsible for:

- Credit assessment and credit insurance

- Credit control and collection

- Litigation, if required, against the debtor

- All communication with the debtor

- Collection and transmission of funds to the export factor

It should be understood that the relationship between the export and import factors is vitally important. The export factor, having prepaid the client, is totally in the hands of the import factor. A poor performance by the import factor will undoubtedly affect the relationship between the client and export factor.

Currency Transactions

One of the particular problem areas identified earlier concerned the difference in currency between the exporting country and the importing country. To maintain a competitive edge, exporters may well wish to sell their goods in the currency of the buyer's country. This, however, exposes them to possible exchange rate risks. Factoring again can assist with this problem.

One way of containing this risk is for the client to enter into a 'forward sell contract' with its bank. This means that it agrees to sell a set amount of foreign currency at a future date for a set amount of, for example, French francs. The client then knows exactly what it will receive when the debtor pays. This does not completely resolve the problem; if the debtor does not pay on time, or at all, then the client may have to buy foreign currency to satisfy the contract. Nor does it give the client the opportunity to benefit from changes in the exchange rate in the client's favour.

The factor can assist in two main ways:

1 Because the import factor has given credit protection, he will normally pay out on a fixed date. The forward exchange contract could be taken out to coincide with this date, though the debtor paying early could still cause exchange rate issues.

2 As an alternative to a forward contract with a bank, the export factor could provide the prepayment in foreign currency, which the client sells at the current spot rate.

In addition some clients may buy raw materials or goods from overseas and have to pay in foreign currency. So it can be cost-effective to maintain a foreign currency account.

Direct Export Factoring

There is one further method employed to handle export business. Basically, the factor does everything without using an import factor. In this case the factor takes over responsibility for overcoming all the difficulties of the export markets. It is normal for these transactions to be linked to debt insurance either via the client's own insurance policy endorsed to the factor or via a factor's managed policy.

The following table summarises the main advantages of using a factoring 'chain' over direct export factoring.

Summary of Main Points of Factoring Chains Versus Direct Export Factoring

Advantages	Disadvantages
Credit cover based on local knowledge.	Not all countries covered.
Usually 100% credit cover – with guaranteed payment 90/120 days after due date.	Service provided by import factor is vital.
	Possible conflicts of interest.
Saving of the costs of international status enquiries.	System delays may slow down payments being received.
Communication with debtors in their own language.	Long communication chain.
Statements in a form common to debtor country.	Can be less profitable for the export factor – there always has to be a 'trade-off' of gains and losses. There has to be an examination of the cost effectiveness of 'doing it yourself'.
Local telephone costs.	
Experienced legal aid available.	
Debtors pay locally.	

Letters of Credit (The Documentary Credit)

The main purposes of letters of credit are to provide a means of payment (for goods/services) between buyers and sellers based in different countries.

A good definition of a documentary credit is:

> ... *any arrangement, however named or described, whereby a bank (issuing bank) acting at the request and in accordance with the customer's instructions is to pay, accept or negotiate.*

Figure 1.12 illustrates the documentary credit cycle. Spend a few moments reviewing it before reading on further.

Figure 1.12: Documentary Credit Cycle

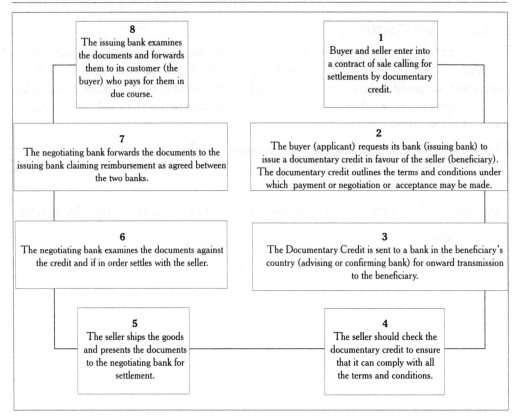

8
The issuing bank examines the documents and forwards them to its customer (the buyer) who pays for them in due course.

1
Buyer and seller enter into a contract of sale calling for settlements by documentary credit.

7
The negotiating bank forwards the documents to the issuing bank claiming reimbursement as agreed between the two banks.

2
The buyer (applicant) requests its bank (issuing bank) to issue a documentary credit in favour of the seller (beneficiary). The documentary credit outlines the terms and conditions under which payment or negotiation or acceptance may be made.

6
The negotiating bank examines the documents against the credit and if in order settles with the seller.

3
The Documentary Credit is sent to a bank in the beneficiary's country (advising or confirming bank) for onward transmission to the beneficiary.

5
The seller ships the goods and presents the documents to the negotiating bank for settlement.

4
The seller should check the documentary credit to ensure that it can comply with all the terms and conditions.

There are very specific rules governing the use of what we should more accurately refer to as documentary credits.

●   The first rule is that payment by this means is contained in the contract between buyer and seller. Only when this is done can the buyer approach its bankers and ask that a credit be issued in favour of the seller.

Once this credit has been issued the seller then knows even before shipping that the bank is promising to pay subject to the correct documents being presented.

One problem is that the seller is relying on the strength of the bank issuing the credit. Should the bank fail to pay legal action must be taken against the bank in the country of the bank – with all the problems of dealing with foreign law. One way around this is for the issuing bank to be based in the same country as the seller – but this is unlikely.

The credit is sent to a local bank; if this is a confirming bank, this strengthens the transaction because now two banks – both issuing and confirming – have promised to honour the payment.

A second important rule to note is:

●   Banks operate under a principle of 'autonomy' of the letter of credit. This means that they have no interest whatsoever in the goods or service *only* interest in the documents. So as long as the correct documents are produced they will pay out.

Types of Letter of Credit

There are two types of letter of credit – revocable and irrevocable. In the absence of a specific specification in the contract they are always regarded as revocable.

Revocable The least common form because it is the least secure. A revocable letter of credit can be amended or cancelled by any party, without prior notice or knowledge of the other parties

Irrevocable Most widely used letter of credit. The issuing bank gives its **irrevocable** undertaking to pay *if all* the credit terms have been adhered to. This type of credit can be cancelled or amended by the issuing bank only if all parties consent to it.

Irrevocable letters of credit can be either **confirmed** or **unconfirmed**.

A confirmed letter means that it has had the 'advising' bank confirm its undertaking and hence add its own undertaking, whereas an unconfirmed letter means that the advising bank only informs the exporter of the terms and conditions.

The message which came via Lloyds Bank London (advising Bank) would have been confirmed as authentic by Lloyds Bank London

To   Lloyds Bank London

From   Lloyds Bank Colon – Panama

Please advise urgently to – CILGWRI INTERNATIONAL EXPORTING LTD (address). We have issued in their favour our sight irrevocable letter of credit No. 24/008 p to the aggregate amount of FF 57,270.00 (Fifty seven thousand two hundred seventy and 00/100 French francs).

By order and or the account of Motta Internacional SA (address).

Available for negotiation in London up to and including end of March 30 1999.

Against their presentation of the following documents:

1. Their sight draft drawn on Lloyds Bank plc Colon Free Zone. Bearing this letter of credit No 24/008.

2. Commercial invoice in English original signed plus 4 copies.

3. Packing list in original plus 4 copies.

4. Full set of clean on board ocean bills of lading consigned to order and blank endorsed. Marked: Freight pre-paid and notify: Motta Internacional SA (address) plus 4 copies Dated not later than 15th March 1999.

5. Weight list in original plus 4 copies.

Insurance will be covered by the buyers.

Covering shipment of the following merchandise: shogun knife set.

To be invoiced CFR.

shipment from UK port to Colon Free Zone via Cristobel.

Partial shipment not allowed; transhipment not allowed.

Special instructions

1. All banking fees including advising commission outside Panama are for the Beneficiary's account

2. Original docs. must be sent via courier by negotiating bank. Duplicate by airmail

3. Kindly acknowledge receipt of this credit, quoting your reference number

4. Documents should be presented within 15 days after the date of shipment but within validity of the credit

5. Please send copy of documents DHL or similar courier service to – Motta Interactional Sa (address)

Copy of courier receipt should be presented upon negotiation

We hereby engage with drawers and/or bona fide holders that drafts drawn and negotiated in conformity with the terms of this credit will be duly honoured on presentation and that drafts accepted within the terms of this credit will be duly honoured at maturity.

Reimbursement instructions

Bills of Lading

These are the document of title to the goods, without which the buyer will not be able to obtain delivery from the shipping company.

They must be clean – that is to say bear no superimposed clauses derogatory to the condition of the goods such as 'inadequate packing', 'used drums' or 'on deck'.

The bills of lading must show the goods to be 'on board'. Bills marked 'received for shipment' are not acceptable unless they bear a subsequent notation, dated and signed stating that the goods are 'on board'.

Under the regulations set out in the Uniform Customs and Practice for Documentary Credits publication No. 400 of the International Chamber of Commerce, the following bills of lading will be accepted:

1. Through bills issued by shipping companies or their agents, even though they cover several modes of transport.

2. Short-form bills of lading which indicate some or all of the conditions of carriage by reference to source or document other than the bill of lading.

3. Bills covering unitized cargoes such as those on pallets or in containers.

    Unless specifically authorized in the credit, bills of the following type will not be accepted:

    1. Bills of lading issued by forwarding agents.

    2. Bills that are issued under and are subject to a charter party.

    3. Bills covering shipments by sailing vessels.

The bills must be made out to the order of the shipper and endorsed in blank. If the sales contract is Cost Insurance & Freight (CIF) or Cost & Freight (CFR), the Bills must be marked 'freight paid'. The general description of the goods including marks and numbers must match the details given in the invoice. The voyage and ship, if named, must be stated in the credit. Unless transhipment is expressly prohibited in the letter of credit, bills indicating transhipment will be accepted provided the same bill covers the entire voyage. Part-shipments are permitted unless the credit states otherwise.

Bill of Exchange

The bill of exchange has been defined as:

> ... an unconditional order in writing, addressed by one person to another, signed by the person giving it, requiring the person to whom it is addressed to pay on demand or at a fixed or determinable future time a sum certain in money to the order of, a specified person, or to the bearer.

It can be used in international trade involving practically all countries of the world and has numerous advantages:

1. It is an instrument long recognized by trade custom and by law, so that it is governed by an established code of practice.

2. It is a specific demand on the debtor.

3. It provides a useful mechanism for granting a pre-arranged period of credit to an overseas buyer.

4. It permits the exporter to maintain a degree of control over the shipping documents by making their release subject to payment or acceptance of the bill. However, it should be noted that the drawing of a bill of exchange does not guarantee payment – bills can be dishonoured and are!

5. The importer does not have to pay for the goods or raw materials until the supplier has despatched them.

In normal circumstances the exporter draws a bill of exchange, attaches the shipping documents to it and lodges them with its bank, giving very precise and complete instructions as to the action to be taken in certain circumstances:

- whether to forward the bill by airmail and ask for the proceeds to be remitted by cable or airmail;

- whether the documents are to be released against payment or acceptance of the bill;

- whether the bill is to be 'protested' if dishonoured;

- whether the goods should be stored and insured if not taken up by the buyer;

- whether rebate may be given for early payment;

- the party to whom the collecting bank may refer in case of dispute. The exporter's bank will forward the bill and documents to its correspondent bank in the buyer's country, passing on exactly the instructions received from the exporter.

Acting as collecting bank, the correspondent will present the bill to the buyer and release the documents in accordance with the instructions received.

If the arrangement called for payment to be made immediately, the bill of exchange will be drawn at 'sight' and the instructions will be to release the documents against payment (D/P).

If it is payable at a fixed or determinable future time it is called a term draft because the buyer is receiving a period of credit which is identified by the tenor of the bill. Hence the bill will be drawn before maturity, which calls for the payment after a certain time interval, usually 30, 60, 90 or 180 days.

> For example it may be '90 days sight' and the instructions will be for the documents to be released against acceptance (D/A) of the bill by the buyer. In this case, the buyer signs his acceptance across the face of the bill, which now becomes due for payment in 90 days, and he receives the documents of title to the goods.

The collecting bank will advise the remitting bank of the date of acceptance and hold the bill until maturity, when it will present it to the buyer for payment. In the event of dishonour, the collecting bank will arrange 'protest' by a notary if it has been instructed to do so.

This procedure provides legal proof that the bill was presented to the drawee and was dishonoured, and enables action to be taken in the courts without further preliminaries. The procedures and responsibilities of banks and other parties are laid down in the Uniform Rules for the Collection of Commercial Paper issued by the International Chamber of Commerce and accepted by major banks throughout the world.

Clean Bills

The method of collecting payment described above is based on the documentary bill, but in certain circumstances use may be made of a 'clean' bill, that is, a bill to which no documents are attached.

This involves the supplier sending the bill for the value of the goods through a local bank for payment or acceptance by the buyer or drawee on presentation.

The supplier or drawer would draw the bill of exchange on the purchase of the goods. Such bills may be drawn for the collection of monies due for services or for any debt, which does not relate to goods. A clean bill may also be used to obtain payment for goods sent on 'open account', especially where payment is overdue. Clean bill collection requires no shipping documents to be attached and is particularly popular in European markets, where the method is also used in internal trade.

The bill of exchange is most likely to be used in a documentary method of payment. This involves the supplier sending the Bill through the international banking system with the shipping documents, including the document of title to the goods, i.e. the original bill of lading. The bank then releases the document on payment or acceptance of the bill by the importer.

The supplier can use the banking system for a cash against documents (CAD) collection. In such situations only the shipping documents are sent and the supplier instructs the bank to release them only after payment by the importer. This method is used in some European countries whose buyers often prefer CAD to a sight draft if the supplier insists on a documentary collection for the settlement of the contract.

2

NEGOTIATING AND STRUCTURING THE DEAL

2.1 Selecting the Market

In this section we shall look at the issues that affect a financier's positioning in the market, including:

- Access to capital and credit
- Cost of funds
- Owners' aspirations

In the UK there has been, although it is rapidly disappearing, a 'negative demand' for factoring and discounting services. This type of negative demand is not uncommon. Most people have a negative demand for the dentist, for inoculations and even work! Before looking at how financiers obtain their business it is important to understand why this should be so.

Working capital finance against debtors and other current assets was introduced to the UK less than 40 years ago. It cuts across the preserves of two of the most conservative of professions – banking and accountancy. Financiers have to work hard to overcome a lack of understanding of what factoring or invoice discounting involves. In the early days, some factors and discounters created a belief that they were the financiers of last resort. The challenge that the industry then faced was to turn this negative demand into positive demand. The asset-based financing industry has matured and it is now recognized that its products play an essential and valuable part in satisfying the working capital needs of businesses. However, it is still necessary to market asset-based working capital finance to prospective clients and introducers by emphasizing a professional approach to their needs and problems.

Very few markets have customers who all have identical needs. This is also true in the market for working capital finance. Therefore, a financier has to decide what proportion of the market he needs to capture and retain if he is to meet his business objectives. He then has to:

- Determine which prospective customers or customer groups might make up this proportion

---

- Identify what is distinctive about such prospective customers or customer groups in terms of their needs for products, services and service levels

- Decide the best way to satisfy such needs

In deciding the last point he will take account of competitors and any limitations on his resources, such as limits on the funds he can obtain. The benefits that a financier will derive from effective market segmentation and a full understanding of such markets are:

- Effective identification of opportunities

- Better targeting

- Being able to tailor the marketing mix (product, price, promotion and place) to the specific needs of prospective customers.

In order to maximize the return from his marketing efforts, a financier should operate in markets and/or with prospects offering the best possibility of a sustained return. In order to do this he needs to find out the following:

- The potential markets and customers that are available

- The criteria for deciding whether a market or a customer is worth pursuing

- The order of attractiveness among potential markets and customers.

This necessitates the creation of a detailed profile of the market showing all its segments. From this analysis suitable and attractive groups of prospects can be chosen. The appropriate marketing strategy can then be devised.

The first decision that a debt financier needs to make is whether the debts of the potential clients are suitable for purchase or for prepayments. In simple terms factors and invoice discounters look first and foremost to the debts to provide the security for the prepayments. The debt should ideally arise from goods or services where the obligation of the client to the debtor ceases upon delivery, with a corresponding immediate obligation on the part of the debtor to pay on the due date. This is sometimes referred to as 'sell and forget'.

Having identified these sectors of the overall market containing potential clients, a financier can then identify the criteria that will determine the attractiveness of individual prospects.

In order to select potential clients that meet its qualifying criteria the financier must next decide what determines:

- Acceptable revenue

- Acceptable profit

- Acceptable risk

Generic selection criteria include:

- Accessibility

- Annual sales levels

- Growth prospects

- Revenue potential

- Cost of acquiring and servicing clients

- Cost of risk control

- Competition

- Internal capabilities and competence

- Funding requirements

Each distinct client group may require a different offering in terms of product, service, price and promotion.

Positioning is concerned with the prospect's perception of the image of one competitor compared with others. It is expressed in terms of relevant product and company dimensions, e.g. quality and price. A financier may need to position itself differently for separate client groups and identify a specific positioning strategy for each such group.

Access to Funding

A key issue, which determines a financier's marketing strategy, is the financier's ability to obtain funding for its prepayments to clients. The financier's financial base and level of external investment affect his target market and the size of the prospects that the financier can attract. A small privately-owned financier with limited capital would have access to only limited credit lines. It will look to spread its risk commensurately with the limited level of funds available for prepayments. In simple terms a financier with £10 million of funds available would be foolish to provide a single facility to one client of £10 million. It should look for a more evenly spread risk across a portfolio of clients. By way of contrast, a major bank-owned financier will have almost unlimited access to capital and credit lines. It will be less restricted in terms of positioning. Accordingly it can attract and write the 'bigger deal'.

Cost of Funds

The size of a financier's capital base also affects its cost of funds. Bank-owned asset-based financiers may have a further advantage in being able to obtain their money cheaper than a small privately-owned institution.

This inevitably drives non-major bank owned financiers into areas of activity where higher returns can be derived through differentiation or niche activities such as:

- Servicing clients with high credit risk

- Concentrating on start-ups

- Dealing only with small businesses

● Financing turnarounds or situations involving high maintenance of collateral

● Creative service levels

Ownership

The owners/shareholders of the financier largely determine its positioning. The owners have their own aspirations in terms of:

● Return on investment

● Appetite for risk

● Strategic objectives

● Product offering

Bank-owned financiers might be positioned in line with their parent company's activities. The greater emphasis on cross-selling products to bank customers will affect the financier's positioning. However a bank parent may see its asset-based finance subsidiary being able to penetrate markets or segments that have traditionally been outside its market territory.

Bank-owned financiers generally have high levels of flexibility in terms of positioning because of their ease of access to funding lines and capital. This enables them to have a broad range of products to offer to a wide range of clients in differing bands of turnover.

Overview

Positioning issues are important when considering the various product offerings and marketing strategies across the entire asset-based finance industry. Some companies have invested heavily in IT and delivery mechanisms in order to be able to handle large volumes of debts. Some have a diversity of facilities to be able to provide a solution-based approach rather than a product-led marketing strategy. There are organizations specializing in providing facilities to specific industries, others promoting a personalized service. Some are prepared to take on higher levels of credit risk or specialize in writing deals that may not be acceptable to the more conventional providers.

Once the financier has determined his position in the market-place and identified his preferred client base he will need to develop a marketing strategy to obtain leads. The following section considers the methods he may use to develop a client base.

2.2   Obtaining Leads and Generating Prospects

Generating Leads

The major avenues used by financiers to promote its services are:

Advertising   Advertising is undertaken in the national and regional press (including radio and television) as well as the trade and specialist press.

Public Relations

This generic heading relates to other promotional work such as relations with the press, articles in magazines/newspapers/books, radio and television appearances of key figures in the industry and specific publicity exercises such as those announcing a new product, or supporting a sporting or charity occasion.

Public relations is aimed at keeping the name of the industry and the individual financier in the minds of both the target audience, i.e. prospects, and the lead generators such as bankers, accountants and finance brokers.

Shareholder Contact

Perhaps one of the largest untapped salesforces that financiers have are their own shareholders. Although in theory leads will be generated automatically by the shareholder, in practice a great deal of work and effort has to be put into persuading the shareholders that the financier's products complement their services rather than stealing business from them. We shall be returning to this topic.

Existing Clients

Probably one of the best possible sources of new business is the existing client who is prepared to recommend the facility to his or her own business acquaintances. The financier should never overlook this source of business. Prospects from this source are more often picked up by client management and operational staff than by new business managers.

Existing Debtors of Factors

All factors maintain large debtor files which contain sufficient information to identify those debtors who may well prove to be good factoring or discounting prospects or even prospects for other financier services. In this connection it is important to remember that every contact with the debtor is also a potential selling opportunity. In particular the way in which the collectors attempt to carry out their function can affect very strongly the view of the debtor to factoring. Every employee on a factor's or discounter's staff therefore will have a marketing and business development responsibility.

Accountants/ Professional Advisors

This is a major potential source of new business and includes a growing number of 'specialist' brokers.

Direct Mail Campaigns

Direct mailing is a useful source of attracting new business and if used intelligently a useful means by which to educate the market. There are two methods of direct marketing:

● Blanket coverage where all companies within specific industries receive a mail shot without further detailed selection as to their financial means or their potential. Many agencies provide such mailing lists.

- Selective mail shots where a mailer is sent only to those companies on whom detailed research has been undertaken ascertaining that there is a strong possibility that the financier will meet their financial and administrative needs.

Direct Enquiries

Direct enquiries arise when the interested party approaches a financier company as a result of simply knowing its name. Very often this arises from a casual contact with a user of factoring or a half-remembered mail shot or advertising campaign from months or sometimes even years before.

2.3   Introducers/Brokers

Before leaving this topic of obtaining leads we need to return to one general area that leads come from, which is the introducer, and explore the rationale for their involvement in introducing business. Into the introducer category we would place three categories:

- the 'professional' introducer, accountants, brokers etc.
- the existing client
- the parent company

Each of these three can have a vested interest in offering business to a financier.

The first, the professional introducer, has both a professional interest in that he or she may well work with the prospect on many other aspects of its business (financial accounting, auditing, insurance, capital equipment purchasing, etc.) and is keen to offer the best solution to the client's financial funding as well as a general package of services. The introducer is also keen to collect commissions on the introductions, and these can be substantial. If the introducer is a firm of accountants it may also be seeking reciprocal business in terms of offering the financier's existing clients specialist accounting services or perhaps having the opportunity of being appointed receivers or liquidators by the financier in the case of failure of clients.

The second, existing clients, have less to gain in terms of increasing their own business but can earn excellent commissions. In this case the benefit is far more on the side of the financier who can gain through client introductions very good quality leads at very little cost (later we shall explore the acquisition costs of new clients).

The third, the parent company, varies depending on who the parent is. Some smaller financiers have a parent whose only involvement in financial services is their financier, so there is little opportunity for leads from this source. At the other end of the scale the bank-owned financier companies have considerable scope for developing leads.

For example, a bank will have many thousands of its customers funded by a traditional overdraft product. If the bank can convert these accounts into financier clients run by their subsidiary, they can make considerable gains

- increased profitability through increased lending – the financier may well be able to advance far more than the bank because they can better manage the asset security on a day-day basis

- improve their risk management
- improve their customer relations by making more money available via the financier
- increase their security by the purchase of an asset rather than standing as a secure creditor (subject to the Insolvency Act restrictions)

There is a general move, in today's industry, by the bank-owned financiers to move much closer to their parent companies and to adopt integrated strategies for delivery of the financial service best suited to the client and the financier/bank.

2.4   Initial Prospect Assessment

Initial information is normally obtained from a screening process and depends on how willing the prospect is to disclose details of its business. The information needed must ideally be sufficient to provide an immediate response on the suitability or otherwise of the prospect. The following information is normally required:

- What the prospect seeks, in terms of facility, financing and service.
- The type of business of the prospect.
- Turnover, both historic and projected.
- Information on the collateral offered i.e. for a factoring/discounting facility.
- Debtor base, including number of debtors, type, largest debtors, total value of debts, terms and conditions of sale etc. Volumes of invoices and credit notes.
- Financial information, accounts.

If the outcome of this initial screening proves to be negative, the reasons for unsuitability should be immediately advised to the prospect. The records, however, are often retained for future reference because it is possible that the reason for rejection now may not exist in, say, six months' time when a fresh contact may be made with the prospect.

If the outcome is positive, an early meeting is arranged for the new business manager to meet the prospect's decision-maker at the premises of the prospect. The nature of such a meeting will be considered in detail later on in this chapter.

2.5   Standard Criteria

It is from this information that the financier will make a judgement about whether it is worth pursuing the enquiry with a visit to gain more detailed information. The facts gained from such a visit are then presented to the financier's underwriters, who will accept or reject the business based on their acceptance criteria.

As can be imagined it is impossible to lay down criteria that would be acceptable to all financiers, e.g. some may not like business related to building contracting or transport, whereas another may like transport and a third building contracting.

What we can do, however, is to draw up broad criteria that the financier is generally looking for. In simplistic terms it is the answer to three questions:

1   Is the prospect an acceptable **risk** for financial investment, including the use of the particular facility being requested (factoring, discounting, stock finance etc.)?

2   Will this business be **profitable** to the financier?

3   Will the prospect and the financier both **benefit** from the arrangement?

When a prospective client is contacted, the financier will seek through its new business managers and/or surveyors to obtain sufficient information to demonstrate to its underwriters that the prospective client and the proposed facility fulfills each of these questions. The information is gathered in a new business visit to the prospect.

2.6   The New Business Visit

This is the single most important meeting to take place with the prospect. At this meeting the prospect will almost certainly form its view as to whether in principle it wishes to continue the application for the facility. The new business manager will also gather more information to enable him or her to decide if the prospect meets the financier's acceptance criteria.

It is essential that the new business manager is 100% professional, imparting confidence and trust to the prospect. The meeting will take the form of a structured discussion with the new business manager having the following objectives:

●   To learn more about the products or services offered by the prospect – to ensure its compatibility with the financier's product. This may involve a review of legal issues, practical issues on how the account could or could not be effectively managed, and identification of any potential security issues (retention of title, ownership of debts, agency arrangements etc.).

●   To discover why customers purchase the prospect's product or service in preference to another suppliers – to assist in assessing the viability of the prospect.

●   To establish the background and current situation of the prospect, both financial and historic – although the financier is more interested in the future prospects of the company than in past historic records, it is interested in patterns and trends because these can illustrate the underlying reasons for the approach for funding.

●   To establish the existing funding arrangements, and to understand the requirements which led to the enquiry – the financier provides working capital so the review must include a careful consideration of the reasons for the request for the financier's services and the impact these could have on existing funding.

For example, it would be of little help to a company that had an existing bank overdraft of £150,000 approaching a factor/discounter for a similar level facility if, on granting the facility, the bank immediately removed its overdraft facility. The company would have no change in its working capital (Criterion 3 'both parties benefiting' would not be met). There may well therefore need to be detailed negotiations with the company's bankers to agree a 'residual' overdraft facility after the commencement of the factoring/discounting financing.

- To review the prospect's future development strategy and how the financier's services will interface with that strategy.

- To assess the character and capability of the management with particular regard for its future plans. Most of the financier's facilities/products and services depend on working very closely with its clients. Trust is therefore a vital element in assessing the prospect and is normally given a high profile in reports prepared for the underwriters.

- To develop an understanding of the way in which the prospect conducts its business in order to establish if there will be operational compatibility with the financier's systems.

- To confirm the prospect's needs and the ability of the financier's facilities to meet those needs.

- To create a high perceived value in the prospect's mind by emphasizing the relative benefits and opportunities to be gained from the financier.

- To agree in principle the most appropriate solution to the prospect's needs. At this stage a discussion will almost certainly take place on the costs and conditions of any facility. We shall be looking at this area later in the course.

If there is an agreement to continue, the new business manager will agree the likely time-scales and outline the next steps in the procedure of gaining acceptance by the financier.

Having gathered this information, the financier's new business manager will be responsible for the submission of the information he or she has gathered for approval, or for a survey (due diligence investigation) of the proposal. The survey, whether carried out as a separate exercise or by the new business manager, would further clarify the prospect's situation, covering the following areas:

- Brief history and description of the prospect's business.

- Comment on and analyse the prospect's financial condition, current funding arrangements, and likely effects of the financier's funding involvement.

- The operation of the sales ledger and its suitability for the financier. An assessment as to the security it provides for the finance facility would also be included.

- Comment on any competition.

- Recommendation as to the offer of the facility covering charges and conditions.

The survey is an extremely important component of the selling function. It is upon the recommendation of the survey team that the final quotation for the provision of the financier's services will be decided. The final responsibility for reviewing the new business manager's and/or survey team's recommendations and agreeing to accept the business will rest with the financier's senior management/underwriters.

2.7   Deal Structuring

Having obtained sufficient information to enable a qualified acceptance (acceptances at this stage will always be qualified because they will be subject to due diligence investigation prior to full acceptance) and to offer the prospect a facility, the financier has then to consider how to structure the offer. At this stage of the acceptance process it is normal to at least send a quotation to the prospect that will outline the deal proposed.

This quotation covers a number of key areas:

● the type of facility to be offered

● quoted fees and other costs

● standard conditions to be attached to the facility

● special conditions to be attached to the facility

● operational conditions

Principles of Pricing

Later we shall be looking in detail at the costing and related pricing of the financier's products and services. At this stage we are interested in how the deal is structured when it is presented to the prospect and the principles behind the setting of quoted prices.

Obviously the pricing is set to recover the costs of the service and provide a return to the financier but this is too simplistic when thinking about how we can structure the deal, so let us explore a few of the vast number of possible combinations of deal structure and pricing.

Example 1   Later we shall look at the acquisition costs of new clients and investigate why it is so important for the financier to retain clients for as long as possible in view of the initial set-up/acquisition costs. If for the moment we just accept this statement, we can immediately see how pricing and the deal structure are closely linked. If we offered a prospect a one-year facility we would set one fee, but if we could agree a three-year deal we could perhaps set a lower fee structure. It is a simple link, but one that illustrates the need to assess each deal separately and to price each based on a wide range of criteria.

Example 2   In a factoring product, workload plays a key component in assessing the pricing, whereas in discounting there is less of a workload element. But how do we relate this to a situation where the client requests, say, a discounting product but the financier, because of security issues or perhaps an 'in-house' policy criterion, will only offer a factoring product? The deal must still be structured in a way that demonstrates how the needs of the prospect are being met despite the difference in pricing.

Example 3   In a packaged financial facility involving perhaps both stock and debtor finance, the costing of two different services must in some way be combined into one packaged price.

What we are talking about here is how to link the financier's services, with the related benefits of the offered deal, to the costing. And if we are to consider benefits of the deal we must start by examining the needs of the prospective client and then link how this can be delivered in terms of a deal structure. We must also recognize that every client situation is different.

2.8   Identifying Needs

In general terms we have already identified why a company should come to a financier – for cash and perhaps for some added element of the financier's service package e.g. credit control. But this is far too broad; companies approach financiers for a whole range of reasons and it against these reasons that the deal must be structured. The following are some of the most common needs.

Working Capital Needs

● To meet the general day-to-day needs of the cashflow, in particular when in rapid growth (classically 'over-trading' when sales grow faster than working capital to support those sales can be generated).

Although it might be a need in the mind of the prospect, financiers will not normally offer facilities to cover urgent cashflow requirements caused through creditor pressure, cumulative losses, withdrawal of current funding (i.e. bank overdraft) or any other situation where they might be seen to be 'the lender of last resort' prior to a probable liquidation.

● To take opportunities offered through obtaining large discounts from key suppliers or to purchase special 'lots' of product at special prices.

● To reduce creditor pressure by releasing cash tied up in debtors or in stock.

● To assist as part of a restructuring package of financial support in MBO's and take-overs.

Credit Control and Sales Ledger Needs

● To take pressures away from owners/managers (particularly in small companies) to enable them to direct their activities towards business generation and profit earning.

● To run a more professional sales ledger operation.

- To control the debtor base.

Risk Protection Needs

- To protect against bad debt.

Obviously there are many other needs but the vast bulk of the financier's business is covered by these prospective client needs.

Structuring Deals – The Why and How

We shall now take each of the above needs and develop a series of models to illustrate how the financier approaches structuring deals.

To Meet the General Day-to-Day Needs of the Cashflow

In example one we shall simply compare the effect of cashflow with and without debtor finance in the form of factoring or discounting.

In both situations we have a new-start company which has prepared a cashflow forecast to identify its cashflow needs for the first six months trading. The company is predicating certain sales levels and in Example 1 anticipates payment around 60 days after invoice date.

Cash Flow Projection – Example 1	Jan	Feb	Mar	Apr	May	Jun
Actual Sales	8,000	8,000	10,000	10,000	12,000	12,000
Sales income			8,000	8,000	10,000	10,000
Total Income (A)			8,000	8,000	10,000	10,000
Expenses						
Directors' salary				2,000	2,000	2,000
Staff wages	5,000	5,000	5,000	5,000	5,000	5,000
Rent and rates	500	500	500	500	500	500
Raw materials paid for	1,000	1,000	1,000	1,000	1,000	1,000
Lighting and heating etc.	200	200	200	200	200	200
Distribution	200	200	200	200	200	200
Total Payments out this Month (B)	6,900	6,900	6,900	8,900	8,900	8,900
Net balance this month (A-B)	(6,900)	(6,900)	1,100	(900)	1,100	1,100
Balance brought forward from last month	-	(6,900)	(13,800)	(12,700)	(13,600)	(12,500)
Balance carried forward to next month	(6,900)	(13,800)	(12,700)	(13,600)	(12,500)	(11,400)

At the end of this period it anticipates an overdraft need of some £1,400 although the overdraft may well peak at around £22,000 (April – anticipating no cash receipts until the end of the month £13,600 overdrawn plus £8,000 due in during the month – can be referred to as 'timing mismatches').

As a new-start company they would have to approach a bank to request an overdraft, of some £25,000, which allows a little for errors in assumptions.

Structuring the same deal with a factor, rather than pursuing traditional overdraft, would change the situation. The factoring deal has been structured to give the client a 70% prepayment as the goods are invoiced with the balance to be paid over as paid by the customer (*for purposes of these exercises we have ignored charges*).

Cash Flow Projection – Example 2 – with Factoring

	Jan	Feb	Mar	Apr	May	Jun
Actual Sales	8,000	8,000	10,000	10,000	12,000	12,000
Sales income at 70% (immediate)	5,600	5,600	7,000	7,000	8,400	8,400
Sales income at 30% (when paid)			2,400	2,400	3,000	3,000
Total Income (A)	5,600	5,600	9,400	9,400	11,400	11,400
Expenses						
Directors' salary				2,000	2,000	2,000
Staff wages	5,000	5,000	5,000	5,000	5,000	5,000
Rent and rates	500	500	500	500	500	500
Raw materials paid for	1,000	1,000	1,000	1,000	1,000	1,000
Lighting and heating etc.	200	200	200	200	200	200
Distribution	200	200	200	200	200	200
Total payments out this month (B)	6,900	6,900	6,900	8,900	8,900	8,900
Net balance this month (A-B)	(1,300)	(1,300)	2,500	500	2,500	2,500
Balance brought forward from last month	-	(1,300)	(2,600)	(100)	400	2,900
Balance carried forward to next month	(1,300)	(2,600)	(100)	400	2,900	5,400

In this example the position at the end of the cashflow period is in credit (bank position) by some £ 5,400.

And although there is still a requirement for some overdraft-type finance, this is very modest at £2,600. (We can largely ignore the timing problems of cash coming in and going out if we make the assumption that invoices are raised throughout the month and that cash should be flowing in steadily.) In fact the requirement is so modest it would be expected that the owners could generate this amount themselves.

Although this is a very simple example it does illustrate how a deal structured under the most common type of factoring agreement can drastically alter the cash position of the client.

To Take Opportunities for Discounts or to Purchase Special 'Lots'

This can either be through factoring/discounting releasing cash tied up in debtors or from perhaps a stock financing arrangement where monies tied up in stock can again be released.

If we return for a moment to addressing the need of the prospective client we can see that finance provided in this way can rapidly alter the business performance of the client. For example:

● the client arranges finance against their debts.

● using the money released it takes the opportunity to buy a larger quantity of stock at advantageous prices (discounts for quantity perhaps) than it would normally buy.

● because of reduced costs it can lower selling prices in the marketplace.

● because of lower prices it attracts new customers, and increases sales to existing customers

● the increased sales generate more cash through the factoring/discounting facility, which means that buying power may improve yet again.

● as the business cycle continues to turn, the client does increasing levels of business with a growing customer base while improving overall profitability.

The previous transactions would have been very similar under a stock finance arrangements although the stock rather than the debtors would have formed the asset base of the transaction.

With transactional finance (trade finance) the finance can be even more closely linked to the purchasing of the goods.

● the client has a customer for certain goods and a firm order can be obtained.

● the client cannot however afford to purchase these goods.

● the financier can purchase the goods direct from the supplier – having satisfied itself that the ultimate customer will go through with the purchase.

● the financier would retain title in the goods after supplying them to the customer, the client invoicing and completing the sale.

To Reduce Creditor Pressure

A very common problem is matching tight terms obtained from suppliers with the longer terms of trade offered to customers/debtors. Again the use of a financier's services can fill the gap.

To Assist as Part of a Restructuring Package

With MBOs and other financial restructuring it is necessary to take a holistic view of a company's financial requirements rather than try to address perhaps many different needs through one type of financial arrangement. It is therefore not uncommon for the financier to become part of a consortium of financial providers providing elements of a mixed package of financial support.

The financier must also consider other issues when trying to structure the deal. Some of these issues will impact on the ability of the financier to provide funding, whereas others will impact on security issues.

Provision of Funding Issues

Companies with very seasonal businesses have cash requirements that vary across the year. The financier may have to structure a deal to take these movements into account. For example:

- during the height of the season the client does a lot of invoicing which creates a rapidly rising debtor base, coupled to a rapidly falling stock position – factoring or discounting would appear to offer a better financing option during this 'growth' phase.

- during the low point in the year the client builds up stocks but has little if any sales – so a stock-financing arrangement would appear more appropriate at this stage of the cycle.

- the role of the financier is to match finance in such a way that its security is maintained while also ensuring that the client is fully supported in its activities.

This raises another deal-structuring issue, that of 'headroom'. Headroom is the concept of ensuring there is always some room within the facility being offered to cope with both 'hiccups' within the plans and also allow for anticipated growth. The flexible and 'open-ended' nature of lending against current assets has a built-in expectation of headroom, i.e. more invoices equal more cash. But that does not take away the fact that the financier may well wish to set some limits to its involvement.

- Simply agreeing a facility that does not fully meet the client's short/medium-term needs creates problems for both client and financier. It is for this reason that the financier will often involve other sources of finance when agreeing a facility, i.e. some level of overdraft via the bank or perhaps the involvement of a leasing or contract hire company.

- Occasionally the financier may structure the deal to anticipate certain actions or plans of the client. For example:

    a client who anticipates that its business may grow very rapidly may be unwilling to accept a costing quotation based on the present turnover levels, while the financier may not be happy just to accept unproven performance levels. The deal could therefore be structured in such a way that as turnover rises over certain pre-set levels, the costing would automatically be reduced. Thus both client and financier achieve their objectives.

- There are situations when the financier is unable to offer a suitable facility to the prospective client. For example:

  the prospective client is seeking a factoring facility for working capital. It is following this route because it has widely exceeded its overdraft facility and can offer the bank no additional security. It also has a debtor base that is very slow paying, and has pressure from creditors, including VAT. The figures are as follows:

Current overdraft limit	£ 100,000
Current overdraft actual	£ 130,000
Gross debtors	£ 289,000
Value of debts over 3 months old (factors will not normally finance debts over this age)	£ 125,000

  Potential funding to be released from factoring.

Gross debtors	£ 289,000
Less aged debts	£ 125,000
Potential approved debts	£ 164,000
At 80% advance	£ 131,200

If the financier entered into a factoring agreement and could actually advance the full amount (this example has ignored the security checking process and assumes that *all* debts are without dispute and payable – which in practice is very unlikely) after repaying the overdraft there would only be £1,200 extra cash generated for the company, pressure would still be there from the creditors. Unless the bank could be persuaded to maintain an element of overdraft after factoring commences, or there are other ways to raise extra working capital, via stock perhaps, the financier would be reluctant to enter into a deal that would not ultimately benefit either party.

Security Issues

An area of real interest to the financier would be a range of issues that can effect the future security of the financier's investment. Such issues affect the structuring of the deal. For example:

- Certain types of service have built-in security problems for a factor/discounter; e.g. newspaper and magazine distribution has a high rate of returns so that a factoring/ discounting deal would be structured to take this into account – perhaps by reducing the initial percentage or arranging a percentage reduction in invoice values (calculated on an average returns rate).

- Contracts that have some prohibition on assigning the benefit of the contract may also need to be considered and the deal structured to overcome these problems.

- Prime debtor accounts may well be restricted in percentage and/or overall financial terms. This can in certain cases create the same situation as above when insufficient finance would be released for the facility.

Service Issues

- A prospect seeking one type of financier facility may prove to be unacceptable for that facility but acceptable for a different facility. For example:

  - A small company may wish for invoice discounting because it wants to retain its own credit control. However it does not meet the discounter's acceptance criteria in terms of size or financial strength. The deal could, however, be structured as a CHOCC (Client Handles Own Credit Control) facility or agency agreement where the client handles its own credit control

- Conversely a prospect who wants a credit control element to the facility may be unsuitable because of the nature of the invoicing. For example:

  - Many thousands of invoices all of the same value to a large number of customers may be costed by the factor at an unrealistic charge. Here a discounting arrangement may well be more suitable.

In this whole area of deal structuring, the financier has to consider every element of the client's business, its operation, its funding needs today and into the future, its relationship with other lenders and then tailor a deal from its own range of products and services that will ultimately deliver benefits to both parties.

2.9   Due Diligence and Credit Analysis

In this section we shall look at the purpose and approach of the due diligence processes covering both:

- Surveying a prospective client;
- Auditing an existing client

Surveys (due diligence) of a prospect's affairs are undertaken in order to find out whether or not the profile, systems, debt and debtor quality, and financial position of the prospect meet the credit criteria of the financier.

In the case of surveying a prospective client, the surveyors produce a report of their findings to their credit committee, recommending or identifying issues within the proposal to be underwritten. This committee then decides whether or not to make a formal offer for the provision of its services to the prospect.

Due Diligence Survey

A key formal function before providing finance to a potential or new client is the on-site due diligence. The length and intensity of the survey varies dramatically between financiers. At one end of the scale small factoring deals are quite often underwritten and transacted by the new business manager as a result of his or her sales activity and written recommendation.

At the other end of the scale specialist expertise is called upon to undertake comprehensive on-site investigations resulting in detailed reports and analyses, particularly where high-value transactions are involved. The industry uses a number of terms to explain the due diligence process. For simplicity we shall refer to 'surveys' in connection with obtaining new business and 'audits' in connection with the ongoing relationship with existing clients.

Confidential invoice discounting is inherently a riskier facility to provide than factoring. Accordingly, most invoice discounting deals are completed following a comprehensive survey provided by the financier's audit department. It is the same department that also regularly visits existing clients to monitor the client and the validity of the debts and/or other collateral.

There are also a few specialist consultants who can provide pre-lending reviews. Some firms of accountants can also assist through the provision of commercial and financial due diligence. However, the specialist nature of a collateral survey is usually outside their standard due diligence routines.

Quotes/Offers

As we saw in the previous section, following a meeting between the financier's new business manager and the prospective client, during which the new business manager assesses their suitability for finance, a written quote or offer subject to survey, setting out the proposed terms of a facility, is sent to the prospect. As previously mentioned some financiers rely entirely on their new business managers assessment of the prospect and may therefore not carry out a separate survey. In such cases the financier may proceed immediately to a formal offer rather than a quote. In either case the letter to the prospect normally specifies:

- in respect of a proposed debt-financing facility:
  - prepayment percentages
  - service rates
  - discount rates
- in respect of a loan against assets other than debts:
  - how the value of the loan is calculated
  - interest rate
  - service fees
- in respect of any facility:
  - security required
  - guarantees and indemnities required
  - any preconditions before funds can be released.

A quote is normally subject to survey and the credit approval of the financier's credit committee. If the quote is accepted by the prospect, a surveyor visits the prospect's premises to conduct a survey.

Quite often a prospect obtains terms with several competing financiers, each of whom is allowed to proceed to survey.

The role of the surveyor is to extract information from the books and records of the company in order to:

- Establish that the collateral can support the proposed funding
- Identify the issues that may affect the on-going viability of the prospect
- Confirm that the prospect's systems and procedures are suitable for the services being offered
- Make recommendations about the above points
- Recommend for or against the proposed deal

The surveyor may also be asked to review and comment on the financial performance of the business. To do so he or she analyses both the audited and management accounts as well as reviewing budget projections and cashflows. The depth of such analyses varies according to the size and complexity of the proposed deal. We will look at the analysis process later.

Risk Identification

The key to successful risk identification is a clear understanding of what a business actually does. This may appear obvious, but if the audit or survey does not have a clear objective it will be of no value.

Survey Objectives

- To confirm the existence of the proposed collateral
- To make sure that the proposed funding is adequately secured
- To confirm that the business is viable by examining:
  - its cash liquidity for its short-term viability
  - its profitability for its long-term viability
- To ensure that the client's operating systems and administration are capable of:
  - delivering sound collateral
  - facilitating the ongoing monitoring of collateral values
- To establish and confirm that management information systems will accurately reflect existing and future trading.

We shall look in detail at the methods and processes financiers use to fulfil these objectives in the section on risk assessment.

Survey Process

A surveyor normally expects to receive a briefing from the new business manager (and on occasion from underwriters and operations staff) together with a copy of the first file, which has been compiled from information already gathered from the prospect.

Included in the first file are:

- Notes of meetings, discussions and negotiations between the prospect and the new business manger showing the nature of the business and including commentary on its historic financial performance and future prospects

- Copies of management accounts, audited accounts, cashflows and budget projections

- Brochures about the prospect together with product information

- A copy of any indicative quote from the financier to the prospect

From the briefing and first file information an assessment of the time required to complete the survey is made. Suitable dates and times are arranged. Survey times vary according to the size and complexity of the deal. Most examinations require at least one day at the prospect's premises. In respect of large and/or complicated transactions the financier normally puts a team of surveyors on site to reduce disruption to the prospect. A prospect that has several group companies or divisions with disparate and /or regional operations will require survey visits to multiple locations.

Once the survey dates have been booked it is usual to confirm the meeting and detail the level and type of information that will be required to complete the survey. The competitive nature of the industry together with the pressing needs of the prospect for funding often create time pressures. This has to be balanced against the financier's need to obtain enough information to determine its risk and whether and on what terms, if any, a facility can be offered.

Below is a list of information that the surveyor will require in order to complete the survey at the prospect's premises:

Prospect Audit Examination Requirements

- Most recent open item aged debtor analysis
- Most recent open item aged creditors purchase ledger report
- Sales ledger daybooks – monthly totals of invoices, credit notes, cash received and adjustments for each month
- Bank statements – for all accounts for the previous 12 months
- Cash book – monthly reconciliations of current account for the previous12 months
- Last four VAT returns
- PAYE returns book (last and current year)
- Most recent audited and management accounts

In addition the surveyor will need access to all:

● Hard-copy invoices for previous 6 months

● Hard-copy credit notes for previous 12 months

● All delivery notes for previous 6 months

● Purchase orders

● Correspondence files with customers

Underwriting the Proposal

Following completion of the survey a proposal, including a copy of the survey report, is submitted to the financier's credit committee for underwriting. It is at this stage that a critical analysis and review of the proposal is made. The underwriting process varies in depth and formality from financier to financier and from deal to deal depending on size and degree of marginality apparent from the survey findings.

Credit Policy

Credit policies vary across the industry and reflect each financier's position, market, product offering, size of client portfolio and appetite for risk.

Many organizations operate a credit policy contained in a manual that sets out the general terms under which business may be underwritten. However, the credit policy is not a strict rule book to determine the merits of every deal. It is to be used as a guide by the underwriters.

It is the function of the credit policy to provide a framework for the financier to meet its financial and strategic ambitions by providing funds to businesses within its target market. The credit policy covers the following issues:

Which products will be offered?	Factoring or invoice discounting on a recourse or non-recourse basis, stock finance, plant and machinery finance, loan against buildings
Debt quality	This affects the ability of the financier to recover prepayments made
Maximum/minimum deal size	Based on turnover or potential funds in use
Industry sectors	Identifying specific industries within the financier's target markets and those that are specifically excluded
Prepayment rates	The prepayment percentage or loan rates for each product
High-involvement criterion	The extent to which any one debtor may be financed as a percentage of the overall debtors' ledger. This is also called the 'concentration criterion'.

Formula limit	Establishing restrictions on the funding of other assets as a percentage of the debtor balances
Client longevity	Minimum length of time that a prospect must have been established
Financial condition	Requirements based on net worth, current profitability and/or cash liquidity
Security	The minimum security required, its type, whether personal or corporate company guarantees are needed
Historical	Any previous insolvency, any existing insolvency procedures
Corporate structure	Type (incorporated or non-incorporated), ownership, relationship with associated or group companies
Geography	Domicile of client, level and type of export trade
Income	Income or pricing criteria based on internal models or policy

It is against the credit policy that each deal is appraised in order to identify any credit policy exceptions, which may require further sanction.

Basic Goals and Purpose of Credit Analysis and Underwriting

These are:

- To identify the suitability of a prospect for this type of funding and the level to which an advance can safely be made.

- To identify and evaluate the underlying strengths, weaknesses and key variables that enable the prospect's business to succeed or cause its failure.

- To ensure that identified strengths exceed identified weaknesses by a sufficient margin to offset any circumstances of which the financier is unaware.

During the underwriting process evaluation of the prospect will be made as to:

- The collectability of its debts and the strength of any other assets taken as security.

- Its past, current and projected financial position, earnings and cashflow.

- Its ability to service both its borrowings from third parties and the financier's facilities.

- The ability of its management to achieve its goals and required performance levels.

- The likelihood of its rehabilitation or insolvency if it is already in a poor financial condition.

Prospect's Intentions

In order to understand the risks involved in granting any facility it is essential to understand the prospect's real purpose behind the transaction. Purposes can include:

- Funding expansion or sales growth
- Funding debt repayment
- Replacing or retiring equity
- Funding purchase of assets
- Funding seasonal requirements
- Funding losses
- Improving the directors' lifestyles

The purpose stated by the prospect and true underlying need for finance are not always the same.

Source of Repayment on Termination of the Facility

Every financier must have a clear understanding of how it is to be repaid if the facility is terminated. The source repayment is either:

- Primary – Conversion of assets, repayment out of earnings or cashflow; or
- Secondary – Realization of security, enforcement of guarantees, workout, placing client into insolvency procedures or refinancing with another lender.

In most cases the source of repayment has to be through liquidation of the collateral and the enforcement of any security.

We shall now look at the various considerations a financier makes when completing its risk assessment.

2.10   Risk Assessment

In the previous section we looked at the approach taken by financiers in completing the due diligence on a prospective client, or carrying out an audit on an existing client. We shall now consider the information that a surveyor would look to obtain from the visit and the information that a financier may have available within its operations department and look at how it could evaluate the information to assist in the risk assessment process.

Factoring and Discounting

In carrying out a risk assessment of the prospect for factoring/discounting facilities the financier is simply trying to establish how closely it fits to its ideal.

Figure 2.1

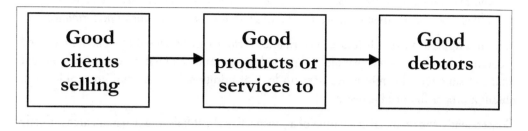

With well-managed trustworthy clients, who sell good products or services to good debtors who can pay and will pay their debts as they fall due, the financier can be reasonably confident that the investment will be safe and that a facility can be offered.

Unfortunately it is far easier to list these three criteria than to establish if they exist in real life. In assessing the risk we must try to make both objective and subjective assessments. These will be based on facts, such as audited accounts, and on intangible areas such as how much confidence we have in the principles of the prospective business.

The key areas that are examined include:

- Evaluation of financial information
- Business plans
- Management quality
- Debtor quality, including
    - Terms and conditions
    - Initial debtor assessment
    - Debt evaluation
    - Bad debt history
- Administration of the business

The risk would also be assessed taking in the full picture of the financing of the company, for example the involvement of other lenders would have to be considered.

Financial Evaluation

Factors and discounters advance money against the purchase of debts, they do not lend money. So we are not trying to establish the prospect's ability to repay a loan or mortgage advance, nor are we assessing the company in terms of the returns we may get as an investor. We are far more interested in establishing the prospect's current financial stability and likely future prospects of success and the current and future cash needs of the business. In general terms we want to ensure that the business will still be running in the foreseeable future and that through our funding, linked perhaps to other lenders, the business can generate sufficient cash for its future needs.

This 'future looking' approach is one of the major differences between the financier and the traditional banker. Bankers have often been described as 'historic lenders' – advancing money based on assessment and projection of past financial performance.

With this approach towards future performance it can easily be seen that looking at audited accounts that may be over a year old will not tell you very much about the company's present financial situation. Therefore, we need to look at additional information to enable us to obtain a proper financial assessment.

Consequently, the financial evaluation of a prospective client falls into two main areas. Firstly an evaluation of its published accounts and of its management accounts, and secondly a wider ranging 'application of common sense' analysis of the information contained within these documents.

The issues and considerations to be addressed in the risk assessment process are detailed below and sample survey working papers are contained in Appendix 1. Study the sample papers as you read through the following section.

Accounts Assessment

We have already seen the range of information obtained through the due diligence stage of the process. The financier would seek to see the following financial information to enable its evaluation to be carried out fully.

- Latest published, and audited, accounts. With the requirements on small and medium-sized enterprises (SMEs) to file only minimal information, we would most likely seek in addition to the published information a more detailed profit and loss account.

- Latest management accounts, including budget figures, profit and loss account and balance sheet

- A copy of current debtors list

- A copy of current creditors list

- The latest bank statements

- Information on the current situation on preferential creditors (Income Tax, National Insurance and VAT)

- A cashflow forecast for the next 6–12 months.

Most financiers use a standard accounts analysis profile, perhaps on a computer spreadsheet, to produce in a standard format a set of accounts analysis information. A typical assessment of the published accounts and the management accounts would generate a number of ratios and other information, most likely including the following. As with all ratio and financial analysis approaches the financier is concerned with trends, movements and comparisons, using these to give a indication of potential risk. Ratios, however, can only highlight potential problem areas, further investigation would be needed to establish exactly what was happening.

- Gross and net profit figures

  $$\frac{\text{Gross profit}}{\text{Turnover}} \quad \text{or} \quad \frac{\text{Net profit}}{\text{Turnover}}$$

  To see figures reflecting industry norms or other clients in the same type of business would be reassuring. Any decreasing trends in either ratio would indicate potential problems and would need to be investigated in more detail to establish the underlying reasons.

  For example, a falling gross profit ratio (and almost certainly a corresponding reduction in net profit) could indicate that the costs of producing the product were rising while the company was unable to increase its prices. This could well put pressure on its cashflow – less coming in proportionately to that going out of the business – ultimately leading to a loss-making situation.

- Gearing

  $$\frac{\text{Long term interest-bearing borrowings}}{\text{Shares and reserves}}$$

  Sometimes called leverage, this ratio indicates the amount of money being borrowed by a company versus the capital supplied by the owners of the business (issued share value, retained profits, revaluations etc.). Analysts generally like to see no more that 30% borrowed on a long-term interest-bearing basis. If greater percentages are seen it means that the large proportions of the company's earnings are going towards paying interest and not into the company.

- Debtor and creditor days

  $$\frac{\text{Current debtors x 365}}{\text{Annual sales on credit}} \qquad \frac{\text{Current creditors x 365}}{\text{Cost of goods sold}}$$

  Extending debtor days or reducing creditor days would indicate potential or existing cashflow problems – debtors paying too slowly (compared to the company's standard terms of trade) or the creditors are being paid too quickly.

  Creditors being paid slower could indicate potential creditor problems – pressure to pay and potential legal recovery actions.

- Stock turnover

  $$\frac{\text{Cost of sales}}{\text{Average stock}} \quad \text{or} \quad \frac{\text{Net sales}}{\text{Average stock}}$$

  This indicates how fast the stock being purchased is being converted into sales. A low figure (or a falling figure) illustrates that the company is not turning stock into sales as quickly as in the past – this can lead to increased cash being tied up in working capital and potential problems from obsolete or deteriorating stock.

- Net worth – The value of the business after deducting liabilities from assets. An invoice discounter may base its facility limit on x times net worth.

An analysis of these figures enables questions to be asked to paint a fuller picture of the company's current and the future situation. Such questions would normally cover the following:

- Sales progress over recent years and months compared to future sales projections in budget and cashflow. This is particularly important because most factoring/discounting fees are based on turnover levels and we have to ensure that the prospect will actually reach the sales targets, otherwise the risk is that we will not make a full recovery through our service fee. (This issue is covered in more detail later under the pricing heading.) Also these trends and projections enable us to calculate the potential investment/funding levels that the prospect will need and evaluate the risk of such investment against the whole picture of 'prospect security'.

- Changes in working capital requirements – linking the cashflow to the projection of funds to be realized from the facilities from the financier.

  At this stage we should consider some of the limitations that may be placed on funding provided via debtor finance. This is a complex area that we will revisit later. At this stage it is necessary to briefly mention three potential problem areas that may reduce ultimate funding levels. In assessing risk the financier builds these issues into its risk evaluations.

- The age of the debtors. Finance is normally advanced for 90/120 days, after which time the finance will be disapproved (withdrawn). If the prospect has an aged debtors ledger with high overdues this will reduce the funding available.

- The creditworthiness of debtors. Depending on the type of facility being discussed the financier would place credit funding limits on all debtors. A prospect with a debtor base of poorly rated uncreditworthy debtors will not receive high levels of funding against such debtors. This is particularly true if the facility sought is a non-recourse product.

- A concentration situation exists, i.e. there is a prime debtor. Ideally a financier prefers a good spread of debtors, so that the failure of one debtor would neither damage the prospect company nor the debtor security of the financier. We have already seen that factors/discounters normally advance between 70%-80% against approved debts. In theory this leaves a margin of safety of 20%-30% to protect against debtor/client failure. If the ledger includes one or two very large debtors, whose failure by themselves would undermine the financier's security and endanger the prospect's survival, the factor/discounter will normally place a funding limit on that/those debtors. This may reduce the total funding available to the prospect.

- This evaluation may lead to questions about the role of other lenders in supporting the prospect's cashflow needs. In particular the role of its bankers and its view of overdraft funding. It is quite common for banks to withdraw or substantially reduce overdraft levels when a company assigns its debts and effectively takes them out of the security held by the bank. However a risk assessment must be made to establish the consequences of such a withdrawal. It would be an unacceptable risk to the financier if the effect of providing funds against the prospect's debtor base was that the overall working capital was less than it was with the overdraft.

We have already seen that 'overtrading' – selling goods quicker than the business can generate the working capital to support the sales – is a problem with traditional banking. The financier is not particularly concerned in seeing potential overtrading trends in the accounts, as the funding it provides is linked directly to sales. More sales = More cash for working capital.

- Debtor assessment questions: from a financial risk viewpoint we are mainly interested in the debtors in three ways:

  - Their age, and any related problems that may prevent or slow down receipt of payment, such as legal actions, disputes, queries etc.

  - How the prospect maintains its sales ledger and runs its credit control. This is particularly important when the facility sought involves the client running its own sales ledger and collections such as discounting.

  - The appearance of debtors that are also creditors. This is the risk of potential set-offs. Debtors will not pay the full amount due against assigned invoices because they wish to deduct the balances owed to them on their creditors' ledger.

- Creditor assessment questions.

  - Ageing of the creditor ledger, including information on any potential legal actions pending or current.

  - Checking the company's latest bank statement against the recently paid creditors. It is not uncommon for companies to try to show a better creditor position by posting payments through the creditors but then not sending them out. From a risk assessment point of view it artificially creates an improved creditor position while maintaining an unrealistic bank overdraft position. This is also checked via the cashbook and bank account reconciliation.

  - Information on the preferential creditors (including the same sort of bank statement review noted in the previous comments to make sure that all cheques have been despatched and/or cleared.

  - Again the financier is concerned about potential contra trading.

  - Retention of title in major supplier terms of trade. Retention of title clauses in supplier terms are designed to retain title in the goods until they have been paid for by the purchaser. From a factoring/discounting perspective this can give problems because the purchaser does not own the goods and if they then assign debts containing goods purchased under retention of title the invoices may not represent good security for the financier. The whole topic of retention of title is covered elsewhere so for the purposes of looking at financial risk it is simply enough to identify whether such a problem exists.

'Common Sense' Financial Assessment

The financial information obtained from the various sources covered above can only provide the risk assessor with a range of questions to be asked. It is the application of experience and a commonsense attitude towards business funding and cash requirements, which will enable the risk assessor to establish the true position. For example, we can take the previous headings and explore what questions the risk assessor would likely want to cover. For each area the owners/directors of the prospect should have answers that stand the test of examination.

The ratios
A review of the ratios will illustrate past efficiency, profitability and liquidity situations. The assessor must be satisfied that the prospect's present position and the projected position (post acceptance) seem reasonable alongside the explanations given by the prospect's owners/directors. For example if the company has been making increasing losses over the past few years, but is predicting that it will move into profit after factoring/discounting commences, it would be reasonable to question why this will occur. Factoring and discounting can certainly assist a company to grow but will not necessarily help profitability.

Sales progress
Again factoring/discounting will not of itself improve sales levels. A projected increase in sales must be capable of justification by the company. Detailed questions concerning where the increased sales are to come from and a review of related increased costs will be asked.

High-Involvement
It may be possible to finance high debtor concentration accounts. But the assessor must be satisfied on a number of key issues, before a decision is made.

- The creditworthiness of the debtor
- The trading relationship between prospect and debtor
- The debtor's attitude towards factoring/discounting (if disclosed facilities)
- The mechanisms that can be used to verify the debt and the willingness of the debtor to cooperate (this can be particularly difficult if not impossible in confidential facilities)
- The impact of a loss of this debtor on the prospects business – would the business survive?

Cashflow needs
Are the cashflow needs as projected going to be met by the funding available from the financier and other lenders? Does the cashflow elements appear in line with other known information, i.e. sales projections, capital expenditure, general expenses and so forth?

Debtor ageing
Can reasons be provided for long-term debt? Will the same trends continue after factoring/discounting commences? If not what will make the trend different? Full service factoring can make a difference to collection performance but relies a lot on client cooperation in areas such as problem and dispute resolution. Will such support be readily available?

Sales ledger   What accounting package is being used? Are audit trails available? These can be very useful to follow recent history through the sales ledger. Poorly maintained sales ledgers can suggest that the prospect is not fully in control of invoicing, cash postings and ledger maintenance. In a discounting facility this can be a real problem, undermining security and presenting unacceptable risk levels. What actions are the prospects gong to take to overcome these problems and do these seem both reasonable and likely to resolve the problems? It is true to observe that, generally, messy ledgers stay messy.

Bank statement   Is any cash arriving from sources other than sales income or any payments out other than to known creditors? Are there any problems with reconciliations? Is there any evidence of other bank accounts? Do the bank figures tie in with cashflow forecasts and management accounts figures?

Preferential   A review of the latest VAT return should confirm that the invoicing in the management accounts is correct, and comparing this to bank statement should establish if the account has been paid.

Contra trading   Establish which are the contra accounts, the values normally seen and the current arrangements for payment. With large balances it may be necessary to approach the creditor and obtain formal acceptance that it will not set-off after factoring/discounting commences. Refusal to give such an undertaking may exclude the debtor from being funded.

Business Plan

Ideally the prospect will have a prepared business plan, although in practice this is most unlikely in the case of smaller companies. Even without a formal business plan document the risk assessor will need to establish that the business is working to a plan. The new business personnel will, within their new business report, have made specific comments on business planning issues. These should cover such areas as:

Marketing and sales – where the sales are going to come from and how they intend to obtain the customers. Possible breakdown of product/services/markets etc.

Capital expenditure – to be spent on what? And what will the new equipment etc. do for the company? How will it be financed? (Working capital finance should not be used for capital purchases.)

Staffing – Numbers, skills, experience – do these match the needs of the company into the planning period or what steps are being taken to recruit/train/develop?

Financial – Once again, the assessor will review this against the other information, confirming that all the information and figures mesh together with no unanswered questions or figures that do not match.

Management Quality

This is a vital area for assessment. But here the assessment is almost totally dependent on subjective feedback from those who have met the prospect's management – the new business staff/surveyors etc.

Assessment must be made on the ability (technical and attitude) of the prospect's management to run the company and achieve its objectives in line with its plans. Weaknesses in terms of limited skills and missing experience must be identified and considered within the full picture.

Factoring and discounting are long-term relationships with the success of the relationship depending on the how well the prospect's staff and the financier's staff can work together. At the assessment stage this can be judged only through personal feelings linked to the experience of how helpful and cooperative the prospect's management is in providing information and answers to questions.

A word of caution is necessary – fraudsters are always helpful, cooperative and believable. The risk assessor must balance the personal feeling issues against the factually substantiated information, with the balance normally going in favour of provable facts.

Customer Failure

A review of the bad debt history and of the credit notes issued over the previous 12 months will reveal the reasons. These can range from the prospect company having:

- Dealt with poor credit risks – this would make the prospect unacceptable for a non-recourse facility.

- Sold to anyone who will buy, because the company cannot find a good market for its product/services. This leads to potential problems for the financier in that the prospect will almost certainly suffer from lack of profitability, resulting in more cash pressures over the short/medium term and could lead to fraudulent action against the financier.

- Poor products/services resulting in excessive claims and resulting debt write off or credits. The very basis of factoring and discounting is the purchase of invoices and the reliance on these invoices for prime security of advances. Claims of any nature reduce the value of this security and excessive claims can completely undermine the whole security of the financier.

Debt Evaluation

Because debtors represent the prime security in a factoring/discounting facility it is vital that a full risk assessment of the debtor base is undertaken. The financier is concerned with a number of issues in addition to those reviewed earlier (bad debts, sales levels, ageing, high involvement). The financier must therefore evaluate the debtor base to establish if, when purchased, it represents full value for the purchase price and offers a margin of safety.

Specific debt risk assessment would cover:

- The nature of the debts and how they arose.

  - Contracts to supply are evaluated to ensure that they contain no legal impediment to factoring/discounting (ban on assignment).

  - Potential risk arising from contractual terms, including possible liquidated damages claims.

  - If there are written orders and the purchase terms and conditions they contain, an evaluation of the impact these may have on financier.

  - Inter-company trading with subsidiaries or companies controlled by those closely involved with the management/running of the prospect. Such debts are impossible to verify/control and are thus normally excluded from factoring/discounting agreements.

- The paper trail covering the debts. From customer enquiry, through quotation, acceptance, delivery and payment, the financier must assess any potential problem issue that might delay or prevent future payments.

- The debt mix is also evaluated to establish:

  - Existing or potential concentrations. The risk assessor must assess the debtor base over the whole business cycle of the prospect's business. It may be that when the debtor base is being assessed the prospect is at its seasonal low point for sales to a major customer. When this customer starts to place orders again as its busy season approaches, a high-involvement situation could easily be created. If the financier is then unhappy and restricts finance on this debtor account, this could give the client problems and possibly result in some sort of fraudulent action against the financier to make up for, in their minds, lost finance.

  - The type of work being carried out by the prospect and the value percentages each different type of work represents. For example, a company may supply a product and also offer a service contract to maintain it. The financier would almost certainly exclude the service contract from the agreement, particularly if it was pre-invoiced, i.e. 12 months service contract covering the next year, because if the service was not completed, perhaps because the client had ceased to trade, the debtor would not pay the debt.

  - If the percentage of such 'non-factorable' debt was substantial this would perhaps make the level of finance that could be generated via the factoring/discounting facility less than was actually needed, which could lead to potential actions by the client that would undermine the financier's security.

Every business is different and the debtor base of each prospect needs very careful assessment to ensure that unnecessary risks are not taken by financier.

Initial Debtor Assessment

In addition to the overall debt evaluation, individual debtors are also assessed.

- Credit checks via an agency or the financier's own internal records of having dealt with that debtor via another client.

- References are generally obtained (in disclosed facilities) from the main debtors (normally the largest ten) to establish their views on the prospect but also to establish that there are not other problems such a potential ban-on-assignment. A ban-on-assignment is normally seen on copies of purchase orders which are checked as part of the debt assessment. The purposes of such bans vary, they may be included in order to stop a supplier sub-contracting work to a third party or may have been deliberately put into the conditions of purchase to stop a financier from gaining good title to the debt. The debtor may do this because:

  - the debtor does not want to be chased by an organization that is more professional in debt collection than the supplier

  - the debtor does not want to risk having to pay the factor again if it pays the supplier in error, which can lead to

  - placing a ban-on-assignment within the standard purchase terms as a direct consequence of this 'bad experience' of factoring/discounting.

Pre-take-on verifications may also be undertaken to establish the current position of the debts, i.e. if they actually exist and will be paid. (Verification will be looked at in more detail later.)

Terms and Conditions

Factoring/discounting facilities are designed with an ideal client in mind. This 'ideal' client sells product/service to other businesses on simple trading terms, normally 30 or 60 days. Any other terms need to be reviewed to establish if they present additional risk. Such terms may include

- Extended payment timescales (90 days plus)
- Offering special discounts for early settlement
- Terms and conditions built in by the purchaser to the purchase orders

  - retrospective discounts to be claimed back once certain turnover levels have been achieved

  - advertising levies that can be invoked by purchaser

Each of these and others can reduce the value of the purchased debt.

  - Supply contract terms and conditions, in particular just in time (JIT) contracts. An overall contract that covers a 12-month supply with each individual supply being separately ordered. If the client were to fail, the overall JIT contract would be invoked and potentially liquidated damages could be claimed against debts outstanding to the financier.

The Involvement of Other Lenders

Factoring/discounting is often taken as one element of a financial package for a company. Other involvement may vary from, on the simplest level, the involvement of the prospect's bank providing overdraft facilities through to complete packages involving stock financing, mortgages, leasing etc. as part of a 'packaged' finance package.

When assessing the risk we need to consider the factoring/discounting facility against the background of these other lenders. The risks we shall examine include

- The continuing role of the bankers. It will not assist the prospect if the bank completely takes all the funds released from factoring/discounting, leaving the prospect with little if any extra cash.

- The nature of charges and other securities taken by other lenders and the impact these have on the assignability of debts.

- The control to be exercised over the prospect company by other investors who may take equity shareholdings as part of their financial package; this may involve linking them into any legal agreements

Risk Assessment Summary

Overall the assessment of new client risk must continually return to the same three simple issues, that of trying to identify if the prospective client is

- a 'good' well-run company
- selling 'good' products and services to
- 'good', well-rated debtors who pay debts as they fall due.

The factor/invoice discounter recognizes that the risk assessment is carried out under difficult assessment circumstances. These include:

- a large dependency on the prospect company to provide accurate information.
- the ability of new business/survey staff to gain truthful answers to all the questions.
- in a relatively short time to assess the character of the owner/manager's of the prospect.
- the competition in the marketplace also places an additional problem in front of the risk assessor/underwriter – to accept marginal deals and run the risk of losing money through a range of potential problems (fraud through to ineptitude) – or to turn down business and loose what could be valuable income streams.

Factoring and discounting are risk businesses, and it is only through taking risks and managing them successfully that the industry continues to flourish. To assist with risk management, factors and discounters enter into legal agreements designed to provide a safety net to the risk assessment process.

Having assessed the risks and agreed the terms of the facility, the financier must now complete the client take-on process. We shall look at this in detail in the next section.

2.11 Taking on a Client

Definition: Take-on is the process by which the collateral is taken up by the financier and the agreement comes into effect.

The process of taking on a client is really the starting point of the whole relationship. The process lays down the ground rules that will bring the parties to the financier's agreement together in a relationship which it is hoped will last for a long time and bring benefits to both parties. The period immediately following the take-on itself is also important because there can be initial 'teething' troubles that need, from both parties' view, to be quickly and satisfactorily resolved to enable the facility to work effectively.

The financier normally does the 'take-on' either by a visit to the new client's premises or on the financier's premises. The take-on includes certain key technical or procedural stages as well as the relationship issues. These include:

- completion and possible additional explanation of the legal documentation, unless already completed.

- review of the roles/obligations of each party, financier and client.

- the procedural and day-to-day administration process activities.

- control processes.

- relationship issues.

This is probably the first time that the financier's operational staff, who will be running the account on a day-to-day basis, have had the opportunity to talk to the client and actually see the nature of the collateral they will be taking on. At this stage it may be that unforeseen information or problems come to light, which may have an impact on the running or even viability of the facility.

Despite previous sales and survey activity it is not until the moment comes to take-on the client that the financier actually knows exactly what it is being offered.

In terms of debts, the debtor base may have changed

- new contractual arrangements could have been entered into

- contra situations may be discovered

- debtor values may be substantially different from those anticipated

- there may be ban-on assignment difficulties

- or there may be an unforeseen operational problem

In terms of stock

- the mix of stock (raw material, work in progress, finished goods) may have altered to such an extent that financing is impossible or will not enable the release of the level of finance required by the client

- the actual stock may not be that which the financier expected – changes in volumes, type of stock etc.

- or retention of title problems could be discovered

The legal agreements may have to be amended or the client may simply need reassurance as to how the facility will be run and the level of finance that will be released.

From this perspective the take-on can be viewed equally as a sales and administrative activity.

Legal Documentation

At take-on stage it is usual that the client will have already seen all the legal documentation and may already have queried areas with the new business manager. Indeed with the consequences of certain legal cases (*Barclays Bank v. Mrs O'Brien* and *Royal Bank of Scotland v. Mrs Etteridge*) concerning the level of understanding of what they (in particular indemnifiers) will be signing, many financiers suggest that independent legal advice is taken prior to signing agreements and related documents. However, it is still not uncommon for clients to query at this stage what certain aspects of the documents mean in practical terms.

Obligations of the Parties

The reading of a typical financier agreement appears to place all the obligations on the client and virtually none on the financier. In fact the financier agreements are written in such a way to protect the financier in case of default or fraud by the client. Consequently, the agreements can appear unduly harsh from a client's point of view. So one of the most important take-on activities, after possibly explaining the agreement, is to place the agreement and the obligations of its parties into practical terms.

Often clients require reassurance on how the operation of the agreement will be carried out.

The financier overcomes these problems by explaining that the agreement is effectively a back-up that is used only if the basic rules of the agreement are broken. The client is usually, at least partly, reassured by the fact that the legal agreements are standard (within each financier) and as such many thousands of companies have signed them and have long successful relationships with the financier.

This 'continual selling' of the agreement is a common element of many take-ons. It may seem that these comments suggest some underhanded business activity on behalf of the financier. On the contrary the financier wants the relationships with their clients to succeed so in practice go to sometimes enormous lengths to keep clients 'alive' when under the rules of the agreement they could have terminated the agreement. The financier tends to look on their agreements as 'trust' documents. They trust the client and do not live day by day with the strictest interpretation of their agreements. However, if the client commits a major breach, the power of the agreement can be put into effect. Getting this message over to the client during the take-on is a vital activity of the process.

Administration Procedures

There are two main elements to the administration procedures:

1. Collecting the collateral information for uploading on to the financier's computer system.

- This is normally done by obtaining an extract from the client's own computer system – this can be done by taking a copy printout of the collateral, debtors list, stock records etc. plus back-up information, e.g. copy invoices and delivery notes. Or it can be done via direct transmission to the financier's own computer.

- This stage of the process can take some time because most financiers will want to carry out, through contacting debtors, a general verification of the information they have been given, prior to making payments to the client. For instance, it is common for the financier to want to verify at least 60% by value of a ledger prior to making an initial payment.

- A financier taking over stock or other assets may well conduct an audit to confirm the existence of the stock or other asset.

- Away from the face-to-face take-on process there are many behind-the-scenes processes.

   - In disclosed facilities debtors must be advised about the assignment of debt

   - Ledgers must be set up

   - Credit checks and verification must be completed

   - Stock values must be entered

It is important that these processes are conducted quickly and efficiently so that the new client is aware only of a smooth transfer from its management of the collateral to the financier.

2. Explaining, discussing and agreeing the operational procedures for the running of the agreement.

- How information will be passed to and from client/financier, e.g. schedule documents, reconciliations, computer links, etc.

- How payments are requested and sent to the client.

- How the financial records are maintained.

- What information will be given to the client – example reports and operational documents will often be given in an introduction pack.

- Full service factoring. It is normal to discuss and agree with the new client how the credit control activities will be undertaken, the involvement of the client in collections, specific information on key debtors, agreeing statement dates, follow up letters etc.

- Discounting – agreeing the format of the monthly reconciliations.

- Reconfirming the conditions in the agreement in respect of, say, the need to forward delivery notes, proof of deliveries, stock movement forms, or other evidence to support the asset value.

- In fact all issues that relate in any way to the day-to-day operation of the agreement.

Control Process

It is also useful at this time when the focus is on the operational procedures to outline the audit procedures of the financier. Doing so at this stage can overcome the problem of audit being only seen as a 'checking up' or distrusting activity. It can be introduced as part of the administrative process of running and controlling the relationship.

Relationship Issues

We have already seen and will revisit frequently the importance of the relationship between the financier and the client. From this relationship stems the security of the financier and the success of both the client and the financier. The take-on process starts to build the relationship originally developed by the new business manager.

The take-on must recognize that new clients have many fears:

- how will my customers take to the new arrangements?
- how will the financier interpret and use the more draconian clauses of the agreement?
- how much cash will we get?
- am I going to lose control of my asset?
- even, will I lose my job?

The take-on is used to allay all these fears, put faces to the people who will be working closely with the client and generally open all lines of communication between financier and client.

Many financiers arrange to re-visit the client approximately 6/8 weeks after the original take-on. At this time at least one complete month's cycle of information will have flowed through the system, both the client and the financier will have experience of the operation of the facility and the time is appropriate for a review and fine-tuning of the original procedures. Also this gives an extra opportunity to meet face-to-face and continue the relationship-building process.

2.12 Content and Effect of the Legal Agreements

Introductory Note

Reference in this outline to a financier is intended to include a factor or an invoice discounter, reference to factoring is equally intended to include invoice discounting and reference to a guarantor includes an indemnifier unless specified to the contrary. These notes apply only to the law of England and Wales. Some provisions may have to change if the client is incorporated elsewhere, e.g. Scotland or the Irish Republic.

Contractual Basis

As you have learnt from the notes on basic contract law three key elements are essential for there to be a binding contract:

- an offer

- an acceptance

- (a) consideration (usually a promise to pay money) or

  (b) a document signed as a deed.

Factoring, like any other commercial relationship, involves a contract between the financier and its client. In every situation, both parties need to know with precision each other's rights and obligations. Because of the complexity of the transactions and their high value, the legal basis of the entire relationship has to be set out in a master agreement signed by both sides. The master agreement may consist of one long document or be comprised of several documents. If it is in several documents it may include some or all of the following:

- Short agreement including a power of attorney

- Standard conditions

- Quotation letter (sometimes called an 'offer letter')

- Supplementary modules covering situations that apply only to certain clients; e,g,

  - Computerized services

  - Export debts

  - Foreign currency

  - Partnerships

- Procedures manual

- Computer user's guide

Each document normally shows whether it is or is not intended to be a contractual document. For example, some financiers do not want the quotation letter to have any legal effect. Others do.

At the end of these notes there is a copy of a master factoring agreement which deals with all the major issues that you or your client would expect to be covered (except for the terms of any electronic service that may be used).

This is a recourse factoring agreement. We shall go through this and explain the purpose of each section. We shall also show how to turn this document into a non-recourse agreement or into a confidential invoice-discounting agreement.

In day-to-day practice, decisions based on the master agreement often have to be made very quickly. It is particularly important for you to have a full grasp of the content and effect of all the provisions in a factoring agreement. They tell you and your client how each of you must act in any given circumstances, together with the extent of any discretions allowed to you. The agreements explain your relationship with your client.

The basic principle behind both factoring and invoice discounting is that they concern the sale of debts to the financier by the original supplier of goods or services in return for the payment of a purchase price. The transfer is called an 'assignment'. This emphasis on the word 'sale' is important. We must at this early stage distinguish another way of providing funds to the client, namely *lending* against the security of the debt. If a financier were to take debts as security for loans he would need to register a charge at Companies House. Without this registered charge the financier would lose the debts to a receiver or a liquidator in the event of the client becoming insolvent. However you must remember that financiers providing factoring or invoice discounting do not take loans or need to register charges. It is also important that the financier does nothing to contradict his purchase through any communication it has with the client, debtor or any other party. Words such as 'loan', 'interest' or 'security' should never be used. A bank is more likely to lend on the security of book debts. However a purchase of debts has certain advantages:

● A financier collects purchased debts without appointing a receiver;

● Discount is payable without deduction of tax. Interest on a loan may be payable net of tax to a non-bank lender.

The Schedule of Variable Items

Because the deal with each client is individually negotiated there are certain provisions that may change from client to client and/or product to product. To avoid having to re-type the main body of text in the agreement for each client these variables are listed in a schedule (sometimes called the 'particulars') and the details inserted once the deal has been structured with the client. It is helpful if these are cross-referred to where they occur in the text. The more important details from the model agreement's schedule include:

Item No.	Heading
1.	Details of client
3.	Debtors covered by agreement
4.	Discounting charge
5.	Prepayment percentage
6.	Administration charge
7.	Additional administration charge
10.	Notices to debtors
11.	Recourse period for unapproved debts
14.	Funding limit

15.   Concentration percentage

16.   Special conditions

We shall deal with their effect when studying the main text of the model agreement.

Overview of Master Agreements

Before dealing with specific issues, you will find it helpful to understand the broad framework of the debt purchase arrangements set out in a master agreement:

● The parties are identified

● Technical words and phrases are explained

● The ownership of all present and future debts of the client is transferred to the financier (lawyers tend to call such transfer an 'assignment')

● The calculation of the purchase price is explained

● The calculations of the discounting charge, the financier's administration and other charges are explained

● When the purchase price is to be paid to the client, including prepayments, once the debt has been notified to the financier

● Certain guarantees are given by the client as to its present position, together with promises as to its future conduct, including the handling of disputes

● The client gives guarantees regarding its present and future debts (often called 'warranties')

● How the financier gets back the prepayment of the purchase price if the debt is not paid before the end of a set period or the debtor becomes insolvent. This is known as 'recourse' and the agreement is often called a 'recourse agreement'

● In a 'non-recourse agreement' the prepayment is not claimed back except for a breach of the agreement. The balance of the purchase price of an approved debt is paid upon the insolvency of the debtor. Some financiers may even pay the purchase price of an uncollected approved debt without such insolvency provided a substantial length of time has passed, e.g. 120 days past the due date for payment

● Certain accounting issues are explained , including the treatment of VAT on bad debts. These are designed to emphasize that the facility is based on the purchase of debts and is not a cash loan by the financier secured against the financier's debts. If it were a secured loan it would have to be registered at Companies House as a charge.

● The right of the financier to contact customers of the client is explained

● The financier's right of access to the client's records is emphasized

● The financier must have the sole right to collect debts

- However the financier may need to act in the client's name and this right is given by the power of attorney in the agreement

- Special provisions for partnership and sole trader clients are explained

- It is vital to know how and when the agreement can be ended

- The financier's rights if the agreement is ended or if the financier has the right to end the agreement but does not do so are clearly set out

- How to give formal notices (e.g. to end the agreement)

- Which law applies

When considering an agreement for the first time each party may concentrate on different issues. We list some of these below. We refer to clauses in the attached model agreement (*see document A annexed to these notes*) to show where the matters are referred to.

What Does the Client Want to See?

- What amounts does he get paid? *(clause 5(1) and 5(3))*

- When does he get paid? *(clauses 5(2) and 5(3))*

- What will the financier's services cost? *(section 6)*

What Does the Financier Consider Important?

- What debts does this agreement cover? *(clause 4(1))*

- Is the purchase price paid on a recourse or non-recourse basis? *(clause 10(1)(i))*

- Is it a confidential invoice-discounting agreement or factoring agreement? *(clause 8.2(v))*

- What fees and charges will be paid by the client, including the discounting period? *(section 6, clause 5(a) and 'Collection Date' in the Schedule)*

- What warranties and undertakings does the client give, particularly as to the validity of the debt and the non-banking of receipts? *(section 8)*

- When can the agreement be terminated? *(clauses 20(1) and 20(2))*

- What are the consequences of a termination event even if the financier chooses not to end the relationship? *(clauses 20(3), 14(2) and 14(3))*

Parties (Clause 1)

Client

It is vital to know with precision who is the client. His details are then inserted in the schedule *(see paragraph 1 of the Schedule)*. Failure to be precise (e.g. wrongly spelling the client's name) may make the agreement unenforceable. To make identification easier most financiers insert the following:

- the jurisdiction where a company is incorporated – 'place of registration'
- its registered number at the Companies Registry

Remember that in the British Isles companies can be incorporated in any of:

- England
- Scotland
- Northern Ireland
- Irish Republic
- Isle of Man
- Guernsey
- Jersey

Clause 22 also prohibits the client transferring or granting security over the benefit of the agreement to anyone else – e.g. the client cannot sell or grant its rights to the prepayments to anyone else. The financier wants only to deal with the client (who it knows and with whom it will build up a relationship) and not some third party. With some well-known clearing banks, the financier may waive this restriction and permit the client to grant security over the agreement and its proceeds.

Financier

The factoring company is called 'the financier' throughout the model agreement. This phrase can apply to anyone who is substituted for the factor if, for example, the portfolio of Clients is sold on *(see clause 22)*.

Definitions *(Section 3)*

Many words in the English language are capable of several meanings. A legal agreement demands precision. In a formal document the most important words and phrases are given precise meanings in order to avoid disputes. These definitions appear in Section 3. In the rest of the agreement these words appear with initial capital letters to remind you to refer back to the definitions section for their exact meaning. We sometimes use italics to remind you that a word (other than 'debt' or 'client') has a precise meaning. The following are worth commenting on:

Approved Debt

Debts are approved for prepayments (and, in non-recourse agreements, also for credit protection). You will note that for a debt to retain the status of an approved debt the client must not be in breach of any warranty or undertaking given to the financier. The financier is entitled to establish an *'approval limit'* for each debtor. Debts above this limit are then *unapproved debts* for prepayments (and in non-recourse agreements also for credit protection).

However some non-recourse financiers may have separate criteria for approvals for funding purposes and for credit protection.

Associated Rights

Where a debt is purchased by the financier, there is also transferred all its 'associated rights' *(see clauses 4(1) and 4(2)*. These are both tangible and intangible matters connected with the debt including:

Instruments	e.g. negotiable instruments, bills of exchange, cheques.
Securities	e.g. charges, guarantees, indemnities securing payment.
Benefits of Insurance	e.g. the payout from credit insurance on a bad debt.
Evidence	e.g. proof of delivery or the order.
Rights under the contract of sale	This could include the right to stop goods in transit, the right to claim interest, the right to sue and give a valid discharge for the debt, or to repossess the goods under a reservation of title or goods which are returned. If the client is unable to satisfy its financial obligations to the financier, the financier may wish to sell such goods to reduce the indebtedness.
Transferred Goods	See below.

Associates

It is important to know who are *Associates of the Client*. Debts due by such people or companies are automatically *unapproved debts* (see the client's warranty at *clause 8.1 (v)*). Experience has shown that such *associates* are more likely to engage in fraud and are less likely to comply with any credit terms. Such *associates* are defined by cross-referencing to Section 184 of the Consumer Credit Act which states:

(1) A person is an associate of an individual if that person is the individual's husband or wife, or is a relative, or the husband or wife of a relative, of the individual or of the individual's husband or wife.

(2) A person is an associate of any person with whom he is in partnership, and of the husband or wife or a relative of any individual with whom he is in partnership.

(3) A body corporate is an associate of another body corporate:

(a) if the same person is a controller of both, or a person is a controller of one and persons who are his associates, or he and persons who are his associates, are controllers of the other; or

(b) if a group of two or more persons is a controller of each company, and the groups either consist of the same persons or could be regarded as consisting of the same persons by treating (in one or more cases) a member of either group as replaced by a person of whom he is an associate.

(4) A body corporate is an associate of another person if that person is a controller of it or if that person and persons who are his associates together are controllers of it.

(5) In this section 'relative' means brother, sister, uncle, aunt, nephew, niece, lineal ancestor or lineal descendant, and references to a husband or wife include a former husband or wife and a reputed husband or wife; and for the purposes of this subsection a relationship shall be established as if any illegitimate child, step-child or adopted child of a person had been a child born to him in wedlock.

Agreements of other factoring companies may use a similar definition from either Section 52 of the Companies Act 1989 or Section 435 of the Insolvency Act 1986.

Collection Date

This is the date on which a debt is treated as being collected. For cash it is the date of receipt. For cheques, drafts and bills of exchange, it is when it is 'collected' from the drawer as determined by the financier. This may be several days after the financier's bank has credited it to the financier's account as uncollected effects. This affects the date of payment of the purchase price *(see clause 5(2))* and the stopping of any discount charge on *prepayments (see clause 5(9))*.

Debt

Note that it includes any tax on duty payable under the supply contract. The word can include a part of a debt. Thus, one invoice to a debtor could comprise partly an *approved debt* and partly an *unapproved debt*.

Delivered

The client gives a warranty that the goods have been 'delivered' prior to notifying the financier of the debt. Delivery merely means the despatch of the goods to the debtor or their collection from the client. Accordingly the goods may not have reached the debtor's premises before the prepayment is made to the client, which may make verification difficult.

Event of Default

This is an event affecting the client that entitles the financier instantly to end the agreement (whether or not the financier actually ends the agreement). After such an event, the financier takes steps to protect itself without actually ending the agreement. e.g. by increasing the charges or disapproving debts.

Goods

This agreement equally applies to the provision of services. To save endless repetition about 'goods *and* services' the agreement treats 'goods' as always including 'services'.

Insolvency and Date of Insolvency

Under a non-recourse facility the financier has to pay the purchase price of a credit-approved debt upon a debtor's *insolvency*. It is important to know what procedures are included within this definition.

Purchase Price

As this is a sale and purchase agreement the monies paid by the financier to its client for debts are for their *'purchase price'*. They are not loans. In a recourse agreement it is the amount collected from the debtor. In a non-recourse agreement it is the amount that would be payable by the debtor but for his *insolvency*.

Transferred Goods

You will have noted from the definition of *'associated rights'* that, when a debt is sold to the financier, there is also sold the *'transferred goods'* relating to the debt which includes goods recovered from or returned by the debtor. Where the financier has a shortfall upon the failure of a client it can recoup part or all of the losses by taking possession of and selling the *transferred goods*.

Transfer of Debts *(Section 4)*

You need to know to which debts the agreement applies. These are set out in paragraph 3 of the schedule. In the example given it covers only debtors in the UK (sometimes called 'domestic debtors'). Debtors outside the UK are often called 'export debtors'. All debts, present and future, to which the agreement applies, are intended to come into the ownership of the financier.

Ownership of debts is obtained in two ways:

- all debts coming into existence after the *commencement date*, shown in paragraph 12 of the schedule, become the financier's automatically *(see clause 4(1))*. Other than signing and exchanging the agreement no other action is needed to give ownership of all such debts to the financier; this type of agreement is sometimes called a 'whole turnover' agreement.

- Debts in existence at the *commencement date* are to be offered for sale to the financier *(see clause 4(4))*. Those it wishes to accept (in practice usually all of those offered) are accepted by crediting their value to one of the accounts kept by the financier, often called a 'Debts Purchased Account', a 'Client Account' or a 'Current Account', depending upon the accounting system in use.

Other factoring companies' agreements may provide for acceptance by the inaction of the financier, e.g. failure to serve a notice of rejection. This offer/acceptance device is designed to avoid stamp duty on the transfer value of the debts at commencement. If the agreement had itself transferred these 'take-on' debts in existence at the commencement date, then stamp duty of between 1% to 3% of the value of the debts would be payable, depending on the total value transferred.

As a back-up provision, debts that do not become the property of the financier under the above provisions (sometimes called 'non-vesting debts') are held in trust for the financier *(see clause 4(5))*. If the client becomes *insolvent*, assets held in trust, including such 'non-vesting debts', do not benefit the client (or its liquidator, receiver or other insolvency practitioner administering the client's affairs) but go to the beneficiary of the trust, i.e. the financier. As an additional security over such non-vesting debts many financiers take a specific fixed charge by way of security over them and register it at the Companies Registry. This has the added benefit of alerting any future person wanting to take security over such debts of the financier's prior involvement. This lessens the risk of the financier having a competing interest in the debt, particularly in a confidential facility, such as invoice discounting.

Prepayment *(Section 5)*

Section 5 headed 'Purchase Price and Accounting' contains the most important part of the agreement that the client will want to see. How much and when will it be paid?

The *'purchase price'*, as we have seen from its definition, is the amount collected from the debtor, including duties and VAT, which is credited to the Client Account on its *'collection date'*, i.e. when the financier obtains cleared funds *(clauses 5(1) and 5(2))*. In a non-recourse agreement it would be the amount that would have so collected but for the debtor's insolvency and in some cases protracted default.

However no client wants to wait until the debt is collected for payment of the purchase price. He wants the benefit of a prepayment facility as soon as he notifies the financier of the existence of the debt. This is provided under clause 5(3). The amount available is calculated at the prepayment percentage (set out in paragraph 5 of the schedule), which typically will be in the range of 70% to 80%, subject to:

- a financial limit on all prepayments and other monies payable by the client, in this case called 'the funding limit' *(see clause 5.(5)(i) and paragraph 14 of the schedule)*. Other factoring companies may call it the 'Limit', the 'Funds in Use Limit' or the 'Review Limit'.

- no prepayment being available for any concentration of the debts being owed by a small number of debtors *(see clause 5.5(ii) and paragraph 15 of the schedule)*.

- no prepayments being available while any *insolvency* proceedings against the client are pending or the financier is entitled instantly to end the agreement, even if it does not do so *(see clause 5.4)*.

Prepayments, any balance of the *purchase price* and any monies that the client owes or may owe to the financier are debited to the current account *(see clause 5(6))*.

Discounting Charge *(clause 5(9))*

So what does it cost the client to have the benefit of a prepayment? The financier takes a discount off the purchase price. But because no-one knows when a debt will be paid to the financier, the discount increases for each day's delay. This is called a 'discounting charge' and is calculated at a margin over the base rate of a named bank *(see paragraph 4(a) of the schedule)* (but subject to a minimum charge). It is worked out on the debit balance on the current account and debited to that account at the end of each month *(see clause 5(9))*. You must clearly understand that this is a discount off the purchase price and not interest. Interest is only appropriate to a loan. Nothing in pure factoring or invoice discounting involves the lending of money. The financier merely makes a part payment of the purchase price earlier than the collection of the debt. For this additional advantage to the client the financier takes a discount off the purchase price via the discounting charge.

Administration Charge *(section 6)*

Apart from early payments of the purchase price, the commercial effect of the agreement is for the financier to provide other services, of which the major ones are:

- administering debtor's ledgers

- collection of debts

- issuing court proceedings to enforce payment of debts.

The client has to pay an administration charge for these services. Other financiers may call it a 'service fee' or a 'factoring fee'. This is explained in section 6 of the agreement. Top Factors administration charge is a percentage of the total value of the debt, including VAT, before any discounts due to the debtor. It is payable upon notification or offer of the debt to the financier. The administration charge percentage is set out in paragraph 6 of the schedule and is also subject to a minimum monthly fee.

If the debt is not collected by the end of the third month after the month date of the debt, a monthly 'additional administration charge' becomes payable. It is calculated at the percentage shown in the schedule of the unpaid amount. Some financiers call this a 'refactoring charge'. Again, it is calculated as a percentage of the notified value of the debt. The percentage appears in paragraph 7 of the schedule. If one of the serious matters listed in clause 20(2) occurs, the financier is entitled immediately to end the agreement. If the financier does not exercise its right to end the agreement, it may continue it under sometimes riskier circumstances. As recompense for the enhanced risks, the administration charge can, in this agreement, rise by 5% of debts existing at the date of the event giving rise to the termination right and all debts thereafter. The discounting charge also rises by 1% *(see clauses 14(6) and 14(3))*.

Charges to the client can be made for:

- payment otherwise than by cheque (e.g. BACS, CHAPS)

- dishonoured cheque charges

- services outside scope of agreement or for variation to the agreement *(see clauses 6(3) to 6(5))*.

If court proceedings are needed, these are usually in the financier's name. The financier passes the costs to the client to pay, including any awarded against the financier (e.g. if it loses the case or any procedural step prior to trial) and has costs awarded against it *(see clause 8(2)(vii)*.

Warranties and Undertakings *(Section 8)*

These are matters that the financier considers of vital importance. While the relationship continues the financier relies on the happening of the background matters set out in Section 8. A warranty is a guarantee by the client. An undertaking is a promise to do something.

Clause 8(1) contains the warranties, including that:

- the client owns the debts with no third party rights attaching to the debts or the *goods* sold

- the client is not technically *insolvent* at the date of the agreement.

Although there are other undertakings elsewhere in the agreement, clause 8(2) attempts to bring together some of the more important which include obligations on the client to:

- to notify the financier promptly when a debt comes into existence

- not to contract with debt payment terms more liberal than those stated in the schedule *(see paragraph 9(a) of the schedule)*

- not to create debts other than in a currency specified in paragraph 9(c) of the schedule (in the example given, this is sterling, although increasingly financiers have to accept debts in euros from multinational clients and in US dollars for clients in the UK offshore oil industry)

- to ensure that no set-off or dispute is raised against a debt

- to give written notice to debtors of assignment of the debt (how this is done is set out in paragraph 10 of the schedule)

- not to finance the debt elsewhere or grant security over it to a third party.

Breach of these undertakings may come to light only after the *insolvency* of the client. However, to the extent that such breach causes loss to the financier, this should be claimable from any guarantor.

Disputes with Debtors *(Section 9)*

A financier wants 'clean' debts that can easily be collected. Disputes dilute the value of the debts purchased by the financier and put at risk the funds in use paid to the client by way of prepayments. Although the client can be forced to buy back disputed debts under the recourse provisions in section 10, this is of little help if the sheer volume of such disputes makes too great a demand on the client's financial ability to pay back funds in use to the financier. To help to avoid such a problem, there must be a well set out disputes procedure. This appears in section 9 of the agreement as follows:

- the client must tell the financier in writing of any disputes and do its best to resolve them

- the financier can also resolve the dispute directly, even if this reduces the value of the debt

- credit notes may need the financier's prior consent.

A disputed debt is normally subject to *recourse* to the client, i.e. the client has to buy it back *(under clause 10(i)(iv))*. However, this could work unfairly against the client where the so-called 'dispute' is merely an attempt by the debtor to get additional time to pay. Accordingly *recourse* is delayed until the earlier of 60 days from the financier learning of the dispute or 90 days from its due date for payment, provided that the dispute is resolved in favour of the supplier *(see clause 9(3))*.

Recourse (Section 10)

'Recourse' is a defined word. From the definitions *(at section 3)* you can see that the financier has a right to insist that the client buys an uncollected debt back at the amount at which it was first notified to the financier. When reading some other company's factoring agreements, be careful of the word 'recourse'. It sometimes means merely the redesignation of an approved debt (approved for funding or credit protection) as an unapproved debt (i.e. with no benefits) but without any requirement on the client to buy back the debt. Such agreements may separately refer to 'repurchase arrangements' or similar terminology.

So what debts can be subject to *recourse* under this agreement? They are:

1. *'Unapproved debts'*. From the definitions you will see that these are debts that are not *'approved debts'*. This is not very helpful! The way out of this conceptual maze is to look at the definition of an *'approved debt'* in clause 3. The result is that a debt will be an *unapproved debt* if:

    (i) it is above an *'approval limit'* (i.e. a limit established by the financier for that *debtor)*; or

    (ii) if the client is in breach of any warranty or undertaking in the agreement relating to the debt; or

    (iii) it is within any class specified in paragraph 2(a) of the schedule.

    Category (iii) is important. Because this is a full recourse agreement the schedule makes *all debts* unapproved at all times (other than for prepayment purposes). If the agreement is to be on a non-recourse basis then paragraph 2(a) will say 'none';

2. debts solely comprising discount, solely wrongly claimed or deducted;

3. debts where debtors claim that they cannot pay because legal restraints (other than *insolvency)* or government action (sometimes called a 'force majeure event');

4. disputed debts (except those subject to a continuing dispute resolution procedure under section 9 above)

You will see from clause 10(I)(a) to (c) that *recourse* in respect of such debts happens on the earliest of:

(a) 60 days after notice from the financier *(see paragraph 11(a) of the schedule)*.

(b) at the end of the third month after the month in which the invoice is due for payment *(see paragraph 11(b) of the schedule)*, i.e. all invoices dated in January which are still uncollected at the end of April are automatically recoursed.

(c) the debtor's *insolvency*.

The recourse price in practice is usually recovered by the financier debiting it to the *current account* which then, for a while, will reduce the client's availability for prepayments from new debts notified.

The above explains how routine *recourse* operates while the financier's relationship with its client is working well. However, if the agreement is terminated upon three months notice by either party *(see clause 20(I))* or is instantly terminated *(see clause 20(2))* because of a serious event listed under that clause (called an 'event of default') or could be so terminated (but is not), then clause 20(3) becomes operative. All debts become *unapproved debts*. Although the word 'recourse' is not used, the effect is the same. The client has to buy the debts back at their notified value. Ownership does not pass until the repurchase prices of all debts have been paid to the financier *(see clause 20(3)(ii))*.

If the financier does not terminate the agreement following an event of default then any newly created debts still come into the ownership of the financier. This adds to the value of the ledger to be collected from which the financier can recoup any prepayments paid for debts. In addition Top Factors can increase the discount and service charges *(see clauses 14(2) and 14(3))*.

Set-off – *Clause 19(2)*

Whenever the financier owes monies to the client (e.g. following collection of the debt) and the client at the same time owes monies to the financier (e.g. for the repurchase price of a recoursed debt), the financier can set the one off against the other, leaving the client only entitled to the balance. Clause 10(2) emphasizes that the client's indebtedness to be set-off can include future amounts, and amounts due under other relationships, e.g. if the financier has entered into an obligation on behalf of the client which the client has guaranteed, or if the client is a debtor to the financier because the client has bought goods from another client of the financier.

However, the client has to pay all monies in full to the financier without any set-off *(see clause 10(3))*. This is to avoid a client, faced with a massive requirement to pay for recoursed debts, making a spurious claim for damages, for some imagined mismanagement in the collection of the debts, and deducting the value of the claimed damages by way of set-off. It must pay all monies due to the financier in full and only then raise the set-off separately.

Credit Balances (Clause 13)

Sometimes a credit balance appears on debtor's ledger. The reasons for this can be numerous, e.g.

- double payment for one invoice
- payment for an invoice that has not been sent to the financier
- a credit note issued which is larger than the invoices notified to the financier.

If a client becomes insolvent, liquidators have been known to make financial claims on the financier for those credits. This places the financier in a difficult position. Some credits may be a liability of the financier to repay to the debtor, some may not. The legal position on many claims is complex and untested. In order to resolve the legal position a great deal of the financier's time may be involved. To avoid such disputes, by clause 13 of the model agreement, the client agrees that it has no right to such credits. This provision should be binding on a liquidator or insolvency practitioner appointed in relation to the client.

Collection of Debts (Section 14)

One of the most important rights that a financier needs is to be able to collect debts in its own name. This right comes automatically by general law as a result of giving notice of assignment to the debtor. It is reinforced by clause 14(1) which gives the financier total discretion as to how and when to issue, defend or compromise any legal proceedings relating to a debt. If the financier wants to sue in the client's name, it can do so under the power of attorney in clause 16. Where the facility is fully disclosed the client's name in practice is rarely needed except where the debtor denies that the debt was ever assigned to the financier. We have already noted that the client is responsible for all legal costs involved.

Client's Records (Section 15)

Clause 15(1) is one of the potentially most dramatic clauses when enforced. If the client is *insolvent* or debtors return goods relating to factored debts (perhaps because the goods were sold, in breach of the client's warranty to the financier, on a sale or return basis) or the client has banked debtor's remittances, then contracts, delivery notes or copies of the client's bank statements may be needed to resolve such disputes. The financier can enter the client's premises, remove the client's records and bank statements, take away any returned goods (in order to sell them as *transferred goods*) or download the client's computer records.

The financier will want to know about its client's financial position. Clause 15(2) of the agreement obliges the client to send in monthly financial statements and annual audited accounts.

The law implies on the financier a duty of confidentiality about its client's affairs. However the financier may be requested to swop information with the client's bank. The client (*under clause 15(3))* expressly permits the financier to disclose such information to the client's bank and also confirms that it has authorized its bank to disclose information to the financier. This can be useful if the financier suspects (but needs proof) that cheques are being paid into the client's bank account rather than being handed over to the financier for collection.

Power of Attorney *(Section 16)*

A power of attorney is the right given to the financier to use the client's name and sign documents on the client's behalf. This power is given irrevocably as security for the performance of the client's obligations under the agreement or to debtors. This means that the *insolvency* of the client does not render it unenforceable. Other purposes are for perfecting the financier's ownership of debts or *associated rights,* e.g. by drawing up formal documentation and signing it for the client. The financier and its officers can also in turn appoint or remove substitute attorneys. This can be useful if an overseas lawyer requires to be appointed with a power of attorney to issue collection proceedings.

Apart from the financier being appointed as the client's attorney each of the financier's directors, its company secretary, its general manager and its officers are also appointed to act as attorneys. 'Officer' is a very wide term and in practice includes any manager or senior executive.

Approval Limits *(Section 17)*

This is the value specified by the financier on a debtor-by-debtor basis to determine which debts are *approved debts* (see definition of *'approved debt'* and *'approval limit'*). As you have seen from clause 5.3 of the agreement, it is only against *approved debts* that a prepayment can be made.

Approval limits are established, varied or cancelled entirely at the financier's discretion. So what happens if there is a limit, the financier learns of adverse credit information about a debtor and cancels the approval limit before the client has notified the financier of a debt which would otherwise have been approved? Will the client be in a position where it can get a prepayment for what is by then an *unapproved debt*? The answer is yes, provided that the goods have been *delivered* or the services rendered before receipt by the client of notice of reduction or cancellation of the approval limit for that customer. Obviously undelivered goods or work in progress for an existing *supply contract* will not turn into an approved debt if there is a withdrawal or reduction in the *approval limit* for the customer before they are *delivered*.

Partnership and Sole Trader Clients *(Section 19)*

Most of the agreement applies equally to clients that are companies, sole traders or partnerships. However, certain extra administrative provisions have to be made for partnerships and sole traders, which are set out here. Examples include:

- the financier's ability to settle with one partner without affecting its claims against the remaining partners

- a demand by one partner (e.g. for a prepayment) can be treated as being binding on all the partners even if not signed by them all

- an undertaking to cooperate in registering this agreement at the Bills of Sale Registry. (See later in this section.)

Commencement and Termination *(Clause 20)*

Each side will want to know when the relationship starts and how and when it can be finished. The start is usually straightforward, being in this case the date specified in the schedule.

Ending an agreement is by:

- a period of notice from one party to the other (often of three months) or

- instantly by the financier if something seriously detrimental occurs (an 'event of default'). This is a phrase often used in commercial agreements, although some factoring agreements call them 'Termination Events'. Top Factors have chosen not to designate them.

Termination with a Period of Notice *(Clause 20(1))*

You should note the strict requirements imposed on the parties under this agreement in giving notice; i.e.

- a minimum of 3 months written notice

- only to expire on the commencement date or any anniversary of it.

If the client wants to go earlier, this potentially could give rise to a claim by the financier for compensation, usually settled by payment of a negotiated early termination fee. In the first year, the financier has to recover its start-up costs through its income stream and such compensation could be substantial.

Events of Default *(Clause 20(2))*

The rights of instant termination by the financier in clause 20(2) break down into:

- those associated with *insolvency*, e.g. (i), (ii), (iii)

- those associated with adverse financial circumstances, e.g. (iv), (viii), (ix)

- those that could adversely affect the basis on which the financier entered into the relationship, e.g. (v), (vi), (x), (xi), (xii)

- breach by the client of the agreement, e.g. (viii).

The most common grounds for the financier terminating an agreement are:

- insolvency

- breach of the agreement by either:

    (a) notifying non-existent debts (a breach of the warranties in *clauses 8(1)(iii) and 8(2)(i)*; or

    (b) banking monies received into the client's own bank account and failing to tell the financier (a breach of the undertaking at *clause 8(2)(vi))*

- retirement from the business of a key guarantor who wants to withdraw his guarantee and is unable to replace it with another guarantor of similar worth (or his insolvency or death) *(see clause 20(2)(x))*.

As we explain below, it is rarely wise for the financier to terminate an agreement.

Effect of Termination

You will have noted that an event of default without an actual termination by the financier puts the financier in a very powerful position because of clause 5(4). The financier continues to obtain ownership of all debts newly created thereafter, but can if it wishes exercise total recourse by:

- withholding prepayments due *(see clause 5(4))*

- demanding back all prepayments made against debts at that time unrecovered *(see clause 5(4))*.

The financier still has to collect the debts and hand over the proceeds (once the above prepayments have been repaid). Usually the mere threat to invoke this clause is sufficient for the client to mend its ways, e.g. it he has been diverting collection remittances away from the financier.

You must be certain of the financier's rights upon termination or his further rights following an *event of default*. They can vary from financier to financier. Clause 20(3) sets out Top Factors' rights:

(i) all *approved debts* become *unapproved debts*; upon a debt becoming an *unapproved debt* then clause 10(1) of the recourse procedure for repurchase normally comes into effect;

(ii) however to avoid the delays and notices needed matters are speeded up by sub-clause 20(3)(ii); this means that the client has to repurchase the outstanding debts at their notified value, with the usual requirement that all have to be paid for before any of them again belong to the client;

(iii) the client has to pay any debit balance on the current account to the financier.

The effect of clause 20(4) is that the financier has a continuing obligation to collect debts until the repurchase price is paid and all debts become revested in the client. In turn, the financier continues to rely on the client's indemnities as to legal costs of litigation and its discounting charge.

To avoid lengthy arguments as to the amounts needed to be paid by a client, clause 20(5) states that a certificate by a director or the company secretary of the financier will be conclusive evidence of the amount due. This will be upheld by the court unless there is an obvious error, e.g. the figures in the certificate do not balance. A similar clause appears in guarantees and saves considerable time in enforcing them through the courts.

Exclusion of Other Terms (Clause 21(1))

To avoid any suggestion by a client that it entered into the factoring agreement because of some statement by a new business executive or some misunderstood letter or advertisement, it is essential to state that only the matters set out in this written document affect the relationship. This means that Top Factors do not intend to rely on any 'letter of offer'.

Giving Notices (Section 23)

Probably the most important notices from a financier to its client will be to terminate the agreement, or to warn the client of unacceptable breaches. These must be sent out correctly. Clause 23(2) sets out that if the notice is given by the financier and is required to be in writing then it must be given by post to the client's address in the agreement or to such other business address as the financier selects. If it is not required to be in writing (e.g. variation of an *approval limit* under clause 17(1)) then in practice it can be given by telephone or fax.

You should note that more stringent requirements are imposed on the client for giving notices to the financier. The most likely is a notice to terminate the agreement. It must be written and sent by recorded delivery or registered post to the office of the financier registered at Companies House or an alternative address designated by the financier for the purpose of receiving notices.

Applicable Law (Clause 24)

It is important to know which law applies to the agreement. In this case, it is English law. For ease of administration, the client accepts that English courts can hear any proceedings brought in respect of it. If the financier is established in Scotland or Northern Ireland it may insist on local law applying to the agreement.

Special Conditions (Paragraph 16 of the Schedule)

It may be that the deal has special requirements, e.g. as the client's recapitalization or new shareholders. In which case, these requirements are inserted in the schedule, usually as preconditions to any monies becoming payable to the client.

Non-Recourse Agreement

A non-recourse agreement is one under which the financier takes the credit risk of non-payment by a debtor under an *approved debt*. It is a comparatively simple exercise to prepare such an agreement. All that is done is to change paragraph 2(a) of the schedule ('Debts within approval limit which are not approved debts') to read:

> *Save for the purposes of clause 5(3) the first £ of Debts owing at any one time by any debtor determined in order of the dates on which the said Debts fall due for payment by such debtor*

This produces a 'first loss' of the value inserted for any debtor with the balance being within the *approval limit* and therefore being *approved debts*. Subcategory (iii) of the definition of *approved debts* then applies only to the first loss, leaving the rest of the debts as *approved debts* so long as the client is not in breach of any warranty or undertaking. You will recall that apart from three minor categories it is only *unapproved debts* that can be recoursed. Thus, under a non-recourse agreement the financier cannot claim back the prepayment made against an *approved debt* and has an obligation to pay the balance of the purchase price on the *insolvency* of the debtor *(under clause 5(2))*, even though the debtor has not discharged the debt.

Once the financier takes the credit risk then certain sections have greater importance so as to enable the financier to recoup its losses. These are:

- Value Added Tax
- Appropriation and division of receipts

Value Added Tax *(Section 11)*

The VAT rules do not allow the assignee of a debt (such as a financier) to claim VAT bad debt relief. Only the supplier of the goods and services can claim. Section 11 of the agreement enables the debt to be reassigned to the client and the client is responsible to the financier for the VAT. The client also has to hold in trust for the financier any dividend received from the estate of an insolvent debtor.

Receipts *(Section 12)*

Where some debts are credit approved and some are not, the financier can take any remittance from a debtor (whatever debts the debtor may be intending to pay) and use it to clear *approved debts* before *unapproved debts*. On a non-recourse agreement this then transfers part of the credit risk to the client for debts outside an *approval limit*.

Invoice Discounting

The principle differences between confidential invoice discounting and factoring is that in invoice discounting:

- no notice of assignment is given to debtors
- the client, as the undisclosed agent of the financier, is authorized to collect debts
- but the financier can step in at any time and collect debts.

Top Factors can easily prepare an invoice-discounting agreement by inserting a revised clause 14(1) as set out below. In effect, some of the provisions of the full factoring agreement are held in abeyance while the client enjoys his agency to collect debts:

> *14(1)   Notwithstanding any provision for notices in accordance with paragraph (v) of clause 8(2) and without prejudice to the provisions of paragraph (vi) thereof, the client shall enforce payment of all debts at its own expense and, for the purpose of such enforcement, is hereby appointed the agent of the financier. However, the financier may at any time by written notice terminate such agency and following such termination, until any debt has become revested in the client in accordance with Clause 10, the financier shall have the sole right to collect the debt and to enforce payment thereof in such manner and to such extent as it shall in its absolute discretion decide, and to institute, defend or compromise in the name of the financier or the client, and on such terms as the financier thinks fit, any proceedings brought by or against the financier in relation to the debt at the expense of the client, whatever the designation of the debt.*

Execution of Agreement

You will note from the last page of the schedule that the document is described as being executed as a deed. This is because it contains a power of attorney, which by law must be executed as a deed. In the case of a company this means either using its company seal (as in the case of Top Factors) or by the signature of two directors or one director and its company secretary (as in the case of the client). Because many companies are now formed without any requirement in their articles of association to have a company seal, the signature of two directors will increasingly become the norm for deeds.

Supplementay Documents

What other legal documents does a financier normally require in order to operate the facility? Each financier has its own requirements but the following are common and examples are set out at the end of this book as Appendix ????:

- Waiver
- Guarantee and indemnity
- Bills of Sale Registry affidavit
- Consent and priority

Waiver (*Document B*)

If the client has granted security, by a charge over its debts, to its bankers or other creditors, the financier cannot buy the debts and the factoring arrangements cannot work. It is essential that such a secured creditor waives its rights to debts, and consents to the client entering into the factoring or invoice-discounting agreement before any monies are paid to the client. This ensures that no claim can be made against the debtors by the secured creditor if the client becomes *insolvent* (*see Appendix 4, the model waiver*). The waiver provides for debts to be released from the charge but that any monies due by the financier to its client remain subject to the charge. The sample waiver ensures that the *'associated rights'* (e.g. *transferred goods*) as well as debts are released from the charge or any trust provisions in favour of the bank. Trust provisions often occur in bank-financed import transactions where pledges to the bank over shipping documents are released in return for the client signing a letter of trust in favour of the bank over the sale proceeds of the shipped goods, i.e. the debt. This could result in the financier and the bank both claiming the debt. Hence the need for a waiver.

Guarantee and Indemnity (*Document C*)

A guarantee is an obligation to pay or perform if someone else fails to do so. It is sometimes referred to as a 'secondary obligation', e.g. secondary to the primary obligation of the client to the financier.

An indemnity is obligation to pay or perform irrespective of whether any demand has been made by the financier on its client. So an indemnifier stands in exactly the same position as the client in relation to the financier for the obligations indemnified. He or she assumes a primary obligation.

There is great diversity in the way in which each financier's guarantees and indemnities are drafted. (*A combined guarantee and indemnity appears as Appendix ???*). To a certain extent this depends on the commercial deal struck, of which the most important features are:

● is the guarantee/indemnity irrevocable or can it be terminated by notice – if so what length of notice is needed? For Top Factors it is 3 months (*see clause 7 of the model guarantee appearing at annexe 6*);

● is there a financial limit on the amount recoverable or is the guarantor's liability unlimited? (in the example it is unlimited).

Guarantees and indemnities are difficult to obtain. There are often commercial pressures to reduce the obligations. It is considered essential that the document states that the following do not relieve a guarantor of its liability:

● any variation of the factoring agreement

● any failure to take a guarantee from someone who was understood to be an intended guarantor

● the settlement by the financier of a claim against any other guarantor

● failure to fully pursue the financier's rights against the client

● any co-guarantor terminating its guarantee.

It is useful for any indebtedness owed by the client to the guarantor to be assigned to the financier as security for the guarantee (under an individual's guarantee) and the right of proof in the client's insolvency (for monies owed by the client to the guarantor) assigned to the financier (under a corporate guarantee).

It is essential to have a certification clause, so that the guarantor is bound by a certificate signed by a director or the company secretary of the financier as to the amount.

Bills of Sale Registry (*Document D*)

You will have noted that all debts that come into existence after the commencement date automatically become the property of the financier. If the client is a partnership or sole trader special registration provisions apply. In the event of the partnership's or the sole trader's subsequent bankruptcy, the assignment will be void against the Official Receiver or Trustee in Bankruptcy handling the insolvent client's affairs unless the agreement is registered at the Bills of Sale Registry as if it were an absolute bill of sale (Insolvency Act 1986). In order to do this the agreement must be executed in front of the prospective client's solicitor, after the solicitor has explained the nature of the assignment to all the partners in the client or the sole trader.

The procedure is that the financier is the first to execute the agreement. He then arranges for all the partners in the prospect, the client or the sole trader to execute the agreement in front of a solicitor.

The procedure thereafter is:

(a) The solicitor should fully explain the nature and effect of the assignment to all the partners or the sole trader.

(b) All partners or the sole trader must sign all prints of the agreement in front of the solicitor, who then witnesses their signatures.

(c) The client's solicitor then swears an affidavit before another solicitor as to the above events (*see the example set out in Appendix ???*).

(d) The affidavit with a copy of the factoring agreement then has to be filed at the Bills of Sale registry at the High Court in London within seven days of the client having signed it.

(e) Registrations are valid for five years and must be renewed before that period expires.

(f) If there is any change in the partnership, e.g. death, retirement, addition, expulsion, amalgamation etc., the above procedure must be adopted in the case of every new partner and a deed of novation is required.

Charge by Way of Security

A charge is a contractual right given to a creditor by its debtor to have designated assets taken and sold to satisfy the debt should the debtor break its contract. It is usually enforced by a receiver appointed by a creditor.

It is normal that most banks and other lenders will insist on security to cover their advances. This security is often taken in the form of a charge over the assets of the company. Charges can be of two main types, fixed or floating. The 'fixed' charge is, as it suggests, attached to a particular asset. That asset cannot be sold or traded without the permission of the chargeholder.

The floating charge is different. It 'floats' or 'hovers' over a category of assets that changes from time to time, such as stock in trade or book debts. The company can change and alter these assets as it wishes and deal with them in the ordinary course of business. The charge only 'crystallises' and attaches itself to the asset in the event of the failure of the business or under some other condition laid out in the charge document. Once it crystallises the charge becomes fixed and the company may no longer deal with the assets without the permission of its lender. The floating charge does not, in theory, affect the ability of the company to finance its book debts. However almost every lender includes conditions within its charge documents forbidding the assignment of book debts. We can consider both fixed and floating charges to be similar in effect as far as the financier is concerned. A waiver is needed, as discussed earlier.

Financiers also sometimes take charges as security for monies that their clients may owe them. This is particularly so with invoice discounters who have greater risk because no notice of assignment is given to debtors. The document containing the charge is called a 'debenture'. Although charges in debentures can cover a wide range of assets, the most usual are over either:

● all assets; or

● non-vesting book debts

If there is more than one charge over an asset and following enforcement there is insufficient to pay all creditors, the normal rule is that the earliest dated charge is paid out first, provided it has been registered at Companies House within 21 days of its creation.

This rule is often varied by a 'deed of priority' between the chargeholders. This can include a financier with a later charge. If a financier takes a charge the priority deed is additional to a waiver, although they are often combined in one document. Priority should also be obtained for *associated rights* (*see the model priority deed appearing as Appendix ???*). The financier takes priority over all assets even though the bank has an earlier charge over the same assets.

3

BASIC LAW OF CONTRACT AND SALES OF GOODS AND SERVICES

3.1 Basic Law of Contract: What is a Contract?

A contract is an agreement made between two or more parties that is binding in law.

Such an agreement gives rise to rights and obligations that may be enforced in the courts. The normal method of enforcement is an action for damages for breach of contract, although in some cases the court may compel performance of the contract by the party who is in default (an action for 'specific performance').

3.2 Types of Contract

Contracts can be classified as either:

'Contracts By Deed'
This must be written, signed, witnessed and delivered. No 'consideration' *(see later)* is necessary in order for the contract to be enforceable.

'Simple Contracts'
All other contracts, whether written, oral or arising out of conduct of the parties, e.g. taking your seat on a bus enters you into an implied contract to pay your fare.

The rest of these notes on basic contract law will deal only with simple contracts. From section 3.14 onwards we will deal with the special features of contracts involving the sale of goods.

3.3 Skeletal Outline of a Simple Contract

In order to form a valid simple contract:

- the parties must have reached an agreement by means of an offer by one party and acceptance of such offer by the other party;

- they must intend to be legally bound;

- both parties must have provided valuable consideration; and

- the parties must have a legal capacity/ability to contract (e.g. not insane or infants);

In some cases, there must be compliance with certain formalities, particularly as to documentation. (e.g. contracts subject to Consumer Credit Act 1974).

A contract consists of various terms, both those expressly set out in the contract and those implied by law or conduct. The most commonly found implied terms are those set out in the Sale of Goods Act 1979 (see later in chapter). A term may be inserted into the contract to exclude or restrict one party's liability but only to the extent permitted by law. i.e. some exclusions are prohibited in certain contracts (e.g. by the Unfair Contract Terms Act 1977 or the Consumer Protection Act 1987).

A contract may be invalidated by:

(a) mistake;

(b) illegality;

(c) misrepresentation;

(d) duress; or

(e) undue influence.

3.4   Offer and Acceptance

A simple contract comprises an offer and an unqualified acceptance of the offer, e.g. a bus company sends its buses along an advertised route to stop at advertised points - this is an implied offer to take you along the route. If you get on the bus at a stop - this is the implied acceptance of the offer obliging you to pay the fare.

The offer:

- must be communicated to the other party before it can be accepted;

- can usually only be accepted by the person to whom it is made; and

- must be unequivocal and not vague.

The following are not 'offers':

- 'Invitation to treat', i.e. where a person merely invites offers which he is then free to accept or reject, e.g.:

    (a) Display of goods in a shop window with prices marked upon them. (This is not an offer to sell the goods at that or any other price).

    (b) Advertisements/circulars/catalogues and price lists.

(c) Invitations to tender. The party submitting the most favourable tender does not thereby enter into a contract.

- a statement of intention, e.g. if a person goes to a concert venue having seen an advertisement with an intention of buying his ticket on arrival then if the concert is cancelled, there can be no action for breach of contract.

- a communication of information, e.g. a statement of the minimum price at which one is prepared to consider negotiating the sale of a piece of land.

Termination of Offer

An offer can be withdrawn before acceptance, or be treated as being withdrawn if not accepted within a reasonable time.

3.5   Acceptance

Until it is accepted, an offer has no legal effect. An acceptance may be by word of mouth, in writing or implied from conduct. If a particular form of acceptance is required by the offer, then the acceptance must be in that form. For example, if the contract states that acceptance must be 'by post to our registered offices not later than 12 noon on Monday 25 September 1999' this does not allow the contract to be accepted orally. A written acceptance on 29 September 1999 is not sufficient unless it complies with the other requirements.

An acceptance must be unqualified and must correspond with the terms of the offer. A conditional acceptance or counter offer rejects the original offer and causes it to fail so that, for example, 'I will buy at your price but subject to an engineer's inspection' is not a valid acceptance.

There must be active acceptance. i.e. a positive communication of acceptance, e.g. a person cannot be deemed to have accepted an offer merely by his inactivity.

So, when unrequested goods are sent to a private individual, they will belong to him after six months, provided he remains silent. (Unsolicited Goods and Services Acts 1972 and 1975.).

Communication of acceptance

Normally, an acceptance is valid only when communicated to the person making offer ('offeror'). There are exceptions to this as follows:

- Where the offeror waives communication either expressly or impliedly, e.g. when a general offer only requires conduct as acceptance, such as the acceptance of offer for sale of a debt under factoring agreement by crediting the debt to the debts purchased ledger.

- Where the contract is made by post, or post is envisaged as the means of communication, then acceptance is complete as soon as it is posted, provided that it is properly stamped and addressed. i.e. The other party will be bound even though he has no knowledge that the acceptance has been posted to him.

3.6   Consideration

In addition to offer and acceptance, and an intention to be legally bound, a further essential element for a simple contract (i.e. not by deed) is 'consideration' (which is often money or the promise to pay money). English law will not enforce a 'bare' promise not supported by consideration.

For example, if 'A' ('promisor') promises to repair the car of 'B' this promise can only be enforceable by B as a contract if B provides some form of 'consideration'. Such consideration would normally take the form of a promise to pay money. However, it could consist of some other service provided by B to which A might agree. Accordingly, 'B' as the recipient of the promise has to give something in return in order to convert a bare promise made in his favour into a binding contract.

3.7   Formalities

As a general rule, no specific written formality is required to render a contract valid and enforceable. However, there are exceptions:

Certain contracts which must be by deed (until 1990 with a seal but now merely declared to be by deed and signed and witnessed) including:

(a) a lease for more than three years;

(b) a gratuitous promise (i.e. without consideration);

(c) a power of attorney.

Because factoring agreements contain a power of attorney from the Client this is the reason that they are signed as deeds.

Certain contracts must be in writing, including:

(a) consumer credit agreements governed by the Consumer Credit Act 1974;

(b) contracts for sale of land which must be signed by both parties and incorporate all terms (Law Reform (Miscellaneous Provisions) Act 1989);

(c) contracts of guarantee. (Statute of Frauds 1677).

3.8   Certainty Needed

Certainty. A contract must be clear in intention. A so called 'contract' is ineffective and unenforceable if:

● it only agrees to enter into a contract in the future ('an agreement to agree'); or

- it only agrees to negotiate a price later; or

- it contains vague terms, such as 'on credit terms'.

However a contract will be enforceable:

- where both parties to the contract have agreed a formula for resolving uncertainties, e.g. they agree to be bound by an arbitrator's or expert's decision; or

- where terms are implied, either by previous usage between the parties or in the specific trade or by statute (e.g. where a contract for the sale of goods does not state a price, the Sale of Goods Act 1979 provides that a 'reasonable price' must be paid.); or

- even if it has some meaningless terms, provided that the main thrust of the contract is clear.

3.9   Conditions and Warranties

A 'condition' is an important term of the contract, breach or which entitles the party injured to consider himself no longer bound to perform his side together with a right for damages.

A 'warranty' is a less important contractual term, breach of which does not discharge the contract and gives a right only to a claim for damages.

Merely describing a term as a condition is not conclusive if, in fact, it is a warranty and vice versa. As to whether a term is a condition or warranty, depends upon the intention of the parties.

3.10   Exclusion Clauses

Clarity needed

It is essential that any exclusion of liability must be written in clearly understandable words. To reinforce this the 'Contra Proferentum Rule' has been developed by the courts. i.e. any lack of clarity in an exclusion clause will be construed as narrowly as possible against the party trying to rely on the clause.

The courts will also strike down any exclusion clause which appears to defeat the main purpose of the contract.

Unfair Contract Terms Act 1977

There are also statutory restrictions on the use of some exclusion clauses.

The most important are in the Unfair Contract Terms Act 1977. This Act does not apply to the contracts for:

(a) property transactions;

(b) insurance; or

(c) transactions of a private nature.

No exclusion of liability for death or personal injury resulting from negligence is permitted. e.g. from defective goods sold.

Where a party either:

(a) 'deals as a consumer'; or

(b) in whatever capacity (including a business capacity) deals on the other party's written standard terms of business

then the other party cannot exclude or restrict his liability for breach of contract except to the extent that such exclusion satisfies the requirement of 'reasonableness'. *Remember that a factoring agreement would be considered as being on written standard terms. Its terms must be reasonable.*

A person 'deals as a consumer' if he does not contract in the course of a business and the other party does contract in the course of a business.

Where a person deals as a consumer, the following implied terms in the Sale of Goods Act cannot be excluded:

(a) description;

(b) suitability for purpose;

(c) satisfactory quality;

Where a person does not deal as a consumer, exclusion of the three above implied terms has to satisfy the test of 'reasonableness'.

Guidelines as to reasonableness are set out in of the Act and include:

(a) the strength of the bargaining positions of the party relevant to each other taking into account the availability of another source of supply;

(b) any inducement to agree to the terms;

(c) whether the customer ought to have known of the existence and extent of the terms;

(d) whether the goods were manufactured, processed or adapted to the special order of the customer.

In hire purchase transactions or contracts for the sale of goods implied terms as to title cannot be excluded or restricted by contract *(whether the buyer is a consumer or business purchaser)*.

The Consumer Credit Act 1974 ('CCA') will set aside any term of a contract subject to the CCA which excludes the protection of that Act.

If a contract attempts to restrict the liability of a party for pre-contract misrepresentations or restrict the remedies available to the other party for misrepresentation then such terms shall be effective only to the extent that they are considered reasonable under the Unfair Contracts Act 1977.

3.11   Duress and Undue Influence

If an agreement has been entered into as a result of improper pressure (either duress or undue influence) which one party has exerted over the other then the contract can be set aside by the courts. However, duress need not be the only or main reason for entering into the contract.

Duress has been defined as 'coercion of the will' such that there was no consent.

Any pressure or coercion, falling short of the very strict rules of duress, such as threats against property, moral pressure or any other improper pressure, may be considered as 'undue influence'.

It must be remembered that where a contract is tainted with duress or undue influence, it is merely a voidable contract (i.e. it continues as a valid contract until the injured party asks for it to be rescinded).

Guarantors sometimes allege that co-guarantors coerced them into signing guarantees in favour of a financier.

3.12   Discharge of Contracts

The discharge of a contract relieves a party wholly or in part from further performing his side of the bargain. Contracts can be discharged by:-

(a) performance;

(b) agreement;

(c) operation of law;

(d) under the doctrine of frustration; or

(e) breach.

Discharge by Performance of Contract

A contract is most usually discharged when performed exactly in accordance with the terms and conditions of the contract. But what amounts to full performance? This is an important question because the price of goods will often does not become payable until the contract is fully performed.

A part performance, even if it is of the bulk of the contract, will not constitute a discharge, except:

(a) where performance is prevented by the other party; or

(b) where partial performance is freely accepted by the other party; or

(c) where the contract is divided into instalments and the parties agree that each delivery is to be separately paid for: or

(d) where the performance has been substantial, i.e. where the contract is as complete as any reasonable man could expect, despite being not strictly in accord with the agreement. This is a matter of fact, not opinion.

Discharge by Agreement

A contract may be discharged or varied by agreement. Whether consideration is needed to make such agreement binding depends upon the nature of the contract:

(a) 'Executory contracts' (i.e. to be carried out in future). Where a contract remains unperformed by either side, then it may be discharged by a simple waiver. A promise by the parties not to sue or enforce the contract is the consideration.

(b) 'Executed contracts' (i.e. performed). When a contract has been wholly or partly performed by one of the parties, then there must be consideration to discharge the contract or a deed is required to effect the valid release of the other party. In the absence of a deed, the other party must provide new consideration (an "accord and satisfaction"). The most usual is a release of an obligation to pay.

Variation of Contracts. There can be a complete or partial discharge by variations with agreements of parties. If, however, one of the parties makes an alteration to what he does under the contract without the permission of the other, then the contract is discharged automatically and an action for damages may arise.

Discharge under Doctrine of Frustration

A contract will be discharged automatically if, without fault of either party, some event occurs rendering performance an impossibility or the contract becomes illegal or there is a radical change in the circumstances so that the contract becomes totally different from that which was originally undertaken. Examples:

(a) Impossibility, e.g. the subject matter is destroyed or becomes unavailable.

(b) Illegality, e.g. trading with the enemy following outbreak of war.

(c) Radical change in the circumstances, e.g. letting a room solely to view the Coronation, which was then cancelled.

The doctrine of frustration cannot be relied upon if:

(a) the frustration is self induced; or

(b) there is express provision in the contract to this effect; or

(c) the event is foreseen or should have been foreseen by one of the parties.

Discharge by Breach of Contract

Breach of contract happens when one of the parties:

(a) denies his obligations; or

(b) fails to perform his part of the contract; or

(c) disables himself from fulfilling the contract.

Such breach can be a breach of warranty or condition. Where there is a breach of warranty (a less important term), the contract continues and the injured party can only sue for damages. Where there is a breach of condition (an important term), the innocent party, in addition to claiming damages, may treat himself as discharged from the contact. This is described as a 'repudiatory breach', i.e. he is not bound to discharge himself. However, the innocent party does not have to treat the contract as discharged and may rely solely on his right to damages.

Anticipatory Breach

'Anticipating Breach' is where a party indicates that he does not intend to perform his part of the contract, in which case the other party can either sue for breach of contract at once ('accept the repudiation') or may await the due date for performance and hold the other party to the contract, thereby preserving his rights as the innocent party.

3.13   Damages

Calculation. Damages are intended to put the injured party into the same position as if the contract had been properly performed and this can include pre-contractual expenses.

Remoteness. However, the plaintiff cannot recover all damages if the court considers that some would be too 'remote', i.e. not in the contemplation of the parties at the time of contract.

Mitigation. The injured party must take all reasonable steps to minimise any loss caused by the breach of contract.

Penalty Clauses. If a contract contains a clause providing for payment of a specific sum upon breach (e.g. cancellation charges in a holiday contract), this is only recoverable if it represents a genuine 'pre-estimate of the loss'. If it is not a genuine pre-estimate, but is more in the nature of a penalty to compel performance, then it will be treated as invalid and the plaintiff may only recover his actual damages.

3.14   Basic Law of Sale of Goods and Services and The Supply of Goods and Services: Statutory Provisions

People constantly buy and sell goods or services and rarely think through the consequences of what they are doing. Accordingly the Common Law relating to sale of goods and services has mostly been codified in:

(a) Sale of Goods Act 1979 ('SGA 1979').

(b) Supply of Goods and Services Act 1982 ('SGSA 1982').

These provide a raft of presumptions about the transfer of ownership, delivery, payment of the price etc. to cover the absence of express agreement between the parties. The SGA 1979 covers the 'sale of goods', which is defined as a contract whereby the seller transfers, or agrees to transfer, the ownership of goods to a buyer for a monetary consideration called the price.

The SGSA 1982 applies when a contract is for 'work done and the supply of materials'.

Tests

The test as to which Act applies is whether the essential object of the agreement is the provision of goods or the exercise of skill. If skill, then SGSA 1982 applies, eg. if a plasterer is employed to plaster a wall, the contract is for work and materials and is covered by the SGSA 1982.

Contracts of barter are also covered by the SGSA 1982 because no money changes hands.

Contrary Intent

The SGA 1979 allows parties to contract contrary to its terms, either:

(a) by express agreement; or

(b) by a prior course of dealing between the parties; or

(c) by trade custom and usage.

But under the Unfair Contract Terms Act 1977, the right to contract out of the implied terms as to title/fitness for purpose/satisfactory quality/sale by description has been severely cut down.

The SGSA 1982 contains similar implied terms in relation to goods supplied under contracts for work and materials/barter/or hire as to title, fitness and purpose, merchantable quality and description as under the SGA 1979. Likewise, contractual terms seeking to exclude liability for breach of implied terms under SGSA 1982 are subject to the provisions of the Unfair Contract Terms Act 1977.

3.15   Terms Implied into a Contract by SGA 1979

Time
Unless a different intention appears from the terms of the contract, stipulations as to time of payment are not deemed to be 'of the essence' in a contract of sale of goods. Whether any other stipulation as to time (e.g. as to delivery) is of the essence in the contract depends upon the terms of the contract.

N.B. In business transactions, stipulations as to the time of delivery are usually held to be of the essence.

Title (i.e. Ownership)

In every contract for the sale of goods, whether commercial or private, there is implied:-

(a) a condition on the part of the seller that he (or she) has the right to sell or that he will have such a right at the time that property (i.e. ownership) in the goods is intended to pass to the buyer;

(b) a warranty that the goods will remain free from any undisclosed encumbrances (such as liens, pledges or mortgages); and

(c) a warranty that the buyer will enjoy quiet possession of the goods, except as to encumbrances made known to the buyer before the making of the contract.

For example, if the vendor buys a car from a thief and the car has to be given back to the true owner, the purchaser is entitled to reclaim the entire purchase price from the vendor.

Description

Where the contract, whether commercial or private, is for sale of 'goods by description', a condition is implied that the goods will correspond with the description.

For example: if a car is sold after being advertised as a '1961 Triumph Herald' but comprises the rear half of such a vehicle welded to the front half of an earlier model, damages for breach of the implied term in the contract as to description would be available.

A sale by description includes cases where the buyer:

(i) has not seen the goods (*e.g. a newspaper advertisement or a catalogue*)

(ii) has seen them but buys them by reference to a description that he relies upon.

If the sale is by sample, as well as by description, then the bulk of the goods must correspond with both the sample and with the description.

The 'description' may include such matters as measurements, methods of packing or quantity.

The vendor may ensure that a transaction is not a sale by description by including phrases such as *'bought as seen'*.

Quality and Suitability

The general rule of law is 'let the buyer beware'. There is *no* implied warranty or condition as to the quality or fitness for any particular purpose for goods supplied unless either:

(a) there is a trade usage to this effect; or

(b) such a term is implied by the Sale of Goods Act 1979 as below.

Satisfactory Quality

Where the seller sells goods in the course of a business, there is an implied condition that the goods shall be of 'satisfactory quality' except:

(a) for defects specifically drawn to the buyer's attention before the contract is made; or

(b) where the buyer examines the goods before the contract, in which case there is no condition implied as to defects that the examination ought to have revealed.

'Satisfactory quality' is defined by the Act as meeting "the standard that a reasonable person would regard as satisfactory taking account of any description of the goods, the price (if relevant) and all other relevant circumstances".

For example, a brand new washing machine should wash your clothes properly, new shoes should not fall apart on the first outing, a meat pie purchased for lunch should not make you ill, a second-hand 'enthusiast's car' should not have previously been written off after having been submerged in water for 24 hours.

Goods must remain of satisfactory quality for a reasonable time. Where perishable goods are sent to the buyer, they must generally remain satisfactory throughout a normal journey and for a reasonable time thereafter.

SGA 1979 says that the quality of goods includes their state and condition and then gives a list of some relevant aspects. These are:

(a) fitness for purpose

(b) appearance and finish

(c) freedom from minor defects

(d) safety

(e) durability

Fitness for Purpose

Where the seller sells goods *in the course of a business*, there is an implied condition that the goods are reasonably fit for any purpose made known to the seller by the buyer (except where the circumstances show that the buyer does not rely, or that it is unreasonable for him to rely, on the seller's skill and judgment) whether or not it is a purpose for which such goods are commonly supplied.

This also applies to second-hand goods.

Disputes mostly arise as to whether the buyer made the purpose known to the seller.

N.B. If the buyer asks for an item under its brand name or lays down detailed specification of requirements, this would make it difficult to prove he relied upon the seller's skill.

These provisions impose a strict liability on the seller who is liable even if someone else, such as the manufacturer, is at fault.

Sales by Sample

A sale by sample occurs where there is a term in the contract to that effect. The mere exhibition of a sample, during the negotiation of a contract, does not of itself constitute the contract as one for sale by sample.

In both business and private sales, where there is a sale by sample the following conditions are implied:

(a) the bulk will correspond with the sample in quality; and

(b) the buyer will have a reasonable opportunity of comparing the bulk with a sample; and

(c) the goods will be free from any defect causing them not to be of satisfactory quality which would not be apparent on reasonable examination of the sample.

If the goods do not correspond with the sample, it is no defence to the seller that by a simple process they can be made to do so.

3.16   When Does Ownership of Goods Pass?

Ownership (usually called 'property' in the SGA1979) and possession of goods must be distinguished. The ownership of goods may pass to the buyer, even though the seller still retains possession of the goods.

The moment when ownership passes to the buyer is important because:

(a) unless otherwise agreed, risk of loss or damage to the goods passes to the purchaser when ownership passes (i.e. if goods are destroyed while still in possession of the vendor but ownership has already passed to the buyer, then the buyer must still pay for them);

(b) if ownership has passed to the buyer, then the seller can sue for the price (unless otherwise agreed);

(c) if the seller becomes insolvent before delivery the buyer can claim possession of goods where ownership has already passed to the buyer;

(d) but if the seller becomes insolvent before the ownership is passed to the buyer, the goods pass to the trustee in bankruptcy or liquidator of the seller; i.e. the buyer cannot compel delivery even though he has paid for the goods;

(e) if the seller resells the goods after the property has passed to the buyer, then the second buyer usually acquires no title unless protected by one of the exceptions to the 'nemo dat rule' (a person cannot give ownership of something he does not own) (*see later*);

(f) similar principles apply when the buyer resells goods before the property is passed to him.

When studying these rules, remember that they apply only to the extent that a contrary intention has not been agreed, i.e. the contract can provide for

alternative rules. This is increasingly common with reservation of title clauses.

SGA 1979 initially and unhelpfully provides that unless the parties otherwise agree, title to goods passes when they intend it to pass. It then sets out the following rules to find out that intention.

Unascertained Goods

Where there is a contract for the sale of unascertained goods (i.e. goods defined by description only and not specifically identified until after the contract is made), ownership does not pass to the buyer unless and until they are ascertained/identified.

For example, if you order 20 tons of steel you do not know which 20 tons of steel in the supplier's yard will be delivered to you until they are set aside with your name on them.

Unascertained goods become ascertained when they are singled out as those to go to a particular buyer by some irrevocable act of the seller.

Specific Goods

If a contract is for the sale of specific goods, the ownership passes to the buyer when the parties intend it to pass. Unless a different intention appears, the Act sets out the following rules, to be applied for finding the intention of the parties.

RULE 1 – goods in deliverable state at the time of contract

Where there is an unconditional contract for the sale of specific goods that are capable of delivery, ownership of the goods passes to the buyer when the contract is made and it is immaterial whether the time for payment or the time of delivery or both are postponed.

For example, on the sale of a haystack, but before the buyer took it away, it was burned down. The loss fell on the buyer who still had to pay the price. Ownership of the haystack had passed to him at the time of the contract. The risk had passed with ownership. Absence of delivery was immaterial.

RULE 2 – goods needing to be put into a deliverable state

Where the contract is for specific goods but the seller is bound to do something to the goods to put them into a deliverable state, then ownership does not pass until this has been done and the buyer has had notice thereof.

For example, any goods where the vendor has to do alteration or repairs (e.g. converting a car to run on unleaded petrol), will not be in a deliverable state until carried out and the buyer has been given notice that the required action has been carried out.

RULE 3 – deliverable goods with price to be ascertained

Where the specific goods are in a deliverable state but the seller has to do something, such as weighing, measuring or testing in order to ascertain the price, then the property does not pass until such act is done and the buyer has notice that the price has been ascertained.

N.B. This is confined to acts done by the seller. If the buyer has to do the weighing or measuring, then ownership would pass upon the making of the contract.

RULE 4 – goods on approval or sale or return

Where goods are delivered to the buyer on approval or sale or return, then unless a different intention appears, ownership passes to the buyer:

(a) when he signifies his approval or acceptance to the seller or he does any other act adopting the transaction; or

(b) when he retains the goods without reasonable notice of rejection within the time fixed or a reasonable time.

For example, pledging goods is an act adopting the transaction, as is reselling the goods. Property then passes to the buyer. But a horse, on 8 days' sale or return, which dies after 3 days with the prospective purchaser is the seller's loss.

RULE 5(1) – future goods

Where there is a contract for the sale of unascertained or future goods by description, then ownership passes when goods of that description and in a deliverable state are unconditionally appropriated to the contract by one party with the assent of the other. The assent may be expressed or implied and given before or after the appropriation.

For example, in a sale of a given proportion of whisky contained in a storage tank, there is no appropriation until the proportion sold has been separated from the bulk and placed in another storage tank.

RULE 5(2) – delivery with no reservation

A seller who delivers ascertained goods to the buyer or to a carrier for transmission to the buyer, without reserving a right of disposal, is deemed to have unconditionally appropriated the goods to the contract and ownership then passes to the buyer.

3.17   Who Bears the Risk of Loss?

Prima facie, the risk of accidental loss or damage passes when ownership passes. This is important where goods are in transit from the seller to the buyer. The buyer bears the risk of damage during of the journey. He cannot complain if the goods arrive damaged. This rule may be varied by agreement or by trade usage so that the seller then has to replace the goods or provide compensation.

However, if delivery is delayed by the fault of either party (e.g. *if buyer wrongfully refuses to give delivery instructions)*, the goods remain at the risk of the defaulting party as regards any loss caused by delay; even if ownership has not passed, e.g. because of a reservation of title clause.

3.18   Reservation of Title ('ROT')

ROT is a contractual device that takes advantage of s.19 SGA 1979. This section provides that where the seller has reserved the right of disposal of the goods by the buyer until some condition is fulfilled, ownership of the goods will not pass to the buyer until that condition is met. This is so despite delivery to the buyer or to a carrier or to anyone else for the purpose of transporting them to the buyer. The most common condition that is imposed is payment by the buyer of sale price of the goods.

The result is that a seller can retrieve his goods and resell them if the buyer defaults in paying for them, e.g. because of the buyer's insolvency. A retention of title clause was held to be valid in the case of *Aluminium Industrie Vaassen v. Romalpa Aluminium Ltd* (1976) and since then retention of title clauses have also been known as 'Romalpa clauses'.

Insolvency practitioners acting for insolvent buyers never accept at face value claims by sellers to repossess goods. They:

(a) look at the ROT clause in the contract and analyse its scope;

(b) question whether it is incorporated in the parties' contract;

(c) consider whether the goods held by the buyer are the ones covered by ROT.

Simplest clause:

> *'Full legal title to the goods shall not pass to the customer until they have been paid for in full.'*

However, if goods are onward sold by a buyer who has possession of the goods, the original seller loses his rights to repossess goods under an ROT clause. This is because SGA 1979 entitles a buyer with possession of goods with the consent of the seller to effect an onward sale to a bona fide purchaser without notice of the ROT. But if the buyer with possession of the goods onward sells under the buyer's own ROT provisions, the original seller can repossess from the end customer if he has not paid the insolvent buyer. This is the 'Highway Foods Principle' and puts a financier at risk of an uncollectable debt, if it has factored the debt due by the end customer from an insolvent client where double ROT is involved.

ROT is best effected on goods with serial numbers or bar codes. Otherwise if the buyer obtains goods of the same type from a variety of different sources the seller will be unable to tell which are the ones he delivered and will lose his claim.

ROT can be drafted with an 'all monies clause', i.e. ownership of any goods sold and paid for will not pass to the buyer until all other goods supplied by the same seller have been paid for. Sample wording:

> *Title in the goods shall not pass to the customer until all sums due from the customer to the supplier on any account have been paid.*

Attempts to trace and reclaim the goods into which the sale goods are converted *(e.g. raw materials into a carpet)* or to trace the proceeds of sale are likely to be struck down by courts:

(a) where the buyer is a company, by determining that it creates a security charge over goods or proceeds of sale, which is therefore unenforceable for non-registration at Companies House; or because

(b) the necessary fiduciary relationship is lacking; or

(c) where the goods sold are then reprocessed by the buyer so that the goods originally supplied lose their specific identity.

The courts are unhappy about a seller trying to assert ownership over something that he has not owned before (i.e. the newly produced goods).

In order for the seller to reclaim goods under ROT it is important that the seller writes into the contract that he has the right to enter the buyer's premises in order to collect.

3.19   Who Can Transfer Ownership?

'Nemo Dat Rule'

The Sale of Goods Act 1979 repeats the Common Law principle of 'nemo dat quod non habet', i.e. that no one can give title to something that he does not own or for which he does not have the authority or consent of the true owner to sell. Accordingly, if a buyer purports to purchase goods from someone other than the true owner of the goods or his agent he cannot usually obtain a good title. It makes no difference that he acted in good faith and without knowledge of the seller's lack of title or authority.

For example, ownership cannot be obtained by purchasing from a thief. Only the true owner can give good title. Anyone so purchasing would be liable to the true owner for damages and restitution of the goods.

Exceptions to the 'Nemo Dat Rule'

There are a number of exceptions to the 'nemo dat rule' (so that a non-owner can transfer ownership), including:

● sales by a person under any special Common Law or statutory power of sale (e.g. under the Disposal of Uncollected Goods Act 1952);

● sales by order of a court (such as a sheriff or bailiff sale when executing a court judgment).

Transactions under the Factors Act 1889

(a) *Disposition by a mercantile agent in possession of goods.*
   A mercantile agent is one having in the customary course of his business as such agent

authority either to sell goods, or to consign goods for the purpose of sale, or to buy goods or to raise money on security of such goods. *Included are auctioneers, factors (in the legal sense, i.e. not financiers), brokers and dealers selling second-hand cars on commission.*

The Factors Act provides that where a mercantile agent is, with the consent of the owner, in possession of goods (or the documents of title to goods) then any sale, pledge or other disposition of the goods made by him, in the ordinary course of his business as a mercantile agent, is as valid as if it were expressly authorized by the owner.

(b) *Second sale by a seller continuing in possession of the goods after sale.*
Where a seller having sold goods continues in possession of the goods, or documents of title, then the delivery or transfer by him (or his mercantile agent) of the goods (or documents of title) by way of a second sale or other disposition is as valid as if it had been authorized by the true owner (i.e. a buyer to whom ownership but not possession has passed) . This is so in favour of a person who takes in good faith without notice of the previous sale.

In order to have the protection of the Act, the subsequent purchaser must have actual delivery or transfer of the goods or documents. While the above rule protects an innocent purchaser, it gives no protection to the double-selling seller. He will still be liable to the first buyer for damages.

(c) *Sale by a buyer having possession of goods.*
Where a person, having bought or agreed to buy goods, then obtains possession of the goods (or their documents of title) with the seller's consent, then a subsequent sale by him to a bona fide purchaser is effective, notwithstanding ownership has not passed to him from the original seller. This is particularly important in nullifying an earlier ROT clause. However watch out for the double ROT problems under the Highway Foods Principle, described above.

The first buyer is still liable to the original seller for the price.

(d) *Protection for purchasers of motor vehicles.*
A hirer, under an HP agreement (or a conditional sale agreement), who sells goods to a 'private purchaser', can pass good title to the purchaser provided that such purchaser is unaware that the goods are still owned by the finance company (Consumer Credit Act 1974).

3.20 Performance of the Contract and Payment for Sale of Goods

It is the duty of the seller to deliver the goods and of the buyer to accept and pay for them. The parties are free to make their own specific arrangements as to delivery and payment. If they do not specify the arrangements then SGA 1979 sets out their obligations, which are summarized below:

Delivery

It is the duty of the seller to deliver the goods and of the buyer to accept and pay for them in accordance with the terms of the contract. *Payment of the price and delivery of the goods must take place at the same time unless otherwise agreed, i.e. the seller can hold onto goods until they are paid for unless credit terms have been agreed.*

Credit is a privilege, not a right.

'Delivery' in the context of the SGA 1979 means '*the voluntary transfer of possession from one person to another*'. Delivery may consist of:

(a) physically handing over the goods; or

(b) handing over the means of control of the goods, e.g. keys to a warehouse where they are stored; or

(c) transferring documents of title; or

(d) where goods are in possession of a third party, an acknowledgment by the third party that he is holding goods on behalf of the buyer.

Place of Delivery

If nothing else has been agreed then *the place of delivery is the seller's place of business, if he has one, otherwise his residence.*

A seller who has agreed to deliver to the buyer's premises will discharge his obligations by delivering at those premises to a person apparently having authority to receive the goods (even though such person is not actually authorized).

If the contract is for specific goods, which to the knowledge of the parties at the time of making the contract are in some place other than the above, then such place shall be the place of delivery.

Incorrect Delivery

Where the seller delivers to the buyer a quantity of goods less than he contracted to sell, the buyer may reject them. If the buyer accepts the goods so delivered, he must pay for them at the contract rate.

The courts will not take into account trivial or microscopic variations. The seller can always protect himself by incorporating into the contract the expressions 'about' or 'more or less'.

Instalment Deliveries

In the absence of a specific agreement no buyer need accept delivery of goods by instalments. Where, however, there is an agreement for instalment deliveries, it is important to know whether it is an indivisible or severable contract. It will only be a severable contract if it is agreed that each delivery is treated as a separate contract and each instalment is to be separately paid for, i.e. part delivery of an indivisible contract gives no right to payment.

3.21 Acceptance by the Buyer

If the buyer accepts the goods, he forfeits his right to reject them as not in accordance with the contract. He accepts them:

(a) when he informs the seller that he has accepted them; or

(b) when he does any act in relation to the goods inconsistent with the seller's ownership, (e.g. sub-selling goods or using the raw materials); or

(c) when, after the lapse of a reasonable time, he retains the goods without telling the seller that he has rejected the goods.

There is no definition of a 'reasonable time'. This depends upon the circumstances.

Where goods are delivered that the buyer has not previously examined, he cannot be treated as having accepted them until he has had a reasonable opportunity of examining them to find out whether they are in accordance with the contract.

Where the buyer lawfully refuses to accept goods, e.g. because of short delivery, he is not bound, in the absence of contrary agreement, to return them to the seller. It is sufficient to tell the seller that he refuses to accept them and the seller must then pick them up.

If the buyer refuses to take delivery within a reasonable time when requested to do so, he is liable to the seller for any loss and any reasonable charge for looking after the goods.

3.22 Remedies for Breach of Contract for Sale of Goods

Remedies of the Seller for Non-payment

'Personal' remedies against the buyer.

(a) he can sue for the price provided ownership has passed or if the date for payment has passed.

(b) he can sue for damages for non-acceptance where the buyer wrongfully neglects or refuses to accept and pay for goods. The seller is expected to mitigate his loss by selling elsewhere.

'Real' remedies against the goods.

(a) he can exercise a lien, i.e. right to retain possession (but not to sell them), until payment;

(b) he can stop the goods in transit to the buyer, regain possession and retain them until paid;

(c) he can exercise a right of resale if:

(i) the goods are perishable; or

(ii) the seller gives the buyer notice of his intention to resell and the buyer does not pay within a reasonable time; or

(iii) the right of resale has been expressly reserved by the contract in the event of the buyer's default.

After resale, damages for loss can also be obtained.

Remedies of Buyer against the Seller for Breach of Express or Implied Terms

If there is an express term in the contract, is it a warranty or a condition? Result:

(a) if it is a condition – the buyer can treat the contract as discharged, reject the goods *and* claim damages or affirm the contract and claim damages only.

(b) if it is a warranty – the buyer can only claim damages.

All implied terms so far mentioned relating to sale of goods are conditions.

Rejection of Goods

The buyer may repudiate the contract and reject the goods where the seller is in breach of a condition. The right to reject is lost as soon as goods have been accepted (see 3.21 above) and he must then limit his claim only to damages.

Action for Damages is Available:

(a) where the seller wrongfully neglects or refuses to deliver goods – any deposits are recoverable; or

(b) where the seller is in breach of a warranty; or

(c) where the seller is in breach of a condition but the buyer has chosen to carry on with the contract and claim damages instead; or

(d) where the right to reject the goods has been lost.

Damages for breach of the condition of satisfactory quality could include:

● cost of repairs or

● extra cost of having to buy goods elsewhere

● damages for personal injury

Action for 'Specific Performance'

In an action for breach of contract to deliver specific or ascertained goods the court may, if it thinks fit, order specific performance of the contract either unconditionally or subject to such conditions as to damages, payment of the price or otherwise as to the court may seem just. Specific performance will only be granted where damages would be an inadequate remedy. Usually it is only granted where similar goods are not available elsewhere.

3.23 Implied Terms in a Service Contract

Where services are supplied under a contract, to which the SGSA 1982 applies, then the supplier must:

(a) provide the service with reasonable skill and care, *(e.g. dry cleaners will not damage your clothes)*.

(b) carry out the service in a reasonable time, if none is fixed by the contract, *(e.g. your car will be serviced by a garage within days, not months)*;

(c) make a reasonable charge if the cost is not fixed by the contract.

Breach gives rise to a claim for damages.

3.24 Sale or Supply of Goods – Other Claims

The above notes explain the rights under contract law between the contracting parties if the goods are defective goods or services are sub-standard. So how does an injured party otherwise obtain recompense from a manufacturer from whom he did not buy the goods? The law is clear that a person putting defective goods into circulation will incur liability to non-contracting parties for his products:

(a) in the tort of negligence; or

(b) strict liability under the Consumer Protection Act 1987 (CPA); or

(c) for breach of statutory duty under of Consumer Protection Act 1987.

Negligence

Under the principles established in *Donoghue v. Stevenson* (1932) ('Snail in ginger beer bottle case'), the plaintiff who suffers damages must prove:

(a) the defendant owed a legal 'duty of care' to the plaintiff;

(b) the defendant was in breach of this duty;

(c) as a result of which the plaintiff suffered injury or loss.

A manufacturer may defeat a claim or secure a reduction in damages by showing an accident was caused wholly or partly by the consumer's own negligence – called 'contributory negligence'.

Strict Liability – Civil

The Consumer Protection Act 1987 introduces strict liability for personal injury and damage to private property caused by defective products. If proven damages are payable. Negligence is not necessary. This overcomes the difficulties of 'thalidomide' type cases. The 'producer' is usually the defendant and is:

(a) the manufacturer of the product; or

(b) the person who obtained or abstracted the product (e.g. *mining company*); or

(c) the processor (e.g. *canning company*).

Persons responsible for paying damages are:

(a) the 'producer' of product; or

(b) any person putting his name on the product, e.g. *own-branders*; or

(c) any person who imports the product into EU in course of business; or

(d) where the producer cannot be identified then any person who supplied the product, *e.g. retailers or wholesalers who cannot identify the manufacturer, importer or own-branders*.

Thus, factors who sell repossessed goods should be safe so long as they keep records identifying the source of the goods.

Defences to a claim include any of the following:

(a) defect attributable to compliance with UK or EEC legislation (but not British Standards);

(b) product never supplied;

(c) product not supplied in course of a business or for profit;

(d) defect did not exist in product at relevant time;

(e) state of scientific and technical knowledge at the time was such that producer could not have been expected to discover the defect;

(f) contributory negligence by plaintiff.

N.B. *Liability under this Act cannot be excluded by contract.*

3.25 Remedies against the Seller of Goods or Services for Misrepresentation

A seller may be held liable for misrepresentation, i.e. a false statement of fact by one party to a contract, that induces the other party to enter into the contract.

A misrepresentation must be distinguished from a mere 'puff' (e.g. extravagantly worded advertising – not actionable).

If there is a misrepresentation the buyer's remedies are:

(a) if the misrepresentation was fraudulent – damages for deceit.

(b) if the misrepresentation was negligent – damages under the Misrepresentation Act 1967 unless the maker proves that he had reasonable ground for believing, and did believe, that the statement was true.

(c) totally innocent and non-negligent misrepresentation – no damages.

(d) in all cases – rescission of the contract provided this is still possible. However in non-fraudulent cases the court may refuse rescission and award damages instead.

4

MONITORING THE RELATIONSHIP WITH THE CLIENT

In this section we shall look at the importance of developing and maintaining the relationship between the financier and the client.

All financiers have to spend money, time and effort in monitoring the relationship with their client. The type and level of monitoring is reflected in the financier's product offering and market position.

Monitoring involves the consideration of:

- General external conditions
- Industry sector and market
- Life cycle of client's product
- Client circumstances

All of these should be covered in the Client Review Report.

External Conditions

External conditions involve the environment and circumstances in which a client operates its business. Although some of these may be outside its control or influence, we need to understand these in order to assess:

- The commercial strength of the client
- Whether the client is vulnerable to these changes
- Alternatively whether these changes create opportunities for the client.

Broad-Based Issues

In order to consider these external conditions we need to be aware of the prevailing economic, political and environmental circumstances. We need to review how these, together with technological innovations and developments, affect a client's business, its products, the cost of its borrowings and its purchasers.

We also need to consider the client's operating environment and take a view as to the client's effectiveness in relation to its competitors, supply chains, distribution channels and the strength of its customers.

Industry Sector and Market

Next we must consider the industry sector in which the business operates and its chosen market. We must ask such questions as:

- Is the market growing or shrinking?

- Who are the dominant players in the market?

- What market share does the client enjoy?

- Who are its major competitors and how are they performing?

- Is the client's product offering susceptible to technological innovation, fashion or seasons?

Product Life Cycle

The product life cycle is a useful means of assessing one aspect of the future prospects for a business. We must recognize that products and services are influenced by changes in external conditions. Such changes may support the development of a product, support a growth in its sales or bring about a decline in sales or even the insolvency of the client.

Figure 4.1: Product Life Cycle

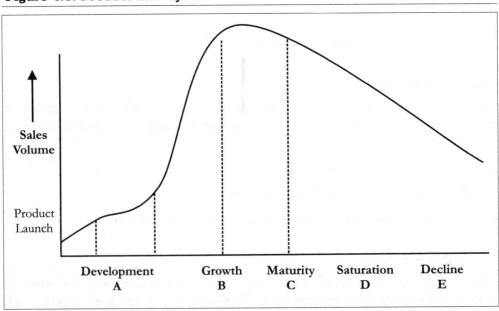

Client Circumstances

Client circumstances that need monitoring include its access to resources, the effectiveness and efficiency of its systems, its management structure and how it manages its culture.

Risk management

The impact of all these elements must be specifically addressed in the report prepared for the client review. We shall deal with the review later. However an outline of the topics and facts to be included in such a report appears in Appendix 8. The report should consider the viability of a client's budgets and forecasts. For example, a client projecting an excessively high sales growth in a mature or saturated market should cause a financier to investigate the basis and rationale behind such projections.

Financiers, who are alert to the opportunities to be gained from changing external circumstances, have helped many growing businesses to exploit such changes in order to gain market share and profitable returns. For example, since 1990 asset-based finance has been widely used in these fast growing business sectors:

● Computer distribution

● Provision of temporary labour

● Distributing and installing air conditioning systems

● Importing and distributing foodstuffs

● Importing and distributing wines and spirits

● Manufacturing sportswear

● Manufacturing and distributing commercial apparel

The development of the affordable personal computer led to an upsurge in demand for hardware and software products. In order to satisfy such demand supply chains have been set up needing access to substantial amounts of asset-based working capital.

As employment and working relationships change, there has been an impressive demand for temporary personnel with a wide range of skills, from packers to software engineers.

We have all experienced the increase in the diversity of imported food products offered in our local supermarkets.

The demand for air conditioning units has grown as a result of changes to our climate and air quality.

Sportswear has become a fashion statement. Corporate logos now appear on everything from baseball caps to office uniforms.

There are of course many thousands of companies that have used a financier for reasons other than financing their product through a growth phase. However, the experiences of the last decade demonstrate that this is one of the most useful features of using an asset-based financier.

Asset-based financing has developed various techniques and protocols in the management of risk with its client base. Important in the monitoring of such risk are:

- Audits
- Client reviews
- Collateral trend analysis

Each financier has its risk management strategy determined by its position, portfolio risk and product offering. Broadly the type of facility gives rise to the following styles of risk management.

Type	Risk management style
Factoring	Responsive
Invoice discounting	Proactive
Financing other assets	Predictive

Let us examine these styles in more detail.

Factoring – Responsive

The very nature of factoring provides for responsive risk management. Factors are heavily involved with their client's sales ledger administration and customers. They receive a constant stream of information, which needs responses. A factor soon knows if, for example, a client's product has deteriorated. Debtors vigorously protest to the factor when pressed for payment for sub-standard goods.

Because factors are immersed in the day-to-day management of their client's ledger management and credit control, there may be a tendency to focus too much on the debtors. Concentrating on credit investigations, credit control and debtor recovery can lead to a failure to recognize that there are other business and financial risks affecting their clients. Monitoring the client's external conditions, product life cycles and business performance are vital.

Many factors, for example, do not visit their clients regularly or perform any audits on their clients after the initial survey. There are differences in risk management cultures between financiers. Some consider themselves proactive in their risk management by monitoring each client's business performance and collateral values. This requires awareness of all the circumstances, which may influence the viability of each client. The financier will not only need to monitor the client's financial performance but also continually to evaluate this performance against projections. It will need to understand the effect of the client's financial performance upon the value of the collateral.

Invoice Discounting – Proactive

Most invoice discounters operate on the basis of regular client contact together with periodic audit visits. The nature and frequency of these visits varies between discounters and is determined by the perceived level of risk that any particular client may represent.

Financing Other Assets – Predictive

Risk management is predictive when the range of assets that are being financed are such that they must rapidly be realized by the financier should the relationship terminate. This can be contrasted with factoring and invoice discounting where the debts should be capable of orderly realization over an extended period for the benefit of the financier.

Auditing as a Monitoring Process

Auditing is a key function of the monitoring process. The sophistication, scope and timing of audits varies. As mentioned above, where only a factoring facility is being provided most financiers rely upon the information gathered through their collection services and the visits of the account manager to obtain information about debts and the client's financial condition.

However financiers involved in invoice discounting or who finance other assets may have a team of specialists who regularly visit clients in order to prepare reports covering the collateral, financial condition, liquidity, systems and procedure.

We have already considered the issues to be investigated and the documents, that have to be produced to a surveyor when visiting a prospect. An audit reviews some of the same information and should be designed to protect the value of the collateral and the funds in use. In order to do so an audit should:

- Compare its test results against the survey or previous audits
- Monitor the client's compliance with its obligations to the financier, its bankers and its creditors
- Monitor the operation of the client's business
- Identify any changes in the client's business that may affect the value of the collateral or the client's future financial performance
- Identify any serious breaches of the facility, such as diverting cash received from debtors into the client's own bank account or notifying the financier of non-existent debts
- Confirm the integrity of the systems and data that the financier relies upon to monitor and manage the facility
- Identify any problems in the service provided by the financier which needs an on-the-spot response or which can be passed back to the account manager to resolve
- Identify any threats to the business

Client Review

An important part of client monitoring is the client review. There are substantial variations in its nature, frequency, level and sophistication among financiers. The responsibility for this procedure normally rests with the account manager.

The client review process gives the financier an opportunity formally to review all aspects of its relationship with the client, including business and collateral performance, income, threats, risks and opportunities.

Variations to the terms and conditions of the facility are often recommended and sanctioned at this time.

Clients are often reviewed at semi-annual or annual interviews, although more frequent reviews may be needed in response to major changes in business conditions or in the client's circumstances.

Collateral Trend Analysis of Debtors

Most financiers use a trend analysis to monitor risks to the collateral and business risks to the client. For example, by monitoring the value of debts notified, the volumes become apparent and can be contrasted against historic sales volumes.

Trend analysis should not be considered in isolation, but applied to the broader picture and used to identify areas for further investigation and explanation.

The table on the next page shows a typical 12-month trend analysis of debtors. The various categories on the left-hand side are explained below.

Assignments

This row shows the monthly values of debts notified to the financier. Growth or decline in sales show up together with seasonal peaks or troughs. Monitoring will identify any anomalies such as disproportionate increases or falls in value, needing further investigation.

It is also useful to compare the value of notified debts against the sales levels stated in the client's management accounts for the same periods. When making such a comparison you must remember that the client notifies debt to a financier inclusive of VAT. A client's management accounts show turnover exclusive of VAT.

Also remember that timing can affect your comparison. Most financiers operate a strict cut-off at the end of each month. A debt that is created towards the end of a month may only be notified to the financier and appear on its records in the next month.

Credit Notes

This row shows the monthly credit note level. Credit note trends are important because they reflect the overall quality of the client's product and administration. This has to be monitored so that the financier can adjust its funding should it consider funds in use to be at risk.

Just as increased levels of credit notes are dangerous, there may also be problems if credit note levels are reducing. This could mean that the client is not notifying credit notes to the financier. Alternatively, the client could be taking longer to raise credit notes. In either case

12 Month Collateral Trend Analysis of Debtors

	Nov	Dec	Jan	Feb	Mar	Apr	May	Jun	Jul	Aug	Sep	Oct	Totals
Assignments	724964	611927	767331	819462	1154445	1037324	788343	605033	737224	559251	624529	693417	9123318
Credit notes	72542	59207	28375	59383	134301	20559	23519	12798	52259	81686	15506	24933	585074
Re-assignments	0	0	0	0	0	0	0	0	0	0	0	0	
Adjustments	2901	44-	2219	2604-	1550-	11317-	2003	122-	28442	2990	6678-	199463	215703
Cash receipts	479546	533811	514948	775908	1051552	517111	813281	859653	505366	678784	680392		7887207
Debt turn (days)	57	63	70	57	68	58	73	79	83	86	90	99	
Pre-payments	592500	593500	693400	564000	943900	838700	885470	577000	797900	376900	560500	820280	8244050
Dilution (month)	10%	9.7%	3.7%	7.2%	11.6%	1.9%	3%	2.1%	7.1%	14.6%	2.5%	3.6%	6.4%
Avg appr'd debts	1069007	1225967	1272237	1337999	1518843	1600449	1660049	1748143	1590527	1497693	1268060	1202335	1299350
Average P/P	829855	954907	982432	1055479	1139677	1233370	1330465	1301668	1189501	984651	947054	1027985	
Avg. P/P rate	77%	77%	77%	78%	75%	74%	76%	81%	79%	77%	78%	79%	
Gross S/L balance	1255259	1254124	1480350	1461916	2003659	1957554	2207296	1986101	1641626	1736667	1926223	2073260	20732607
% Reserves	11%	11%	9.1%	13%	14%	21%	12%	17%	17%	20%	24%	22%	16%
Monthly P/P bal	798741	868037	1057986	856816	1336581	1336718	1520546	1300519	1258941	970893	1040457	1198069	13344310
Funds available	71732	20760	18428	151955	29221	93617	27848	17015	46588-	77944	40667-	4989-	416279

the value of the debts held by the financier is being diluted. Looking at the debt turn trend can identify this. For example, if credit note levels are falling and the debt turn is increasing, it is reasonable to assume that customers are refusing to pay because of a failure to deal with sales ledger and product queries.

Conversely if credit note levels are falling and the debt turn is consistent or improving, it is reasonable to believe that product queries and /or the client's sales ledger administration are improving.

Reassignments

These are debts that have been transferred back to the client because the financier no longer wishes to have them on its books. A large level of reassigned debts would require further investigation to determine why debts previously assigned were subsequently passed back to the client.

Adjustments

High-value adjustments in any month, whether credit or debit items, usually require further investigation.

Cash Receipts

This row shows the monthly level of cash collected from debtors. It should be analysed with the debt turn and assignment levels. If the cash trend declines this will be reflected in current debt turn. This may be the result of problems with the products sold, credit control or sales ledger accounting. In extreme circumstances reductions in cash levels can be evidence of a client collecting cash from debtors and fraudulently failing to hand it over to the financier.

Debt Turn (days)

This row shows monthly debt turn calculated on a roll-back method. Debt turn is used to calculate how quickly a client collects the outstanding debts. This is achieved by deducing the value of 1 day's sales.

i.e. Annual sales including VAT = £500,000

£500,000 ÷ 365 = £1,370 = 1 day's sales

1 day's sales are then divided into the total sales ledger amount outstanding, say:

Sales ledger = £120,000 ÷ £1,370 = 87.6 days

Debt turn can also be calculated for shorter periods on the same basis:

3 month's sales ÷ 90 days = 1 day's sale etc.

By using a roll-back method we can establish a monthly debt turn and analyse trends. Debt turn is one of the most key trends a financier uses to monitor the sales ledger performance. The speed at which the sales ledger converts into cash reflects the performance of the debts from which the financier's funding has to be recovered.

As well as analysing a client's debt turn against historic performance, peer group analysis is also conducted. For example, a financier will know that a company providing temporary recruitment staff to blue chip customers will achieve a debt turn of 40 to 50 days. If the debt turn averages 70 days or more there is cause for concern and further investigation. Debt turn also provides a strong clue to how quickly the debts can be realized if the facility is terminated.

Prepayments

This row shows the value of prepayments made each month. This will show whether the client's use of the funding facility is reducing or increasing. It should be analysed in conjunction with other trends.

Dilution

Dilution is a word used to describe the proportion of the assigned debts that are credited or credit journaled within any given time period. For example, if a client assigns £100K of invoices and £10K of credit notes, then the dilution is 10%.

Monthly dilution is based upon transactions included in a specific month. Annual dilution describes the relationship between credits over a 12-month period.

The dilution level is an important factor in determining the prepayment rate offered to any client. For example, a financier is unlikely to offer a prepayment rate of 80% if dilution averages 20% because this would leave no margin between the prepayment and the level to which the sales ledger dilutes or is erased in value terms.

Average Approved Debts

This row shows the monthly average approved sales ledger balance. Debts that are not approved for financing are called unapproved debts and are deducted from the gross sales ledger to arrive at the approved sales ledger. It is only against the approved balance that funding can be made available.

Average Prepayment

This shows the average amount in the month that the client has taken by way of prepayments.

Average Prepayment Percentage

The percentage shown in this row is in the proportion that the average PP bears to the average approved sales ledger. This percentage can be compared to the contracted prepayment percentage. If the average PP rate is close to the contracted PP rate we know the client has taken full advantage of the funding available under its facility. If a client always takes the full amount of its availability, the financier may be concerned with the cashflow position of the client.

Gross S/L Balance

This row shows the gross sales ledger balance at each month end. It includes all unapproved debts.

% Reserves

Reserves are debts on the sales ledger against which the financier will not make prepayments. Reserves are also described as unapproved debts. Always remember that approved debts are available for prepayments. Unapproved debts are not available for prepayments.

The entry on the collateral trend analysis shows the value of the reserves (i.e. unapproved debts) converted to a percentage.

Reasons for reserves can include:

Age	Debts over 90 days old.
Dispute	Debts where the debtor is claiming a dispute about the goods, the account balance, or specific invoices.
Contra	Where debtors are also suppliers and have the right to offset the amount they are owed by the client against what they owe to the financier.
Credit limits	Reserves may be held in relation to a client trading with a customer over the debtor's credit limit.
High involvement/ Concentration	A reserve to reduce the exposure of the financier to a debtor over an agreed concentration limit.

Monthly Prepayment Balance

This is the total value at each month end of the finance taken by the client.

Funds Available

This is the amount available at each month end, which the client can, but has not, taken. This information, when read in conjunction with the PP and the average PP rate, assists in identifying the quality of the assigned debts together with the level and usage of the funds available.

The above profile indicates a number of worrying trends and data.

Assignments

Based on total debts notified over the year of £9,123K, the average monthly assignment is £760K yet the client has achieved this level only once in the last 6 months.

Credit Notes

Credit note levels appear to be volatile. There is no obvious trend emerging although the levels for September and October appear to be too low.

Adjustments

October adjustments of £199K stand out and should be investigated.

Prepayments

There is no obvious trend. However the overall level of prepayments is declining.

Debt Turn

This trend is very significant. Debt turn has deteriorated from 57 days to 99 days. This could indicate a real reduction in either product quality, customer quality, credit control or sales accounting/administration, or a combination of any of these.

Prepayment Rate

Over the last four months the client has become fully advanced between 79% to 81%. Note that funds available are negative or overadvanced for 3 out of the last 4 last months.

Reserves

Note that the level of reserves between November and October has doubled from 11% to 22%.

4.1   Monitoring – Indicators of Problems or Possible Fraud

The Factoring and Discounting Industry do not lose money as a result of fraud, only through failure of its own polices, systems and procedures.

Managing Director of a major UK factoring/discounting company

Perhaps the above statement is a little simplistic, because there is indeed an increasing volume of evidence suggesting that the industry is now being targeted by the professional criminal whose sole intention is to defraud the financier. However it is also very true, if the financier sets clear policy, effective risk assessment and management systems, and follows good operational procedures, there is no reason why fraud should not be a minor issue.

Before starting our study of this area we must briefly consider a number of vital risk/security issues.

Firstly, it is not acceptable to remain within an area we know well and take no risks – asset-based financing is after all a risk businesses.

Secondly, the general 'rule' to follow is only to take risks where you know you can take the loss – so the financier lays down financing limits at various levels of debtors, client etc. to control the overall risk as well as often registering charges over the assets of the client company.

Thirdly whenever possible adjust the odds as much in your favour as possible. Recourse factoring, for example, has this as a main principle – the risk of specific debtors being spread over the strength of many debtors.

Having established that we have a risk situation when faced with financing decisions, we then consider a range of other issues such as:

- our relationship with the client
- the type of agreement we have (recourse/non-recourse/discounting)
- the expertise of the client in its business
- the current ledger experience
- the commercial expedience of saying no! to the client

From the client's viewpoint risk can look very different:

When there is nothing to lose we can afford to risk all.

This saying is perhaps a truism but unfortunately this is not an uncommon attitude of the businessman under pressure. At the root of most of our fraud cases is the client desperately seeking a way out of a problem – normally financial.

Their attitude towards the risk of discovery/punishment, may well be one of

Well, we are in so deep now we might as well press on.

Insolvency legislation tries to cover this situation by taking away some of the protection of limited status of directors who deliberately trade while insolvent. But we still have many sole traders, partnerships and indeed directors as factored/discounted clients who see the fight for possible survival as outweighing the law.

So we must become a reader of human nature and skilled in understanding all the communication signals given out by those we meet. No one can tell for sure what someone else is thinking or feeling or what his or her needs or desires are. All we can see is people's behaviour, what they do and what they say. So when we meet/talk to clients we must use their actions and words to identify these hidden thoughts and feelings to assess their attitudes to their current situation, and then interpret them correctly if we are to take successful decisions and anticipate potential frauds.

That is not to say that the trust, between financier and client, which has been built up perhaps over a long period of time should be abandoned at the first sign of trouble. Rather the financier must recognize the facts of the current situation and sift these from the emotions, both his own and those of the client.

It would be easy for the financier to take Draconian action under the agreement to stop any possibility of risk. This, however, can easily produce the opposite consequence to that anticipated, e.g. disapproving an account when there has been information from a debtor of a dispute seems a reasonable course of action to protect the financier's position. However, if in the process of doing this the client is upset, placed under increasing financial pressure because of the disapproval and starts to look at the financier as an enemy rather than a friend, we lay ourselves open for potential fraud action against us.

> *The approach when looking at fraud protection is to '... be part of the solution not part of the problem ...'*

It is also true that the vast majority of clients are honest trustworthy people who wish only to succeed in their business activity. However the moral balance of business survival by defrauding the financier is not really different to a car driver speeding. We can always give excuses; we are in a hurry, we haven't been caught in the past, we won't do it tomorrow etc. The client who needs cash for wages today may be tempted to send in an invoice although the goods will not go out for a few days. Their argument will be that everything will be OK tomorrow, it will not happen again etc. – not really that much different from the speeder.

In recognizing the problems leading to potential fraud we must consider two areas:

● External problems arising from the client's business activities

● Internal information indicating potential security risk and possible fraud.

External Problems

The subject of business failure is very large and in the context of this book we can hope only to touch on some of the main causes and their effects and to put together a framework against which we can consider the risk relationship between client and financier. It is a key element in the 'policing' role of the financier that we should at least recognize symptoms of decline, and then use that knowledge to protect ourselves.

Beyond this level of awareness there may also be opportunities to identify the causes and perhaps even to suggest recovery to the client's directors/owners – without stepping over the barrier and becoming shadow directors (*Re 1986 Insolvency Act*).

We are a service industry and it is not sufficient for us, having identified symptoms of decline, to abandon the client by taking Draconian measures to protect our security. It is far more beneficial, within the framework of protecting security, for us to work on assisting the client to resolve the problems. This will hopefully help to retain a stronger client who may even be more pro-factoring/discounting than before its problems.

We have already seen that when assessing prospective clients a financier places high emphasis on the ability of the owners and managers of prospect companies to run their business in a 'businesslike' way. We make enquiries as to whether they have the experience and skills needed and evaluate their commitment to the business. In summary, we try to reassure ourselves that we have good management in control of our prospects, before acceptance.

The change from good management to bad management does not happen suddenly overnight. The indications are always there for a long period, growing ever stronger until even the most unobservant cannot miss them. There are signs in the way the business is being run, in the reactions of management to their daily problems and activities, and in their relationships with all their external contacts (bankers, factors, suppliers, customers etc.). Protection against business failure really commences with the initial acceptance of the client, and as we have seen there are procedures and systems to evaluate prospects. This detailed assessment of a client and the approach taken in setting up the initial agreement and related security documents is absolutely vital in reducing future risk.

Although a financier will try to identify problems and relate these to its funding position, it must be acknowledged that it is often difficult to distinguish between symptom and cause. In fact it could be argued that almost anything a business does wrong is an indicator of a potential problem. The normal observable signs of potential business failure include:

Financial information	decreasing profitability, falling sales income, increase in creditors, changes in certain key ratios, changes in owner's drawings.
Management	panic in crisis situations and an increase in the number of such situations. Rapid staff and management turnover, particularly worrying with senior managers/directors.
Marketplace	redundant products, decline in sales (easily seen though the fall in factored/discounted debts), falling market share, increased competition/loss of customer base.
The future	lack of any long-, or even medium-term planning, or planning that appears to ignore the problems of today.

Because factors and discounters work very closely with clients through their account management and operational staff, it ought to be possible to identify more precisely business problems that can lead to business failure and the related security risk to the financier. Such indicators may arise for the following reasons.

'Poor' Management Reasons

Inadequate management, covering a range of poor management from the criminal to those with lack of interest.

The 'one man band' is often a problem for factors and discounters who often deal with small businesses, run by one person. The pressures on this person to take all the decisions, cope with day-to-day problems, plan for the future while doing the thousand and one activities needed to keep the business running are certainly high. This pressure increases as problems from other areas increase. The distraction from profit-making activities into fire-fighting further distracts the manager and ultimately weakens the business.

Then we have ineffective directors, such as directors who have other business interests that keep their attention turned away from our client company

Many smaller clients suffer from an in-built management problem: lack of common skills.

We have directors who are interested only in their own part of the business, the sales director who fights with the financial director, the production director who is concerned only with his or her department and the research director concerned with inventing the world's best 'widget'

– even if no one could ever find a market for it.

'Poor' Financial Policies

The need to borrow to run a business is normally regarded as sound business sense, within limits. It is when the company starts to exceed the accepted levels of equity/debt ratios that problems occur. The financial policy of 'borrowing' to get out of trouble is fraught with danger. This is, however, one of the easiest signs for the financier to spot. We all know that constant requests for early prepayment or increased advances against assigned debt is a sure sign that a client has problems.

Almost as bad, but taking longer in effect, is a conservative financial policy that does not look towards the future. In good times salting away reserves rather than investing in equipment, technology, sales and marketing activities designed to increase business. It is a truism that businesses cannot stand still; they either grow or die.

The type of financial support may also in certain cases be helping in the decline of the business. Borrowing on long term at high fixed interest rates is building up problems for the future, as is obtaining investment with punitive repayment requirements. A careful balance is always needed between the borrowings and the lendings (debtor investment) of a business.

'Poor' Spread/Big Contracts

It is always exciting for a company to be offered a 'big contract'. There are, however, considerable risks in accepting such contracts. Sir Kenneth Cork laid down a simple rule when he said that ...

> No company should ever enter into a contract which, if it went wrong, would by itself cause the company to become insolvent.

It is, of course, very hard for third parties such as factors/discounters to, in the eyes of its client, pessimistically advise against such deals. The factor or discounter may well bring their own policies into play, limiting finance by imposing high involvement criteria/limits. Even though the factor may protect itself against the direct threat of investment risk in the debt, the threat of loss of the client and the problems which that can bring still remain.

Added to this we must also consider the problems of a damaged relationship with the client who we 'refused to help'.

'Poor' Profitability/Overtrading

In theory at least the problem of overtrading (sales growing faster than finance is available to support those sales) should not be one faced by companies using factors/discounters. The services we offer are based on finance that matches the growth of our clients. In practice, overtrading can also be looked at as the situation that exists when management pursue sales growth regardless of profitability.

In this instance the problems can stem from two sources:

- Firstly, the company that wishes to increase its market share.

- Secondly, from those who are suffering financial problems and see sales as the panacea for solving them.

Financial Reasons

Lack of financial control

Second only to poor management and perhaps arising from it, lack of financial control is one of the most common characteristics of a declining business. It is important because weak controls normally indicate that the management is actually unaware of what is really happening within the business. It cannot differentiate profitable and loss-making activities. It cannot see where money is being tied up in the business, producing cashflow problems. It cannot readily answer questions raised by bankers and other lenders/investors, which starts to destroy its credibility.

Market Reasons

Competition (price and product)

- Both price and product competition are common causes of business decline. A business that does not respond to its changing market or responds too late to changing needs is often starting down the slippery slope to failure.

- Price competition is even more likely to be a cause for business decline. There are normally four possible threats to price:

    - Buyers demanding keener prices.

    - New direct competitors.

    - Suppliers increasing raw material prices, with a knock-on effect to the selling prices.

    - Possible use by customers of substitute products or services rather than those of the client.

Changes in Market Demand

Lack of sales/marketing effort

When we are busy we don't bother selling because we have more than enough business. When times are hard we put every effort into sales.

This is unfortunately a common attitude. The well-run business recognizes that sales take time to generate. It also knows that in difficult times people are more likely to stick with the supplier they have been using, unless give-away prices are being offered, than switch to someone new trying to break into a shrinking market. Ongoing sales activity is essential to help in maintaining a future order base. Recessions have in the past seen many companies go into liquidation for no other reason than their market disappeared. These businesses have been described as being like 'the froth on top of a cup of coffee' – businesses with no body.

Failure Patterns

Business failure always seem to follow a pattern and the financier should recognize this pattern, read the signs and start to become involved in assessing the risk level and taking appropriate action:

- The first stage normally involves a fair degree of complacency. The symptoms are ignored, and the problems not recognized.

- Secondly the crisis is explained away. There is a belief that it will by itself disappear. There is considered to be no need for any action.

- Thirdly there is, at last, some recognition of the problem.

- The seriousness of the problem is underestimated.

- Action taken is too little, and too late.

- Problems start to build on problems.

- Time and effort is being diverted to problem solving rather than to running the business.

- Finally, as the business nears total collapse, management often suffers from an inability to do anything to sort out the problems.

People and Personal Issues

The real key for the financier lies with the account manager recognizing the human emotions at play in the process. Crisis induces stress, which has a negative effect on managerial behaviour. This negative behaviour will show itself in a variety of ways.

These range from survival actions such as 'bending' the rules (passing fictitious invoices and including fraudulent activities) through to depressive actions (ignoring the problem, giving up before putting up a fight and even in extreme cases to suicides).

Note: It should be recognized that there is also considerable pressure on the financier's own management which is trying to protect its company against loss (financial or client). It needs to think clearly and be decisive about the actions needed. Business failure has a tendency to gain momentum and we are not often afforded the luxury of lengthy consideration of the problems before taking action. Stress has a spiral effect. The problems of the performance of the business affecting the client, which in turn affect those charged with looking after that client, are often overlooked.

It is probably fair to draw the conclusion that in those situations where management is generally poor/weak, the prospect of failure will severely reduce the management's ability to make effective decisions to resolve their difficulties. The message – beware of poor management in difficult times!

Fraud

It is against this background that fraudulent action occurs.

Fraud is often described as a slippery path, down which clients go when under pressure. The responsibility of the financier to try to stop the slide both for its own and others' protection is a vital account management activity. The protection that the financiers take under their various agreements and other legal forms is designed to minimise the possible effect of fraudulent activity. But it is in reality the work by account managers and others in whom the protection of the client's security is vested that the real protection work takes place.

In the UK during 1991 member companies of the Association of British Factors and Discounters (ABF&D) – the forerunner of the FDA – provided information for the ABF&D Diploma Course by supplying details of fraud cases they had experienced. A detailed analysis of all this information shows up one outstanding feature of almost every case. This information clearly highlights that the major problem is one of carelessness within the member companies themselves that account for most fraud losses. The most common contributing factors being:

- not following laid-down procedures and policies
- not ensuring documentation is fully up to date
- lack of training in awareness (what to look out for, particularly for junior staff)
- commercial expediency overwhelming common sense!
- ignoring pre-take-on conditions
- not recognizing the signs (often caused by being too close to situations and under pressure from clients – service outweighing security)

The information also confirms that it is only very rarely that a client enters a factoring/discounting arrangement with the intention of defrauding the financier. The industry has in its past experienced attempts to assign debts twice, to hide previous criminal records, and to carry out larger scale fraud both directly against factor or discounter and where the factoring/discounting arrangements represented only a very small part of the fraud. It must also be recognized that fraud is extremely difficult to prove. Someone planning a well-thought-out fraud can hide his or her steps, particularly in the confusion created by the failure of the business.

Internal – Reading the Signs

The key to fraud protection is based in the information network within the financier, normally centred on an account manager. All information of any significance concerning a client should be channelled through this person.

That information, coupled to the account manager's own first hand knowledge of the people running the client, ought to enable the manager to stand back and take an overview of any given situation. In other words an effective account manager is in a position to prepare a kind of balance sheet of good and bad points which will provide a true picture of the factor's security, as well as indicating any necessary action to protect that security.

The 'cycle' of monitoring performance starts with a need to have an understanding of what are normal and acceptable levels of business performance and the specific goals, targets, standards etc. that the client has set itself.

Large companies may have laid-down strategic plans, which detail those goals that they intend to achieve in the next planning period. A company's corporate plan will also contain such information. It is normally part of the role of the account manager to obtain information on the planned activities of clients. It is only by fully understanding the objectives and performance needs that any monitoring can take place.

Once we know what the company expects to do, and regularly update our information whenever we have contact with the client, we can then start to compare actual performance to projections. At the start of a financier's arrangement the new business manager will almost certainly obtain business projections and plans from the prospect. These would include budgets and cashflows etc.

While these are mainly intended to be used for initial assessment and costing of the prospect, the financier can also use them as a starting point for monitoring the performance of the client. It is very important to re-emphasize the importance of the financier (via operational staff) listening to a client and observing what is actually happening.

Security and Fraud

Having seen many of the warning signs of client business problems we must also be alert for attempts by the client to breach the conditions of the agreement in order to make a financial gain. These gains are usually only of a temporary nature, although it must be recognized that a desperate client fighting for survival will do almost anything to delay the end. There are also many cases which illustrate that the saying that 'fraud is a slippery slope' is absolutely true.

The client that raises a fictitious invoice one day to assist in easing a pressing financial problem will, unless stopped quickly, be doing the same again next time a problem appears. As the level of problems grow so does the need to raise more and more fictitious invoices. So let us now look at some of the most common problems that undermine the factor's security and can be viewed as individual stepping-stones along the route to fraud.

How Are Factors and Discounters Defrauded?

There are a vast number of ways that a client can reduce the value of the financier's security and ultimately lead to fraud. These include:

Pre-Invoicing

Invoicing prior to the delivery of the goods or the supply of the service is usually done for short-term financial gain with the intention of delivering the goods as soon as possible. The financier pays out against a 'fictitious debt' which has no value until the goods/service delivery is completed. This is the most common fraud. Only careful cross-referencing between delivery note dates and invoice dates reveals what is happening, unless the invoice was verified on receipt. The fraudulent client, however, often knows the 'trigger' level for verification/credit checks and pitches the invoice value below that level. Even if discovered it can claim a mistake by the carrier or by 'someone in the office'. Factors and discounters are constantly looking for patterns of behaviour like this to help to identify when such actions are taking place.

Banking Funds

This is often considered the worst fraud. It occurs when the client who has already had funding against an invoice banks the debtor's cheque in its own account, thus having up to 180% of the value of the invoice (80% prepaid by the financier and 100% from debtor). Besides the financial benefit the financier may be forced, in cases when the client goes into liquidation prior to handing over the money to the financier, to chase the debtor for payment. The additional damage is to the reputation of both the financier and the industry as a whole – this is one of the main causes of companies placing ban-on-assignments on purchase conditions.

Identification of this fraud may come about in a number of ways:

● Factors may be told by debtors when they are making collection calls.

● Factors may see a client's 'own cheque' being sent through the system – this can be checked against the client's bank statements comparing date of receipt by the client compared to date of receipt by the factor.

● Discounters have to rely on regular audit checks, again comparing bank statement receipt dates, this time comparing the discounting trust receipts against receipts and payments in the client's own bank account.

Holding Back Credit Notes

The client who does not advise a financier that it needs to issue credit notes breaches the factoring/discounting agreement. The financing is being maintained on invoices that will never be paid.

Identification of this fraud may come about in a number of ways:

● The factor may be advised by the debtor when making telephone collection calls.

● The client will perhaps issue the credit note shortly before age disapprovals are put into effect, and the financier may spot a trend of credit notes being issued for invoices that are nearly at this point in time.

Non-Advice on Debit Notes

The same problem as holding back credit notes: the debtor will not be paying these balances but if not informed the financier will continue to finance them.

Incorrect Cash Allocation

This is a common fraud in discounting, because all information on receipt and allocation of cash comes from the client to the discounter. The client advises that cash received relates to old disapproved invoices, thus releasing 100% of this figure from the discounter. In fact the cash was paying more recent approved invoices which, had they been paid, released only say 20% (balance of entitlement) to the client.

Identification of this fraud may come about in a number of ways:

● A careful examination of remittance advices sent by debtors to confirm that a correct allocation has been carried out.

● Via verification

False Invoicing

There are many ways in which a client may attempt to pass false invoicing to the financier. The simplest one is just sending an invoice and then issuing a credit note to clear it some weeks later before it is disapproved for age.

A variation on this is to 'roll invoices', that is to send through false invoices but arrange to pay them, again before age disapproval, at the same time replacing them with new invoices. The financier's records will show only a debtor account that is being paid regularly.

Double invoicing occurs when the client invoices exactly the same goods/service twice, with different invoice numbers and on different dates. If it is lucky the debtor may pay twice in error. But even when the debtor realizes that there is a duplicate, it often advises only the client who does not tell the financier. Only when the duplication is spotted by the factor's credit controllers or the client clears the account with a credit does it come to light. If caught the client's easy defence is that "...someone in the office made a mistake...". Once spotted the factor must make sure that the pattern of behaviour is not repeated.

Contrivance with a third party, either a 'real' debtor or a friend of the client, is also used to defeat the factor's/discounter's verifications. Every contact with supposed debtors is greeted with confirmation of the existence of the debt. Such contrivance has been seen with both willing assistants and under criminal threat.

All these false invoicing situations are difficult to spot and the client has that easy line of defence, "... someone in the office made a mistake...", at least the first time. Also, as previously stated, the fraudulent client may often knows the 'trigger' level for verification/credit checks and will pitch the invoice value below this level so that often it is only discovered by chance.

The financier's protection is to watch for patterns in credit notes and maintain a good verification process.

Invoice-Based Problems

Free issue goods Beware of the invoice including the value of the free issue material which is subsequently claimed as a set-off by the debtor. Also the financier should carefully check the insurance of the materials while it is in the possession of the client because any loss or damage to it will certainly result in a contra claim.

Abnormal sales If the client starts to invoice goods that are not normally sold by the client, the client manager needs to establish why there has been such a change in the client's business.

The risks include:

- the inability of the client to fully and adequately service the new goods.

- the client is desperate for income, so has seized any opportunity without full research.

- the extra efforts needed to promote the new products may distract the client from its main business activities, resulting in poorer administration with the knock-on effect to resolving debtor problems.

Part orders Any invoice that refers to a part order must ring an alarm bell and require investigation. The possible problems include:

- the debtor is unlikely to pay until it has received all the goods.

- there may be some contingent liability on the client if all the goods are not supplied. This could result in contra claims against the factor even if the goods have been paid for.

The account manager should negotiate with the debtor that each part of the order will be treated as a separate transaction and that payment will be made against each invoice as due and that no contra claims will be entered. All this must be in writing.

Returnable Beware of clients who provide goods, parts of which are returnable, such as pallets, spools or parts to be reconditioned. Such goods will be the subject of either a subsequent credit against the invoice or a contra claim. The account manager should negotiate a reduced prepayment with the client to maintain the financier's overall margin. A very careful control should also be kept on the account to prevent the build-up of large numbers of credits due to debtors, which will undermine ledger security.

Discounts Invoices that allow for a large early settlement discount to be deducted by the debtor for quick payment reduce the financier's safety margin. Such invoices also suggest that the client is desperate for money and is prepared to give away profit margins.

Terms of trade Changes in the client's terms of trade can also be a sign of problems. A shortening of credit terms suggests a need for cash from the debtors. A lengthening of the credit period suggests an attempt to attract new debtors with special terms.

There are other areas of potential invoicing problems, which can effect the financier's position, that we have already seen. These include:

- Retention of title clauses (ROT)
- Contra accounts
- Sale or return (can be called consignment stock)
- Self-billing accounts.

Structured Frauds

Structured frauds are those where there have been deliberate attempts to defraud the financier. Because of the difference in acceptance levels for factored and discounted business and the additional difficulties in controlling and monitoring invoice-discounting clients, most structured frauds take place in an invoice-discounting facility. That is not to say that factors do not also suffer. There have been a number of sophisticated frauds committed, including clients installing high-tech telephone equipment routing all telephone calls to their own offices so that they could verify debts and manage the factor/debtor relationship.

Almost all these types of frauds also involve the duplicate or triplicate factoring/discounting of the same debtor ledger.

Fraud Case Study 1 – Make-It-Up Publications Limited

The following case study has been supplied by a UK factor. Although certain facts have been altered to ensure confidentiality, the events described are true.

Background History

Make-it-up Publications was taken on as a full service factoring client at the end of June 1997. The company had two separate trading activities:

a) **Makefile** – A folder designed to act as an additional cover to a popular weekly magazine with advertisements for local businesses. The folder was to be 'wrapped' around different magazines each week.

b) **On-the-Make** – A free newspaper distributed locally on a weekly basis combined with a distinct but separate employment paper on the reverse side (this combination was to take advantage of split distribution costs).

The new business manager in his report noted the following comments:

Strengths

1. Innovative products exploiting niche market

2. Enthusiastic management

3. Cost-effective distribution due to split costs with paper

4. Greater market coverage due to the diverse elements of the split paper

5. Telesales staff who were full time and salaried, as opposed to commission based

6. *On-the-Make* was a free publication and so had a good circulation

Weakness

1. Lack of general management experience

2. No experience in a similar market environment

3. Lack of net worth

4. Low invoice value

5. Vast customer base including individuals

6 Short period of trading (3 months)

7. No signed order forms. Orders were taken over the telephone by telesales staff

The factor offered a facility on the following basis:

The Proposal

'Makefile' was to be excluded from the agreement due to the contractual product nature.

'On-the-Make' invoices were to be factored but not for private individuals. Invoices relating to private individuals were to be kept on a separate sales ledger operated by the client.

Order copies were to be provided for all factored invoices. Invoices were to be accompanied by a copy of the 'On-the-Make' publication.

General

The prospect was visited before take-on to assess their operation.

A system run on a PC was seen giving information on pricing, costs, commission payable, insertion dates etc.

Orders were seen to be confirmed by customers returning signed copies of draft advertisements within a specified time period. If these were not received the advertisement would not be inserted.

The directors of the company were found to be pleasant people who readily gave information and assistance. Two had proven track records in sales, and all appeared to have a good awareness of the financial side of the business and very definite plans for the future.

Factoring Agreement

Recourse agreement full service

Initial advance	70%
Factoring charge	3%
Factor's discount (over base)	+ 1.5%

Operational Factors

From the outset the deal proved difficult because of the incomplete nature of their records. Reconciling the control totals took several man-hours.

Take-on customers numbered 377, climbing subsequently to 524 in one month.

Within 10 days of initial funding and the despatch of confirmation of balance letters, the first query list was compiled. This contained 16 queries and was despatched on 3 July.

Within the first month of operation it was discovered that the client had banked over 12% of the gross ledger balance.

The number of queries began to mount:

Query list dated 27/07 had 48 queries broken down as follows;

Disputes on charged amounts	12
Incomplete addresses	15
Frequency of advertisement disputes	3
Fictitious ('fresh air') advertisements	10
Misc.	8

The number of queries increased by 71 between 1 and 9 August.

The factor now had queries generated in two weeks of 119, i.e. 22.7% of the customer base.

No queries were resolved by the client during this two-week period.

The Meeting

A meeting was convened on 2 August to discuss the operational problems. It was attended by the assistant general manager, client manager and the three directors/indemnifiers of the client.

The meeting covered the following areas:

a) The unacceptably high level of queries and the underlying reasons for those queries, i.e. maladministration on the client's part relative to incorrect addresses on invoices, names of customers etc.

b) The lack of order confirmations. The client agreed that confirmation of orders would be provided either by fax or post, thus placing the onus on customers to refute those orders if necessary. These confirmations were to be available to the factor.

c) It was agreed that query lists would have to be dealt with within 7 days by the client. A response was expected to all disputes raised.

d) The client was warned that unless the situation was resolved during the month the provision of a factoring facility would be reviewed.

Following the meeting all areas discussed were confirmed in writing. On receipt of this letter the client advised the factor of an employee who was interested in investing a substantial amount in the business. This did not happen.

Terminating the Agreement

During the next two weeks it became apparent that virtually no queries were being resolved and further queries were coming to light, especially those regarding unauthorized advertisements.

Serious discrepancies appeared between prices quoted to customers and those appearing on invoices.

After two months' operation on 21 August 1997, a letter was sent advising the client of termination of their facility and a separate letter was sent to each indemnifier notifying them of their responsibilities as personal indemnifier.

On 22 August a firm of accountants was called in by the client to advise them as to their options.

They wrote in their report

Clearly the company is insolvent both on a cash and balance sheet basis.

They also advised that the only option available to the client was

some form of formal insolvency proceedings.

The Fraud

Following notice of termination and subsequent meetings at the client's premises at the end of August, the managing director disclosed that he was currently serving a two-year suspended sentence for mortgage fraud. This was later verified by independent sources.

Collections continued to prove both slow and difficult. By mid-September 188 solicitor's letters had been despatched.

During this time the level of queries rose substantially to over 57% of the gross ledger.

It subsequently became apparent over the course of numerous meetings with the directors that they had been aware that fresh air invoices had been factored. It also transpired that 30% of the gross ledger contained 'Makefile' contractual invoices.

The factor had been advised at take-on that all such invoices were on a separate ledger and had been shown evidence of that ledger. While all subsequent invoicing had been checked for evidence of 'Makefile' work, the factor discovered that they had been on the ledger from take-on.

The confirmation of balance letters had not revealed them because the work had been requested and most customers knew 'Makefile' to be a trading style of 'Make-it-up Publication'.

Makefile invoices were raised on a contractual basis and were invoiced one year in advance.

In most cases the artwork for these 'Makefile' advertisements had not even been completed. All 'Makefile' invoices were included as part of the take-on balance.

Of the 188 solicitor's letters sent, only one case went legal, such was the inability to prove the debts.

The majority of the disputes arose as the result of one telesales employee who single-handedly raised invoices, which ultimately appear to have been complete fabrications of sales. His aim appeared to have been to attempt to mistakenly enhance his standing in the sales team.

The fraud perpetrated by this client could be summarized as follows:

1) Non-disclosure of information relative to the granting of a factoring facility, i.e. conviction for fraud.

2) The factoring of invoices clearly excluded from the factoring agreement, i.e. Makefile invoices.

3) Fraud as a result of the banking of cheques relating to invoices that had been factored.

4) Fraud relating to negligence on the part of the directors, i.e. trading while insolvent and failure to fulfil their warranties to the factor over the debts.

5) Employee fraud – the telesales employee deliberately raising invoices for debts that did not exist and which were subsequently factored.

Update

As the 'collect-out' continued it was discovered that one of the directors had returned to the Netherlands. (She was a Dutch National and subsequent investigation proved she had no assets.)

Another of the directors was also found to have no assets and shortly after termination had his house repossessed. The third director and indemnifier had two properties with very little equity.

This third director had threatened to bankrupt himself if the charging order was registered. He requested he be allowed to raise the finance himself and make a final payment to his creditors. This was not considered likely to be productive and in the event the factor went ahead with the orders.

Personal guarantees were given by the directors as security to the printers, fax supplier, car lease company, bank and to the factoring company.

A decision not to bankrupt the first two directors was taken because it would be unproductive.

To date there are currently 347 customers still on the ledger disputing their indebtedness.

Of these approximately 100 have agreed to settle after negotiation.

Only one customer has had judgement entered against him and is currently paying monthly instalments.

The factor continued to collect, albeit slowly, and hopes to recover any shortfall from the remaining indemnifier.

Questions to consider – In retrospect it is always easy to see the problems and say why they happened. In this excellent report on an actual fraud case, how do you think the financier could have acted differently to prevent the situation happening? (Please do not forget that commercial expedience must also be brought into play.)

Fraud Case Study 2 – Procedo/Balsam Fraud Case

Although this is an extremely complex case it does illustrate one overwhelming lesson to discounters is to check that your debts are **REAL** and **HAVE VALUE**.

Balsam AG (Germany) was the producer of the world renowned 'Astro-Turf' used in major sports stadiums around the world.

The owners of Balsam bought a 17.7% share in Procedo, (one of Germany's largest factoring companies).

Balsam and its subsidiaries then entered into factoring agreements with Procedo all on a NNF basis.[1]

The main factored activity of Balsam was the erection of very large sports arena.

The case is subject to legal action in the German courts, but it is a matter of public record that the entire business ventures of Balsam were totally fictitious. Other than producing Astro-Turf they never built anything.

The sad story is that the factor never accurately checked the validity of the invoices it financed, and this ran over a period of 10 years.

And the value of fictitious invoices issued by Balsam?

By June 1994 it was clear that 141 stadium contracts representing **1,960 Billion DM** had been forged and factored by Procedo.

Remember the quotation 'The factoring and discounting industry does not lose money as a result of fraud, only through failure of its own polices, systems and procedures.'

---

[1] NNF is Non-Notified Factoring. In the UK we would call it Confidential Discounting.

Fraud and Security Risk Warning Signs

The financier is dependent on reading and interpreting warning signs as its first line of defence against fraudulent clients. Factors have an advantage in that they have regular contact with debtors who will, unless they are also involved in the fraud, give information that can illustrate many of the problems. The confidential discounter, however, operating at arm's length from the debtor, has internal information, occasional verification to spot problems and the regular audit process to spot frauds. Statistics are also generated by most financier computer systems (see Information Technology section later in the course) and these can be used to follow trends and to identify potential problems.

Some significant warning signs include the following.

Lengthening Debt Turn

The financier's security is vested in the debts, so any signs of lengthening debt turn can be considered worrying. An examination of the reasons for this lengthening may provide indicators of potential or existing problems such as:

- debtors paying slower because the nature of the debtor base has changed and the client is selling to poor debtors. This leads to increased debtor-based risks and may result in funding being reduced because of credit limit reasons and place more pressure on the client who may seek other ways, including fraud, to replace lost funding.

- poor collections by the client (in discounting or CHOCC or agency facilities), or due to inefficient collection activity or deliberate late reporting of receipts of cash (banking in own bank account and then transferring to discounting account) to maintain maximum cashflow.

- problems caused by the client's goods or services not being up to standard and debtors not paying, linked to credit/debit note issues covered earlier.

- fictitious invoicing only being 'paid' at the last moment (rolling invoices) or cleared by credit note prior to disapproval.

- changes in the client's terms of trade beyond what were agreed in the agreement. This could illustrate that the client is finding business difficult to obtain and in an attempt to bring any business in to the company is offering extended terms to persuade customers to buy. This is a good indicator of client panic.

- Internal poor performance by the factor's own collection staff.

Dilution of the Value of the Sale Ledger

Ideally every invoice assigned to the financier is fully paid without any deduction. This is not, however, the case. With any business there are 'dilutions' to invoiced amounts that can be caused by faulty goods requiring replacement return, incorrect invoicing, legal actions and many more. The financier normally considers three areas of dilution.

Asset-Based Working Capital Finance

Credit notes   every invoice that is financed and then credited reduces the financier's security. However credit notes do help to keep the sales ledger clean and assist in the assessment of its true worth in non-fraud situations.

Reassignments   debts are reassigned to clients for a number of reasons, normally because in the financier's opinion they are for one reason or another uncollectable (failed legal actions, liquidated debtors, considered not worth chasing any more etc.). Debts should never be re-assigned until it has been uncontroversially established that they are worthless.

Discounts   some debtor discounts, quantity or early payment may be recognized and allowed within the agreement, but when these amounts become excessive, the value of the debts is undermined. There are also certain buyers (supermarkets in particular) who have rights under their purchase terms to claim retrospective discounts, based on volumes of purchases over a period.

In each case the effect is to dilute the value of the debts held by the factor and discounter. Statistically it has been shown that you can multiply by three the normal dilution levels of a client if the client does fail.

Dilution example

Normal dilution rates:

Credit notes	5%
Reassignments	2%
Discounts	1%
Total	8%
Client in liquidation	8% x 3 = 24%

Against an Initial Payment of 80%

a possible shortfall of 4% (100% - 80% - 24%)

Increasing Demand for Additional Funding

When a prospect is assessed for factoring/discounting facilities, one of the areas investigated is the financial needs of the prospect and how factoring/discounting, perhaps together with other lenders, can address this need. Although needs do change from time to time, the nature of factoring/discounting as an open-ended source of finance that grows with the needs of the company, so the financier would not normally expect to have demands for additional funding from clients.

Demand for extra funding can stem from a number of reasons.

- inappropriate factor/discount product offered at wrong terms, or facility restricted at lower than needed initial percentage, perhaps based on old assessment of client. This problem will create in the client's mind an image of an unhelpful financier, develop lack of trust both ways – financier and client and visa versa – and may prompt client to take action (fraudulent invoicing etc.) to fill the funding gap. The financier must continually assess and re-assess the client's needs against its own security.

● cash pressures from outside the agreement such as:

- poor collections.

- changes in supplier terms. Either suppliers wanting payment quicker or a move to a new supplier means that the client is purchasing perhaps at better prices but on more restrictive terms.

- to cover cash pressures for such things as holiday pay in times of poor sales (Christmas) and annual shut-downs when expenses remain high but sales are nil.

- to finance client's lavish lifestyle.

- to finance other business or activities of the directors away from the factored/discounted business.

- to cover capital expenditure programmes that should be financed in other ways than through working capital.

- financing losses.

The commercial difficulty of handling these requests for additional funding is that they are always short-notice, high-pressure requests, against tight time deadlines- '...we need wages today...' and it is very easy for the financier to be hassled into making quick off-the-cuff decisions without taking time to examine all the issues. This is most probably the main reason why financiers fall for frauds.

Remember – Fraud is always to do with cash!

The financier can see this problem even clearer if it takes the time to look at other information and place the request for additional funding into proper context to the whole business situation. For example, within the conditions of the agreement the financier has a right to financial information, management accounts etc. from the client at regular intervals. If these management accounts include the cashflow forecasts, which almost every business prepares, it is a relatively simple matter of comparing the current requirements against predicted figures and establishing exactly where the pressure within the business arises.

Unrealistic Sales Ledger Performance

Comparing actual sales levels against both predictions (from cashflows and budgets) and against a knowledgeable view of what the client can reasonably produce/deliver (because of the staffing, equipment, purchase level etc.) will again give an indication of possible fraudulent activity. For example, a manufacturing client who appears to be achieving growing sales with little evidence of either purchasing or holding raw materials, nor having the machine capacity, must ring warning bells. Likewise a client supplying temporary staff who cannot show matching payment records highlights a problem.

One of the most common and easily conducted tests of whether a client's sales ledger is fictitious is to compare assigned debt against the same period's VAT quarterly return. Although clients may send fictitious invoices to the financier it is most unlikely that they pay the VAT on such fictitious debts.

Deteriorating Stock Profile

One of the most common reasons that gives rise to cashflow problems are stock issues.

- too much stock can mean that cash is unnecessarily tied up on the shelf and create cashflow difficulties.
- values of stock, particularly 'commodity' driven raw materials like plastics and steel, can raise and fall, creating loss situations
- obsolete stocks can build up which have no real value
- short-cutting on process to speed up the sales cycle can have drastic effects on the quality of the goods sold, e.g. timber that is not kiln-dried before manufacture to save costs and time.

Client Turnaround Situation

All of the issues we examined in the early part of this section of the course concerning business failure and decline must be taken as warning signs that the client is under pressure. Any and all financial pressures on a client could see them turn towards the factoring/ discounting facility as a route to easily obtainable money. Without mistrusting the clients, factors and discounters constantly walk the high-wire between fraud protection and client service.

5

RETAINING AND DEVELOPING THE CLIENT

In this section we shall review the attributes for successful account management. The relationship with the client will be enhanced by the information it receives from its financier and the effective resolution of any problems.

5.1 Relationship Management

Managing the relationship with the client is an integral part of a financier's operations. It is carried out primarily by an account manager, whom some financiers call a 'client manager' and others a 'relationship manager'.

Although an account manager's responsibilities vary between financiers, his or her principal responsibilities are to protect the financier's funds in use and to maintain and develop the relationship with the client. In carrying out these responsibilities the manager has to:

● Reduce the risks from the relationship

● Maximize the return to the financier

● At the same time meet the client's aspirations and expectations of the facility.

Account Manager Profile

A successful account manager needs a wide range of skills in order to successfully perform the job. The most important are described below. (For the sake of this account we shall assume that the account manager is a man; the remarks apply equally to a woman.)

Knowledge of Collateral

He must have a thorough understanding of collateral. Effective financing decisions can only be made if he can accurately assess the realizable value of the assets against which funding is made available. He must be aware of the circumstances that influence and effect such value. He must be able to rapidly spot movements and trends in asset values.

Sectorial Knowledge

He must understand business practices and protocols across a wide spectrum of industries and sectors. It is only through an in-depth knowledge of his client's business and circumstances that he can make successful judgements about the security of the funds in use or spot potential threats to the viability of a client.

Skilful Negotiating

An account manager has to be a skilled negotiator in the day-to-day operation of the facility and in determining the ongoing structure and terms of the relationship.

Financial Interpreting

In order to identify risks, it is vital that an account manager can interpret and analyse balance sheets, profit and loss, accounts, cashflow statements, budgets and projections.

Ability to Communicate

Account managers are at the centre of a communications junction, involving clients, seniors, peers, junior staff, auditors, business development managers, surveyors, credit underwriters and bankers, together with external professionals such as accountants and lawyers.

The account manager receives a constant flow of information which he needs to be able to rapidly sort out and prioritize. In this way he can be an effective team member. He must be able to communicate effectively and coherently on the telephone, during face-to-face meetings and in writing both internally and externally.

Interpersonal Skills

A high degree of interpersonal skills are essential in order to successfully interact with the diversity of individuals and organizations with whom he will come into daily contact.

Understanding the Law

Account managers need a broad understanding of legal issues that affect the financier, under company, contract and insolvency law. He must be up to date in his knowledge of collection procedures through the courts and be able to give clear instructions in litigation issues that arise in defended cases.

Sound Judgement

Most financiers, including their credit committees, base their operational strategy for clients on the recommendations of their account managers, while leaving their manager with substantial discretion concerning day-to-day financing decisions. Provided that the account manager uses sound judgement with a clear strategy in mind, the funds in use should be secure from any internal failings of the financier.

Relationship Parameters and Issues

Asset-based financiers do not have to enter into agreements for minimum levels of service, even though they are commonplace in other industries. They have been fortunate in being able to rely on contracts that are heavily biased in their favour. Even so, a debt financier has to provide his client with substantial amounts of data on a regular basis.

The client can expect a monthly statement of account detailing all charges and information relevant to the facility. In addition the financier sends out a monthly movement report. This shows all the movements in respect of payments, debts notified, adjustments and cash receipts. With factoring facilities the accounts also shows:

- A monthly sales ledger report
- Daily cash receipts and allocation report
- Debts or balances which are unapproved for age, dispute, concentration or in excess of credit limits
- Debtor approval limits, ratings and any changes.

On a daily basis the financier provides information in respect of funds available, gross values of debts or other assets, details of unapproved debts and any other matters that affect the funds available. Most financiers now provide clients with online access to this information via Internet technology or a dedicated phone link.

The immediacy of access by the client to information from the financier produces pressure for delivery of both funds and data within the shortest possible timescale.

A well organized financier has internal performance standards in respect of the availability of funding and time limits for responding to queries and requests for information. Often these are the basis of disclosed commitments to the client.

Successful account managers must constantly review the facility with the client to ensure that agreed service levels are being maintained and that the facility continues to meet the requirements of both the clients and the financier.

A major feature of debt financing is that the nature of the facility creates the potential for conflict. This becomes magnified in a factoring relationship because of the high degree of involvement that the financier has with a client's customers through credit control management.

Let us consider this in more detail by taking some examples such as:
- Disputed debts
- Funding limits

Disputed Debt

Discovery: The financier discovers that a debtor is refusing to pay a significant account

Response: The financier may withdraw finance in respect of this debtor by designating all his debts as unapproved. The client is notified of this fact.

Reaction: The client believes that all the goods have been sold and delivered in accordance with the contract. He correctly believes that the debtor is only using the dispute to obtain extra time for payment and that the financier is penalising the client who has done nothing wrong.

The financier under these circumstances is in a difficult position. He has to consider whether the value of the debtor's disputed account is significant in relation to the total funds in use. If the answer is 'no', then he may give the client time to resolve the situation before withdrawing finance.

If, however, the answer is 'yes', the financier may attempt to gain further information about the current credit standing of the debtor. At the same time he should investigate the dispute. If the situation cannot be resolved quickly the financier will have to consider withdrawing finance until the debtor agrees that all or some of the balance is due or the client accepts the validity of the dispute.

Debtor Funding Limit

Debtor funding limits are also a major cause for conflict. A client receives a large order from a major customer and needs finance against the resulting debt. However, the financier may not wish to approve the entire debt for prepayments either because of the customer's credit standing or because the debt will represent a significant proportion of the entire sales ledger balance. This is usually described as a 'concentration'. The amount of any concentration against which prepayments may be made is usually determined by the financier's credit policy and set out in the formal debt purchase agreement with the client. Let us look at how the financier can deal with this issue.

If the customer's creditworthiness cannot be established or his credit rating is low, the financier has no alternative but to restrict funding, discourage the client from taking on undue risk or requesting that the customer provides security or a third-party guarantee.

If the customer's credit standing is satisfactory, financing is subject firstly to the financier's credit policy and secondly to obtaining a full understanding of the risks involved. To do so the account manager needs to examine the purchase order, delivery, documentation and assess the likelihood of something going wrong. It may be that further assurances can be gained by a dialogue between the financier and the potential customer with full consent and involvement of the client.

5.2   Restructuring the Facility

Debt financing is fluid. The profile and make-up of the debt changes daily and reflects the client's business performance and external conditions affecting the client. A successful account manager must be able to react effectively to the client's changing circumstances. This may lead to a restructuring of the facility.

As we saw earlier, at the outset of the facility the client and financier will have completed legal documents including a contract, setting out the terms under which financing is provided for financing debts. It will include details of:

Review limit The maximum amount of funds in use that the financier will permit at any time.

Prepayment rates The maximum percentage that the financier will pay against approved debts.

Concentration limit The percentage of the entire sales ledger owed by any one debtor above which funding will not be available.

Type of facility Factoring, recourse or non-recourse, invoice discounting, confidential or disclosed, stock financing.

Discount charge Usually expressed as a percentage over the base rate of a specified bank.

Service charge Usually expressed as a percentage of the notified value of each debt, although fixed fees are sometimes used.

Annual minimum service charge. The minimum income from the percentage service charge that must be achieved.

Other charges Agreement fees, variation fees, payment transfer fees.

Many facilities are provided for an agreed minimum period of one year with an ability on either side to terminate on three or six months' notice expiring after the initial period. It is becoming more common for longer-term facilities to be put in place, particularly in respect of large and complicated deals.

Restructuring the Facility – The Process

An account manager when resolving problems may find that the facility needs restructuring. This may be caused by:

● Turnover growth

● Cashflow problems

● Competitive pressure from other financiers

In turn the causes of cashflow problems can include:

● Bad debts

● Cancelled orders

● Large orders

● Client acquisitions

Let us look in detail at the above circumstances and the evaluation process involved before restructuring can be offered.

Client Turnover Growth

The client's turnover has grown significantly, resulting in a request to exceed the existing financial cap on the funds in use.

Evaluation Questions

● Was the increased turnover level predicted and forecast?

● Why was the review limit set at the agreed level?

● Has the turnover growth been profitable?

● Will an increase in the review limit alone be sufficient to meet the existing and future working capital needs of the client?

● What has caused the increase in turnover?

● What will be the effect of the turnover growth on the client's business in terms of resources, production, finance, facilities and systems?

● How has this turnover growth affected the financier's security?

● Has this turnover growth been achieved by sales to poorly credit-rated customers?

● Have the debts become more or less concentrated?

● Has the debt turn increased or decreased?

● Has the client changed its terms and method of doing business to increase sales performance?

● Is the increase the result of new products or a change in the sales mix? If so how does this effect the quality of the purchased debts?

● Is this increase sustainable or just a blip?

● How has this increase affected gross margins?

● How does this increase affect the viability of the client in both the short and long term?

● How does this increase affect the type and level of stock held?

The answers to these questions will enable the account manager to decide whether an increase in the funds in use will be in the financier's interest. The risks and rewards of continuing to do business with the client will be fully understood and evaluated.

Client's Cashflow Problems

The client has turnover problems and wants an increase in the prepayment percentage.

Evaluation Question

● What has caused the problem?

Possible Causes

- Poor sales performance
- Reduced gross profit margin
- Capital expenditure
- Shareholder's drawings and consequent lifestyle issues
- Increased sales performance
- Customers paying slower
- Suppliers demanding faster payment
- Increased holding of stock
- Other financiers reducing or withdrawing facilities
- Production or supply problems
- Bad debts
- Product obsolescence
- Economic conditions
- Market or sectorial circumstances

A critical analysis of cause and effect is required before any long-term decision can be taken. Temporary support of the client may be needed in order to identify the effect of the client's cashflow problems on the security held by the financier and the continued viability of the client's business. Such critical analysis must investigate the following issues:

- Is the problem short or long term?
- Should the problem be solved by increased borrowings or financings, increased investments or reducing costs?
- Do we know the length and value of the cashflow shortage?
- How does this affect the financier's security?
- Can the collateral support the increase in funding levels?
- Is the business viable?
- Can the financier gain sufficient reward to compensate for a higher level of risk?

There are many circumstances where a financier will give a favourable decision in order to assist a client through cashflow problems. Such circumstances may include:

- Bad debts
- Cancelled orders
- Large orders

We shall look at each in turn.

Bad Debts

A manpower services company that provides temporary computer contractors suffers a huge bad debt, which causes an immediate cashflow crisis. A critical evaluation reveals that:

- The underlying business is profitable

- A full and growing order book will ensure that the loss can be replaced

- Future trading will repair the damage to the balance sheet

- Collateral to support any increase in the prepayments is sufficient

- The financier will be amply rewarded

- The client will fully cooperate

In this real-life situation, the financier helped the client by increasing the prepayments and after nine months the business reverted to profitable trading. The financier then reverted to the previous funding facility.

Cancelled Order

A provider of security personnel receives confirmation from a major supermarket to put security staff in over 100 stores. Following a change in policy the supermarket cancels the order. The client, however, in the meantime has increased resources, hired staff and purchased uniforms. A critical evaluation reveals that this is a short-term problem. By negotiating with creditors, including the landlord and the Inland Revenue, the client is able to trade out of the position with the help of the financier who increases prepayments in return for additional security offered by the client.

Large Order

A distributor of electrical components invoices at the rate of £200K per month and makes modest profits. He has funds in use from his financier of £300K with a prepayment percentage of 80% against debtors. There is a limit of the funds in use of £400K.

The client negotiates with a blue-chip customer to deliver £1m of goods, to be shipped over a two-month period with credit terms of 30 days from delivery. The client is unable to get its own supplier to extend credit above existing levels.

The cashflow and budget projections suggest that:

- The client will make an additional £250K profit with minimal additional costs

- A prepayment percentage of 90% is needed

- Funds in use will reach 600K

- Debts outstanding will peak at £500k

- The blue-chip customer will represent a 55% concentration

A wise financier under these circumstances may look to finance the transaction by a temporary restructuring of the facility to accommodate a £500K review limit and a 90% advance rate subject to:

- Receiving copy orders and delivery notes in respect of the transaction

- Obtaining satisfactory credit agency ratings or credit insurance on the customers

- Taking additional security from the client such as a charge over assets other than the debts

- The client allowing the financier to pay the supplier direct

- Obtaining confirmation from the debtor of the validity of the debt together with an acknowledgement of notice of assignment and an undertaking to pay the debts to the financier

- Strict adherence to the revised funds in use

- An increase in service fees and/or a one-off facility charge

As an additional service the financier could consider providing a loan facility against the security of the client's stock.

Other circumstances that may require the facility to be restructured can include:

- An acquisition

- Competitive pressures

Acquisition

A client may wish to increase and develop its business through an acquisition of assets or by purchasing the shares of another company. In these circumstances a financier can increase its business by restructuring the facility and providing additional finance. As a result a client may come to rely heavily on a financier both in terms of financial support and commercial expertise.

When presented with an acquisitions proposal from a client a financier needs to

- Ask why the client wants the acquisition

- Review the client's existing business

- Evaluate the target company

- Review the proposed financial structure

Why does the client want to make this acquisition?

The obvious answer is to make more money. If so how is this to be achieved? Will it be by:

- An increase in sales?

- Increasing or protecting market share?

- Diversification into other sectors or products?

- Securing essential suppliers?

- Vertical integration through the supply chain?

- Remedying existing trading problems?

- Increasing manufacturing or sales capacity?

Once the financier has satisfactory answers to the basic questions it will move on to the next stage of the evaluation process.

Review Existing Business Conditions

The financier must review the client's business performance compared with:

- The client's expectations

- The client's historic performance

- The market in which the client operates

If the existing business is experiencing trading difficulties, an acquisition may compound or exacerbate the problem.

At this stage the financier should enquire whether this acquisition is consistent with the client's stated objectives and corporate strategy.

Evaluation of the Target

If a financier is happy with the client's rationale and its existing business conditions, a critical analysis of the target company must be undertaken. This analysis will follow the same principles as those involved in gaining new business for the financier and underwriting the deal. In order to undertake the analysis the financier needs to know the following about the target:

1. Its current and historic trading positions

2. Is it solvent?

3. Is it subject to any type of formal insolvency procedure such as receivership. administration, winding up or voluntary arrangement?

The financier will then conduct a SWOT analysis to find out the inherent *strengths* and *weaknesses* of the target.

A financier should find out why the target company's shareholder wants to sell. Shareholders may want to exit as a result of:

- Trading problems

- Retirement plans

- To maximize return on their investment

- A strategic decision by the group parent to sell a subsidiary because of economic, political or financial conditions affecting such parent.

The financier will next look at the operating conditions of the target. The buzzword when people talk about acquisitions is synergy, as in the question 'will the business come together synergistically?'

To answer this question the financier has to look at:

Logistics – locations, buildings

Culture – executive, management, staff

Market – the likely market reaction to the acquisition

Resources – the resources and ability of the management team to effect and manage the transition

Financial Structure

The all-important issue is whether the acquisition will be a financial success. This will be determined by the answer to these questions:

- How will the deal be financed?

- Is new capital being introduced?

- Does the transaction involve a sale of shares or a sale of assets?

- Will the acquired company be integrated or become a subsidiary?

If the financier is satisfied that the acquisition makes commercial sense it can assist by restructuring the existing facility to generate more cash or by providing such restructuring facilities against the assets of the target company. Such restructuring can include:

- Increasing the funds-in-use limit to reflect increased sales activity

- Increasing the prepayment percentage

- Providing loans against other assets such as stock, plant and machinery or buildings

- Providing temporary bridging facilities

Competitive Pressures

Increasingly financiers find themselves competing for business. A client who is aware of this will try to get a better deal either from the existing financier or a competitor. The cost to the financier of replacing an existing client is such that any potential loss of a client to a competitor requires sensitive and careful consideration. These questions need satisfactory answers:

- Does the client really want to leave?
- If so what are the reasons?
- Does the client provide sufficient reward for the risk?
- Is the existing facility meeting all of the client's requirements?
- Can the facility be restructured to meet the client's requirements while still providing a sufficient reward for the financier?

Typically negotiations with an existing client will centre on:

- Service
- Price and prepayments
- Product

Service   This is the most difficult area for an existing financier. If the client believes that he has received consistently bad service it will not stay. How many of us will continue to visit a restaurant that has provided bad food, poor service and charged us for the privilege? Conversely a financier who has consistently met the client's needs in terms of service levels will find its negotiating hand stronger.

Price and prepayments   If service levels have been acceptable a client may want to move away only because a better financial offer has been made by the competition. If everything else is equal the existing financier will normally match a competitive price structure provided it can maintain an adequate reward for the risks to be undertaken. If the proposed reward is unacceptable then the client will be encouraged to move to a competitor. However, many competitive quotes involve both an increase in facilities coupled with a reduction in price. It is under these circumstances that a financier will find it needs to substantially restructure the present facilities.

Product change   A financier must remember that a client will find it attractive to change to a competitor who can solve the client's need for finance with less intrusion by the financier with the customers. For example, a competitor may offer invoice discounting to a client with a factoring facility. This may appear very attractive to a client who wants to regain control over credit management and sales accountancy functions in order to remove the obtrusive nature of a factoring facility. In this case, if the existing financier has the facilities and considers the risk justifiable, it may counter the competitor's offer by suggesting a similar invoice-discounting facility. This is only possible for a client who meets the stricter requirements of an invoice-discounting facility.

If an invoice-discounting or asset-based client is offered a return to bank funding, this can be attractive. A bank's reporting requirements are likely to be less obtrusive than those of an asset-based financier. Banks write commercial business with greater emphasis on the client's accounts and financial statements so that the bank does not have to use its resources in managing and monitoring collateral.

The fact that a financier relies largely upon the strength of the client's financed assets rather than the client's financial statements can often persuade a client to stay. The financier may remind the client that banks have, in the past, been accused of withdrawing their umbrella as soon as it starts raining. An asset-based financier usually supports a client through difficult times as long as the underlying collateral continues to service and support the funds in use.

A financier who proactively offers to restructure a facility in line with the client's existing and future working capital requirements can strengthen the relationship with the client to their mutual benefit.

5.3   Contractual Provisions for Protection of Funding

Most commercial transactions rely upon a large dose of trust between the parties. This is particularly so in factoring. The financier is buying an intangible asset for a very large upfront payment with little opportunity to inspect what it is purchasing. It is unlike buying a motor car where the shiny new vehicle is paraded for inspection and testing before any money passes.

So, how does the financier protect the investment in prepayments made against uncollected debts? The protection measures break down into the financier's rights against:

(a) the client

(b) the debt

(c) the associated rights

(d) the guarantors

(e) non-contracting third parties

In the last resort, a financier wants protection against an insolvent client unable to pay back monies overdrawn from the financier. Such requirement to pay back may happen because:

(a) the notified debts are non-existent (fraud)

(b) the debtor is insolvent

(c) the debts are disputed

(d) the debt turn extends causing a greater proportion of debts to be recoursed.

The financier's rights are largely found in the documentation and to a lesser extent in the general law. The most important documentation for the protection of funding is:

(a) the factoring agreement

(b) guarantees and indemnities

(c) charges

In an earlier chapter we have already examined the factoring agreement in detail. However, it is necessary to revisit this major document when helping to protect the funds in use.

Rights Against the Client

A financier often sets out pre-conditions before funding commences. In the case of the Top Factors' agreement these are set out in paragraph 16 of the schedule. Such conditions can cover any additional matters that the financier considers necessary for protection, such as the assignment of the client's credit insurance policies or an increase in the paid-up capital.

Such special conditions could also cover matters to be continued during the relationship.

If there is a breach of the special conditions or any other term of the agreement during the relationship, Top Factors can invoke clauses 5(4) or 5(10) relying on a breach of clause 20(2)(vii) (i.e. the client has broken the agreement). Under clause 5.4 Top Factors in their absolute discretion can withhold all prepayments and demand repayment of any prepayment previously made together with all present and future liabilities. Under clause 5(10) monies due by the client are set off against collections and the debit balance is immediately payable by the client to the financier.

This would leave Top Factors merely with an obligation to collect the debts. Funding would cease and the financier could claim recovery of the exposure. As the agreement is not terminated any further debts created belong to Top Factors but with no obligation to increase the funding through further prepayments.

Apart from breach of the agreement the financier can likewise protect himself if any other event of default under clause 20(2) occurs.

The events of default listed in clause 20(2) should be fully understood. They break down into:

(a) insolvency related events	(i), (ii), (iii)
(b) enhanced credit risk of the client	(iv), (v), (vi), (viii), (ix)
(c) breach of the agreement	(viii)
(d) change in third party positions	(x), (xi), (xii)

Once the financier is aware of his rights under an event of default such as appear in clause 20(2), how does he protect his funding in addition to his rights in clause 5(4)? The answer is found in clause 20(3). The most usual demand by the financier is for repayment of the current account debit balance under clause 20(3)(iii). The financier retains the debts as security for such payment.

If there is a breach of a client's warranty about a debt (e.g. that the goods have been delivered), the debt becomes an unapproved debt and can then be recoursed under clause 10(1) or the prepayment must be repaid under clause 5(4).

If the financier considers that his funds are at risk this usually arises because of an event of default. If Top Factors consider that the exercise of the draconian rights explained above would cause the client to fail, they may have no alternative but to claw back the funding on a gradual basis. It may then be some consolation that in such riskier circumstances the financier's charges to the client increase under clauses 14(2) and 14(3).

Apart from the rights under a factoring agreement some financier take security over the other assets of a client through an all-assets debenture. If the client is unable to repay the funds in use following proper demand, the financier may appoint a receiver to the client. The receiver will realize the client's assets and make distribution to the creditors (including the financier) in accordance with insolvency law and priorities.

Rights in Respect of Debts

You will have noticed from clause 4(1) of the model agreement that all future debts vest in the financier immediately upon their creation. This is often called a 'whole turnover' arrangement. This gives excellent protection to the financier because:

1. all the debts of the client, whether or not notified to the financier, are the property of the financier. This is useful in insolvent situations when the client may have sold goods without telling the financier about the debts; they are automatically the property of the financier and not of the liquidator;

2. there can be no claims from subsequent debenture holders to the client's debts because they are owned by the financier (provided the financier is the first to give notice of assignment).

To prevent a client overtrading a funding limit is often established which puts a ceiling on the total value of prepayments at any time in respect of outstanding debts *(see clause 5(5)(i) and paragraph 14 of the schedule)*.

Credit notes can rapidly dilute a financier's investments in debts. Clause 9(4) enables the financier to insist that credit notes are issued only with the financier's permission.

The amount that the financier is prepared to pay as a prepayment (or in a non-recourse facility by way of payment of the purchase price) is determined by the approval limit. This is set out in the financier's absolute discretion *(see definition of 'approval limit')*. In the chapter about the factoring agreement we have pointed out that an approval limit already set can be varied or cancelled under clause 17.

The strongest right of the financier in respect of a debt is to be able to sue for its collection. As the assignee of the debt a financier can give notice of assignment, sue for and/or give a valid discharge for a debt. This includes the right to compromise any dispute. These rights, which exist in general law, are also spelt out in the model agreement at clause 14(1).

With disclosed facilities, such as full factoring, the debtor is told of the financier's purchase of debts by a 'notice of assignment'. This is affixed to invoices when they are sent to the debtor. This notice is also repeated on statements. Typical wording states:

> *Our sales accounts are factored to TOP Factors Ltd to whom the benefit of this account has been assigned and to whom all cheques should be made payable. This account can be discharged only by payment to TOP Factors Ltd and not to any other party. Cheques should be sent to them at ...*

This notice of assignment is important for three reasons:

1. To prevent the debtor paying the client and gaining a good discharge of the debt.

2. To avoid set-offs arising (see below).

3. To avoid the obtaining of priority by subsequent charge holders.

The financier often experiences the situation in which the debtor has ignored the notice of assignment and continued to pay the client direct. A payment to the client by ignoring a notice of assignment does not discharge the debt. The debtor can be made to pay again. However, it is important that the financier makes a particular point of advising the debtor of the correct procedures for discharging debts to avoid the time and expense of suing the debtor.

Provided that the financier can prove that notice of assignment was given of the specific debt prior to the payment to the client, the financier is entitled to demand payment again. This is important where the client fraudulently demands payment from the debtor and then goes into liquidation or the client and the debtor conspire to avoid paying the financier.

All financiers have stories of bitter, unhappy debtors forced to pay twice. Such debtors are likely to cause ongoing problems for financiers by placing a ban on the future assignment of debts.

A 'set-off' occurs when a debtor tries to reduce the amount of money owing to the financier by the value of a debt owed to the debtor by the client. The date of notifying the debtor of the assignment of the debt is critical in establishing the rights in such cases. Once the notice of assignment has been served on the debtor, it effectively draws a line under the preceding transactions.

If the claim, by the debtor, against the client arose prior to receipt of notification of assignment, this claim, whether it arises from the contract or elsewhere, can usually be set-off against any claim by the financier. However, it must also be due and payable before the assigned debt is payable. For example:

- On 1 January 1999 notice of assignment is given to the debtor on a £10,000 debt due for payment on 30 January.

- The client owes the debtor £7,000 under a loan repayable as to £4,000 on 15 January and £3,000 repayable on 15 February.

- The debtor can off-set the £4,000 from the £10,000 assigned debt due to the financier but must recover the £3,000 directly from the client.

If, however, the claim arises out of the contract or subject matter of the assigned debt (e.g. damages caused by faulty goods supplied), the debtor can claim the set-off. In this case the dates of notice of assignment are immaterial. But the debtor can only set-off against the financier a sum equal to the debt assigned and no more. Any claim in excess of the debt is called a 'counterclaim'. It can be claimed by the debtor only against the client. It cannot be claimed against the financier.

Referring to Appendix ??, you will note that under Top Factors' agreement debts can be notified to the financier once the goods are placed in transit to the debtor, even though they may not have reached the debtor. Problems can arise if the client then becomes insolvent before paying the carrier. Carriers have a right to hold goods if there is money due to them from their customers for freight charges. If an insolvent client fails to pay its carrier the goods may not reach the debtor and the debt will be worthless. The financier may have to pay the freight charges to release goods to the debtor. This is particularly important in export markets.

The financier has what lawyers call an 'equitable assignment'. This is an assignment procedure that does not fully comply with section 136 Law of Property Act 1925, which would give a 'legal' or 'statutory' assignment. The only result of having an equitable assignment is that in court proceedings the debtor is entitled to call for the client to be joined as a party. If the client's relationship with the financier is good this is not a problem. The client willingly joins in. If there is any doubt the financier will use the client's name under the power of attorney in clause 16 of Top Factors' agreement. This avoids any client-induced delay in court proceedings to collect a debt.

Associated Rights

A financier not only buys the debt but also its 'associated rights', which are defined in the agreement. Upon the insolvency of the client disputes with debtors increase in frequency. Financiers find it valuable to be able to take possession of the client's ledgers, computerized data, proofs of delivery and contractual documentation as soon as such insolvency looms. These assist in resolving disputes. These documents are within the definition of 'associated rights' purchased and owned by the financier.

Following the insolvency of the client there are requests by debtors to return goods (*e.g. not in accordance with the contract or sold on sale or return*). The financier can accept returns and sell the goods for the credit of the client's current account under clause 14(4). The right of access to the client's premises to recover returned goods or documentation is given by clause 15(1). Any net proceeds are to be credited to the current account to reduce any funding by way of prepayments and charges.

Rights Against Guarantors/Indemnifiers

Guarantees and indemnities are used to protect the financier against loss under a recourse agreement when the value of debts held does not realize the full value of prepayments made against them and the client becomes insolvent.

A guarantee and indemnity may be held by a non-recourse financier to protect it against breaches of the client's warranties about debts.

Guarantees and indemnities can:

- cover everything that the client is obliged to do; or
- be limited to cover certain aspects, e.g. any or all of:
    - the client's warranties;
    - wrongful banking of remittances;
    - fraud;
- be of unlimited financial value or limited to a specified figure, plus interest and costs;
- be irrevocable or revocable by a period of written notice.

In the model guarantee and indemnity (Appendix ??) the most powerful clause is 1.2, under which the surety (whether corporate or individual) undertakes immediately on demand to pay amounts due by the client to the financier. Prior termination of the factoring agreement would not be necessary before claiming under this guarantee. The amounts due by the client could arise under clause 5(4), 5(10), 10(1) and 20(3) of the model factoring agreement.

The financier may have taken security for the guarantee, e.g. by an all-assets debenture from a corporate guarantor. Failure to comply with a demand under the guarantee allows the financier to appoint a receiver to the guarantor in order to recover amounts due. Personal guarantors can also be asked to provide security, such as a charge over a home.

In the absence of security the financier would normally issue proceedings against the surety for the amount due by the client. The amount due would be conclusively certified under clause 10 of the guarantee.

The guarantee document also gives rights to the financier in respect of monies owed by the client to the surety (*see clause 8 of the guarantee*).

Rights Against Non-contracting Parties

Under confidential invoice discounting arrangements, the client receives payments from debtors discharging debts. In factoring situations debtors sometimes continue to pay such funds to the client. The financier must trust the client immediately to pay over such funds to the financier. The client must not bank them into its own bank account. In the model agreement the client specifically undertakes in clause 8(2)(vi) to deal with debtor payments by handing them unbanked to the financier. In addition the client undertakes *'to hold such remittance in trust for the financier and separate from the client's own monies'*. Clients in financial difficulties have been known to bank debtor payments into the client's bank account to reduce an overdraft (and thereby reducing the directors' personal liabilities under guarantees given to the bank). The financier is then left with a shortfall upon the client's insolvency. If the defaulting director has also given a guarantee to the financier demand can be made for the shortfall. If he has not given a guarantee he can still personally be sued for the tort (a civil wrongdoing) of conversion of funds belonging to the financier, plus interest. The limited liability of an incorporated client will be no protection to the defaulting director.

5.4 Compliance with Contractual Requirements

The complexity, value and structure of any facility usually determines the range and scope of the financier's legal requirements. These requirements usually cover four areas:

● Documentation and security

● Changes to the client

● Financial reporting

● Additional terms tailored for a specific client

Documentation and Security

There is a legal obligation on the part of the client always to ensure that the collateral remains unencumbered. For example, a factor expects clean title to any debts he purchases; they must not be charged to a bank or other lender.

The legal documentation addresses the fiduciary duties of the client and its directors in relation to assets assigned to, or held as security for, the financier. It emphasizes that the cash received from debtors belongs to the financier. It is essential that the copy invoices supplied evidence valid obligations of the debtors to pay.

Other fiduciary issues may include prohibitions in respect of dealing with assets such as stock, plant and machinery and buildings if they provide security for the facility.

The legal documentation specifies how often debts should be notified to the financier. The frequency of draw downs or prepayments is specified as is the frequency with which information regarding the composition of stock and its movements are needed.

The legal documentation usually sets out the financier's reporting and documentary requirements and also deals with the rights and remedies available to the financier should the client fail to comply.

Where non-debtor based assets are financed, the agreement determines the frequency under which assets such as stock, plant and buildings are valued. The level and type of financial information required by the financier during the currency of the facility is also covered. Standard reporting requirements are likely to include:

- Audited accounts within 6 months of the financial year-end

- Quarterly management accounts within one month of each quarterly reporting period

- An aged purchase ledger to be provided monthly within 10 days of each month end

- An aged sales ledger to be provided monthly within 10 days of each month's end. This is not required under a factoring facility because the factor will already have this information

Changes to the Client

Changes to the control of a client or its business can seriously prejudice a financier. If there is a material change in the client's trading activity, ownership or control then the financier can usually change the terms of the facility or even terminate it.

Financial

With large financing facilities it is common for an asset-based financier to introduce financial covenants. These impose minimum financial performance criteria on the client, which reflect the risks involved in granting the facility.

Such covenants can cover:

Turnover	Minimum sales performance.
Gross profit	Minimum margin as a percentage of value.
Net profit	As a percentage or value.
Net worth	As a value.
Gearing	Expressed as a ratio of debt over net worth.
Total debt	Expressed as a value.

The covenants applied reflect those issues that the financier believes to be critical to the client's success.

For example:

Distribution Company

	Current Performance	Projections
Sales	10 M	15 M
Gross Profit	3 M /30% of sales	4.5 M /30% of sales
Overheads	2.9 M	3.5 M
Net Profit	0.1 M	1.0 M

This prospective client has demonstrated a £100K profit from its existing activities. However, it projects that sales will increase from £10M to £15M without any significant increase in overheads. It could be that the critical success factor is its ability to increase sales. Therefore the financier may apply a covenant related to sales performance.

Additional Terms and Conditions

These are agreed at the outset of the relationship in addition to those terms and conditions included in the standard legal documentation. These terms are specific to an individual client and relate to the type and content of information to be supplied to the financier to monitor the ongoing collateral. These could include:

● Copy purchase orders in respect of customers whose outstanding debts exceed a specific value

● Copy delivery notes in respect of individual invoices over a specific value

● Documentation about critical suppliers or liabilities to the Inland Revenue or Customs and Excise

● Specific reports in relation to stock movement or composition

● Any other information required by the financier

Conclusion to Relationship Management

It is the account manager who has to ensure that a client complies with its contractual obligations. In this he or she will be supported by the audit team and other operational staff.

It is important that the client does not see the client relationship function as a policing role. Although close monitoring of the value of the assets funded and the client's compliance with his legal agreement is essential, it has to be carried out with the least possible disruption to the day-to-day running of the client's business.

Over-obtrusive risk management can be self-defeating.

6
DETERMINING AND MANAGING THE EXIT STRATEGY

A successful exit from a relationship and the recovery of the funds in use will usually only result from a professional approach to the monitoring process. Skilful monitoring of the clients' circumstances will assist the exit and recovery. A financier must never be caught out by changing circumstances that affect the existing and future viability of any client within its portfolio.

In order to manage a recovery strategy effectively it is necessary to understand what happens when a company becomes insolvent and what options are then available to the company. In the following section we shall consider the various of the formal insolvency arrangements and the effect these would have on an asset-based lender.

6.1 Insolvency

In practice some form of formal insolvency of a company, partnership or individual occurs either when:

● Its liabilities exceed its assets with no reasonable prospect of the situation being reversed; or

● It is unable to repay indebtedness as it falls due.

If a client ceases to trade no further debts will be generated.

The client will, almost always, enter into a formal insolvency shortly thereafter. The most common forms is either a winding up (sometimes called a 'liquidation') for a limited company and a partnership or bankruptcy for a sole trader client.

Corporate Insolvencies

The formal insolvency procedures we shall look at that involve corporate clients are:

● Liquidations

● Administrative receivership

● Administration

- Company voluntary arrangement

Liquidations

There are three types of winding up:

- Members voluntary
- Creditors voluntary
- Compulsory liquidation

Members Voluntary Winding Up

This procedure is rare. It is a way of realizing the assets of a solvent company for the benefit of its shareholders. They initiate the process and appoint a liquidator to realize all the assets and discharge all liabilities. Any surplus is returned to the shareholders. A declaration of solvency is needed and all creditors must be paid within 12 months.

Creditors Voluntary Winding-Up

This is used when the directors believe that the company cannot continue on a solvent basis. The directors approach a licensed insolvency practitioner to assist them in calling a creditors' meeting and in preparing a statement of affairs for circulation to the creditors. The shareholders pass a resolution placing the company into liquidation and appoint a liquidator. The creditors vote at the creditors' meeting for the shareholders' nomination to remain in office or to be replaced.

Compulsory Winding-Up

This occurs where a petitioning creditor presents a winding up petition to the court. After a hearing the court issues an order for the company to be wound up. The Official Receiver automatically becomes the liquidator but he may be replaced by a licensed insolvency practitioner.

Liquidator's Responsibility

It is the responsibility of a liquidator to dispose of a company's assets in order to maximize the return for the benefit of all the creditors.

Financier's Position upon Client's Liquidation

The financier rarely gets involved in the winding-up process other than to notify the liquidator of assets that have been charged or assigned to the financier.

However, a financier who is confident that the funds in use can be recovered from the assigned debts has no right to vote at a creditors' meeting. A factor continues its collection efforts but an invoice discounter has a number of choices. He can either:

- Give notice of assignment to the debtor and use his own collection departments or a collection agency; or

Or

- Ask the liquidator, as his agent, to collect the debts in the company's name. This avoids giving notice of assignment.

Where a very high level of prepayments against debts was required or where a financier is financing assets other than debts, he usually has formal security over all the assets of the company. Upon insolvency or failure to repay the facility, the security can be enforced by appointing an administrative receiver. Alternatively, a liquidator can realize the assets subject to the security and make payment (net of costs) to the financier.

Administrative Receivership

Receivership occurs following the appointment of an administrative receiver under a charge by way of security over substantially all the assets of a company. It is also possible to appoint a receiver over specific assets, such as non-vesting book debts or a Law of Property Act receiver over real estate property.

Appointments of administrative receivers are usually either:

- Passive

- Aggressive

A passive appointment occurs when the company asks the debenture holder to appoint an administrative receiver to protect the assets of the company. This may follow lengthy discussions and negotiations between the parties, where ultimately the appointment is seen by all to be the most appropriate solution.

An aggressive appointment results from a debenture holder realizing that he must act quickly to protect the secured assets, which form the security for his funds in use. There will be a formal demand for repayment of such monies as are due on demand. Sufficient time only to visit a bank to draw a draft is allowed. Typically only a matter of hours passes before the receiver is then appointed.

Reason for Appointing a Receiver

An appointment is likely to be made for either of the following reasons:

- To obtain and retain control of the secured assets where the company is likely to enter into any other form of insolvency.

- To facilitate an orderly realization of the company's assets for the benefit of the debenture holder.

In each case the secured creditor is entitled to put his or her interests before that of the insolvent company or the unsecured creditors.

Third Party Appointed Administrative Receiver

A financier who is merely providing finance under a debt purchase agreement and is not involved in financing other assets may often find that a receiver is appointed to his client by a third-party security holder. The third party is often a bank, which has waived its rights to the debts to enable the financier to offer factoring or invoice discounting.

As with a liquidator appointment, the financier will continue to collect debts in order to recover his funds in use, using the same methods.

There are a number of circumstances in which a financier may benefit from an appointment. If through the appointment of a receiver the business continues to trade, there is less disruption to the customer base. This should make it easier to recover outstanding debts. Successful credit management is about establishing a debtor's willingness as well as his ability to pay. Financiers find customers very reluctant to pay outstanding debts when the client is no longer available to service the debtor. This scenario is particularly common where the assigned debts arise from goods sold or services delivered with a continuing obligation on the part of the client to provide after sales maintenance or a guarantee period. If through an administrative receivership the business is onward sold so that the debtor perceives a continuity of service, the financier should enjoy a seamless recovery of his debts.

Financier Appointing an Administrative Receiver

It can be expensive to appoint an administrative receiver. The insolvency practitioner usually asks the party appointing him to guarantee the cost of the receivership, should there be insufficient assets in the company to pay such costs.

If the financier has lost faith in the existing management and is concerned with its integrity or possible breaches of trust, he may appoint a receiver if he can see it as the most effective way of recovering his funds in use. This may be more likely when financing assets other than debtors, particularly if the client is unable to continue trading. An appointment would put an end to the existing corporate governance. The administrative receiver, as agent of the company, has full powers over the company's assets.

Administrative receivership may facilitate a short period of ongoing trading, which may well enhance the realizable value of the company's assets. One of the most valuable assets a company has in recovery terms can be its goodwill and customer base. A business that has been established in its sector for a number of years and enjoys a large and loyal customer base quite often has a hidden asset that may be realized only if the customers continue to be serviced through the company's continued trading. So the sale of this asset out of receivership may benefit a financier in three ways:

- Receipt of the proceeds of goodwill (if charged).
- Ongoing trading should assist the financier's recovery of the debts.
- Any stock held as security for the financier's facility should achieve a higher realizable value.

Also other assets such as plant, machinery and buildings are likely to achieve higher recovery values if these assets remain active and maintained as opposed to being mothballed and sold at auction.

There are circumstances where a business has not been able to achieve its potential and fails. However, if the company's assets are of interest to its suppliers, customers and competitors the receivership may be able to achieve an all-assets sale. Under an assets sale they are, with a few exceptions, purchased from the receiver free of any liabilities. This may be very attractive to a purchaser who is looking to extend its existing business, without taking on the old liabilities built up by a company through its previous adverse trading activity.

The quality of the assets and the business as well as the number of interested parties determine the value a receiver gets for the assets. From a financier's perspective an all-assets sale has many attractions, including the ability to exit cleanly from an insolvent client with a seamless recovery of the outstanding debtors. If the assets under receivership are sold to a purchaser who at the same time pays the financier for a reassignment of the debts, this can assist the financier to obtain an early recovery.

Administration

An administration is an appointment that protects an insolvent company from its creditors. It is a rescue mechanism to protect a company's business and assets.

Its directors contact an insolvency practitioner who assists with the company's application to the court to obtain an administration order. The court has to be persuaded that the administration order is likely to achieve one or more of the following purposes:

1. the survival of the company and the whole or any part of its undertaking, as a going concern;

2. the approval of a company voluntary arrangement;

3. a more advantageous realization of the company's assets than would be effected on winding up.

Client in Administration

Where a financier has a charge over all of his client's assets, including a floating charge, then he must be notified of the intention to apply for an administration order. This gives him a short period in which to appoint an administrative receiver. If he does so this will put an end to the application. If he does not appoint a receiver he cannot do so while an administration continues. Because administration is a ground to terminate most financing facilities, most proposals to enter administration involve the financier's agreement to continue funding.

Upon appointment the administrator assumes full control over the company's affairs and assets.

As with administrative receivership, control of a company is taken away from the incumbent management or shareholders. This may give comfort to a financier who has lost faith in them.

Administrations are financed from the company's resources. They do not require the financier to give an indemnity, which he may have to provide if he appoints an administrative receiver. Financiers quite often see administrations as an opportunity to continue to provide finance to a client while a longer-term solution to its difficulties is found.

As with an administrative receivership a financier is likely to benefit from a controlled and orderly disposal of the company's assets rather than the assets being sold under the forced sale conditions of a winding-up.

Company Voluntary Arrangements – 'CVA'

A CVA is an arrangement with creditors to reduce and or delay the repayment of debt. An administration often precedes a CVA. However a CVA can also be instigated by a company approaching an insolvency practitioner to act as a supervisor.

Here is a simple table to explain the potential benefits of a CVA to an insolvent client :

Insol Co Ltd

Assets		£000s	£000s
	Plant	250	
	Debtors	400	
	Stock	200	
	Other	50	
Total assets			900
Liabilities		£000s	
	Trade creditors	(600)	
	Prepayments	(300)	
	Loans	(100)	
	Other	(50)	
			(1050)
Negative Net Worth			(150)

Insol Co Ltd is insolvent to the extent of £150K. If, however, the trade creditors can be persuaded to accept 50p in the £ in full settlement of all claims, the balance sheet will return to a positive position.

Insol Co Ltd

Assets		£000s	£000s
	Plant	250	
	Debtors	400	
	Stock	200	
	Other	50	
Total assets			900

Liabilities		£000s	
	Trade creditors	(300)	
	Prepayments	(300)	
	Loan	(100)	
	Other	(50)	(750)
Positive net worth			150

Why, you may ask, should creditors accept a reduced amount?

Firstly you need to consider the break-up value of the assets if the company goes into liquidation. As part of every insolvency procedure the insolvency practitioner will produce an estimated statement of affairs showing the book and realizable value of the assets on the company's balance sheet. In the case of Insol Co Ltd its estimated statement of affairs would look like this:

Assets	Book Value £000s	Estimated to Realize £000s
Fixed-charge receipts		
Plant and machinery	250	100
Debtors	400	300
Other	50	0
	700	400
Distribution to charge holders		(400)
Surplus from fixed-charge assets		0

Other realizations

Stock	200	50
Cost of liquidation		(50)
Distribution to creditors		0

This shows that if the assets were to be realized through liquidation the unsecured trade creditors would take a total loss. So an offer of 50p in the £ under a CVA provides an opportunity for the creditors to reduce their loss by 50%. In addition, the creditors will earn future income from continuation of supply.

CVA Procedures

An insolvency practitioner upon a nomination from the company notifies creditors of the proposal and calls a creditors' meeting. At this stage the practitioner is called the nominee. For the scheme to be approved by the creditors a majority vote of 75% of value of creditors voting is required.

If the proposal is approved, the nominee is appointed as the 'supervisor' of the scheme. His responsibility is to supervise the payment of monies by the company into an account, which is then held and distributed to creditors.

Not only does a company under CVA benefit from a reduction in its indebtedness to creditors but quite often the arrangement allows for repayment over a substantial period of time. One to three years is quite common.

If the scheme fails, the supervisor arranges for the company to be placed in liquidation. Any funds in the supervisor's account are distributed in accordance with the winding up rules.

Financiers and CVAs

Financiers often see a CVA as providing time to improve its security as the client continues to trade. Financiers may well be asked to continue providing finance through factoring or invoice discounting. Some financiers specialize in financing CVAs. The combination for an ailing company of both reducing debt and increasing its working capital availability is very attractive in a turnaround scenario.

Failures of CVAs

Many CVAs are unsuccessful. This can be because:

- The supervisor under a CVA has few management responsibilities in relation to the day-to-day running of the company. Accordingly the same management team that brought the business into an insolvent state is left in complete control of the company's affairs.

- Many suppliers who have to accept a reduced repayment of their debt are reluctant to deliver further goods on previous credit terms. This strains the company's working capital resources, particularly if the suppliers demand payment in advance or on delivery or on very short terms. However, any proposal should recognize this and adequate provision should be made for this increased funding requirement.

● Some suppliers see future trade as an opportunity to recoup their losses by increasing their prices for new supplies.

Personal Insolvency

Where the client is a sole proprietor or a partnership, a financier will have to deal with personal insolvency matters. It is important to understand that a person carrying out business as a sole proprietor or in partnership is personally liable for the debts incurred and that under insolvency conditions both business and personal assets may be seized in order to meet the liabilities of the insolvent business.

From time to time a financier has to deal with the personal insolvencies of some of his sole trader or partnership clients. The opportunities and issues are similar to those in respect of an insolvent company. The principal procedures are:

● Bankruptcy

● Individual voluntary arrangements

A financier may have to pursue a director of a client for payment under his or her personal guarantee supporting the facility. If judgement is obtained and no monies are forthcoming, the financier may decide to petition for the director's bankruptcy.

Bankruptcy

This occurs where an individual declares himself insolvent or is placed into bankruptcy by a court order following a creditor's petition. His estate is wound up by a trustee in bankruptcy. Any funds realized are distributed to creditors by way of a dividend.

Individual Voluntary Arrangement (IVA)

A voluntary arrangement in respect of an insolvent individual is similar in its effect to a CVA. It presents an opportunity for an individual to avoid becoming a bankrupt by making an arrangement with creditors.

6.2   Proactive Client Termination

A financier who feels uncomfortable with an existing client may be unwilling to see if the client can trade out of a looming insolvency. He may act proactively and terminate the facility to avoid the problems of collecting out when the client is in formal insolvency. The situations in which he would be wise to do so include:

- Deteriorating financial conditions
- Deteriorating collateral
- Deteriorating management and control
- Commercial problems
- Fiduciary problems
- Serious breach of the legal agreement
- Accumulating failures
- Insufficient rewards
- Third-party changes

We shall look at each of these in turn.

Deteriorating Financial Conditions

This occurs where a financier believes that the client is in danger of going out of business and there is no ability and or willingness by the directors or shareholder to take action.

Deteriorating Collateral

Changes in external circumstances, business direction, product offering or client administration can have a seriously detrimental effect on the financier. Examples include the sales ledger becoming unacceptably concentrated, increasing levels of customer delinquency, higher levels of returns, customer quality deterioration and increasing debt turn.

Deteriorating Management and Control

The departure of key staff can cause the client's financial and operational controls to deteriorate to the extent that a financier feels that his funds in use are at risk.

Commercial or Business Problems

A financier may recognize impending problems with a particular sector or industry that cannot be corrected.

Fiduciary Issues

The financier must be alert to fraud, lack of integrity by the directors or conduct adverse to the financier's interests. If the financier loses confidence in the client to such an extent that he no longer trusts the client, there is little point in continuing any facility.

Serious Breach

A serious breach of the facility may be described as an action of the client giving the financier cause to doubt the client's integrity and which seriously affects the collateral.

Continual Failure

A client may continually ignore requests for information or fail to comply with other conditions of the formal agreement. On an individual basis these may be minor but on an accumulated basis the financier may well question why he should continue with the facility. Examples include:

● Continually withholding small amounts of debtor cash received

● Failure to deliver audited or management accounts on time or at all

● Failure to complete schedules of debts, formal assignments, or other documentation on a timely basis or at all

● Continual delays in issuing or notifying credit notes

● Failure to resolve customer's disputes in a timely manner

● Failure to provide purchase ledger information

● Consistently failing to deliver sales ledger information within agreed timescales

Any of the above taken in isolation could be viewed as day-to-day operating issues to be resolved through diplomacy and negotiation. However, where a client is obviously acting on a continual basis in disregard of the agreement, a financier would be justified in terminating the agreement or reducing the prepayments.

Insufficient Reward

There are circumstances under which a financier decides that the risk associated with the provision of the facilities to a client does not justify the reward.

These can include:

● Pricing of the facility based on the clients' projected business activity which fails to materialize

● Deterioration in the client's financial performance which increases the likelihood of business failure

● A change in the client's business activity which seriously damages the collateral

● A deterioration in the client's financial control and sales accounting functions which causes the financier's workload to increase

Under these circumstance a financier can:

1. Increase the return; or

2. Reduce the risk; or

3. Terminate the facility and recover his funds in use

If a financier is able to turn the situation around so that sufficient reward can be generated from a client, termination need not be considered.

However if the risk cannot be reduced, or the cost of increased management resources needed to monitor and maintain the value of the collateral cannot be recovered, the financier may decide to part company with the client.

Changes to Third-Party Situation

A related party's activity or operation may have a significant adverse effect upon the success of the client and the security of the collateral. These are circumstances or actions beyond the financier's control that may well cause him to terminate the facility in order to protect the funds in use.

For example:

- A client is part of a group of companies whose financial fortunes have deteriorated. The financier finds that the funds in use are being used to support loss-making activities elsewhere in the group, despite the financial stability or success of the client.

- Action taken by another financier, such as a bank, causes a client failure which forces the financier into vigorous action to collect his funds in use.

Methods of Managing Exit Strategies

We have already considered the role of an insolvency practitioner in the recovery of the funds in use. Although insolvency procedures can help a financier in his recoveries, they are not a panacea for every problem that may face a financier. A financier is often able to act independently of any formal insolvency procedures. In this case the design and management of the exit strategy is entirely in the hands of the financier. His only aim will be to collect his funds in use as quickly, cheaply and profitability as he can.

The procedures that follow from a financiers decision to terminate the relationship with the client include:

- Collect out
- Inter-factor transfer
- Return to bank finance
- Managed exit

We shall look at each of theses in turn.

Collect out

The financier's primary method of recovery of his funds in use is from the debts assigned . With a factoring facility this is achieved through a continuation of the existing collection process until such time as the financier has recovered all prepayments, discount, fees and expenses. Any surplus monies recovered and the remaining debts (if any) are then transferred back to the client, whether solvent or insolvent. The factoring agreement is then terminated.

Where invoice discounting is provided, the financier gives notice of assignment to the debtors, loads the information on to its factoring system and recovers the prepayments through factoring collection procedures.

Under insolvent conditions some financiers may allow the liquidator or administrative receiver to collect the debts on its behalf for a fee. Alternatively a financier can call upon collection agents or specialist firms of solicitors to effect the collect out for fixed fees.

Inter-Factor Transfer

Under an inter-factor transfer the outgoing debt financier is repaid his funds in use by another financier who is offering a debt financing facility. The debts are then transferred back to the client in order that they can be dealt with under the incoming factor's legal documentation. Although these procedures are usually called an 'inter-factor' transfer, it can also be applied between a factor and an invoice discounter and vice-versa or between invoice discounters.

Members of the Factors and Discounters Association operate under a set of guidelines for transfers between members.

Such transfers can occur for a variety of reasons, including:

- The client outgrows its existing facility and no longer fits the preferred client profile of its financier

- The client requires a change of facility, e.g. from factoring to invoice discounting, which the outgoing factor is either unwilling or unable to provide or the terms are unacceptable

- The client no long fits into the financier's risk profile

- The client is unhappy with the service provided or the price charged by the outgoing financier

- The client wants an additional service which its existing financier cannot provide, such as stock or import finance or finance against export debtors

- There has been a complete breakdown in the relationship

Transfers between financiers are becoming more common as the financing market matures and businesses become more aware of the range and diversity of services being offered by competitive asset-based financiers.

Return to Bank Finance

Once a client has achieved its objective in using the financier it may then decide to return to its bank for finance. This may be because of reduced bank charges offered or less intrusion by the bank into the client's day-to-day operations of its sales ledger and collections.

Managed Exits

A financier should be able to spot that the client's future viability or the collateral is at risk.

Supporting evidence can be found from:

● Adverse collateral trends

● Adverse financial trends

● Adverse business trends

Adverse collateral trends may be evidenced by:

● Lengthening debt turn

● Increased levels of customer disputes

● Deterioration in customer quality

● Increasing problems with product quality

● Falling stock levels

● Slowness or absence in reporting collateral movements

● Increase in sales ledger ageing

Adverse financial trends may be evidenced by:

● Monthly sales levels in decline

● Reducing profitability or recording losses

● Lack of or slowness in producing financial statements

● Increasing pressure from suppliers

● Increased usage of finance facilities

● Bad debts from customer failures

● Building up of arrears in VAT, PAYE, taxes.

Adverse business trends may be evidenced by:

● Key staff leaving

● Principals becoming difficult to get hold of

● Backlog in administration and finance function

● Production problems

Collateral Evaluation in Crisis Management

Having spotted the risk to the client or the collateral, the financier then has to engage in crisis management. To determine the financier's strategy in managing the crisis he must undertake an examination of assets supporting the funds in use.

A critical evaluation of the collateral must be made. Initially this is undertaken through a desktop evaluation, i.e. a review of both the collateral control data from the financier's operating system and the raw data submitted by the client in relation to the facility. This evaluation includes reviews of:

- The debt trend report
- The current aged debt report
- The collateral movement report
- The debtor concentrations
- The last debt reconciliation
- The current cash collections
- The stock movement report
- The stock mix between finished goods, raw material, work in progress
- The last audit visit by the financier's team
- The client correspondence file
- The most recent account management submissions
- Legal documentation
- The latest management accounts
- The last independent audited accounts and valuations of buildings and other assets.

On-Site Investigation

The next step is to visit the client for the following purposes:

1. To meet the client's principals and decision makers to find out their views on the current situation and their strategy for successful ongoing trading.

2. To carry out in-depth analysis of the debtors by investigating source documentation including:

   - Invoices and credit notes
   - Delivery notes
   - Sales ledger accounting data
   - Bank statements

3. To verify the value and collectability of the assigned debts by:

   - Reviewing credit control activity
   - Identifying customer disputes and collection problems

4. To verify the existence and value of any other assets forming the financier's security by:

   - Conducting a physical stock check

- Conducting a walk-through observation of plant, machinery and buildings.

5. To assess the client's liquidity from the following documents:

    - VAT returns and payments
    - PAYE and NI declarations and payments
    - Accounts payable review
    - Bank accounts and facility letters
    - Cashflow statements and forecasts

The liquidity evaluation will also want to identify any immediate or potential threats to the business from key suppliers withholding supplies, landlords threatening distraint, creditors taking legal action, utilities being cut off, or staff leaving because wages and salaries cannot be paid.

The size and complexity of the task determines the number and type of people required to conduct the evaluation process.

Typically the account manager orchestrates the on-site investigation and conducts the initial meetings with the client. Internal audit staff and specialist external consultants are used to evaluate the client's liquidity.

Quite often the evaluation is hampered by the absence of essential data. This can result from breakdown of the client's sales accounting and financial reporting systems. Specialists may be needed to investigate, identify and retrieve essential information or assist with the on-site monitoring.

In the initial stages of crisis management, answers are needed to these key questions.

- Do the assets against which the facility has been made available have sufficient realizable value to repay the funds in use?
- Is the business likely to fail in the short term?
- Is the business viable or can it be turned around?
- Does the client's existing management team have the integrity, ability and resource to continue trading and maintain the value of the collateral?

If the assets can repay the funds in use the financier is in a position to consider potential turn around scenarios without jeopardising its secured position.

Next, consideration is given to the immediate and short-term cash position to determine if the business is able to continue to trade and to look at opportunities for the company to generate new cash from its existing owners or external resources.

If there is insufficient funding available to continue operations, a financier is well advised to take action as soon as possible to realize the collateral.

If the business is viable but is suffering from a lack of cash, consideration may be given to the use of an insolvency procedure as described earlier to enable the business to continue to trade while being protected from pressing creditors. Also a fundamentally viable business provides the opportunity to look at the exits, including a sale of the business or its assets; again, the ability to generate cash in the short term is a critical success factor.

Fundamental criteria for continuing to support a client under crisis management conditions are the existing management's integrity, ability and resource.

Any turn around/recovery strategy that involves ongoing trading of the business is likely to fail if the company's management are found wanting.

Hopefully the crisis management investigations reveal that continued or additional funding, can be generated either from the existing collateral or by the taking of new security. If a decision is made to continue or increase funding, it will usually be on the basis that intensive monitoring of the client will be needed for a considerable time.

Type of Exits

1. The client repays funds in use

2. The client is re-financed

3. The client is sold

4. The client's assets are sold

5. The financier collects out

All of the above, excluding 1, may arise under crisis management conditions. The financier may even find that the 'bigger fool policy' operates in his favour. In this case he will be paid off by another financier.

What Happens When it Goes Wrong?

If a financier fails to get satisfactory answers to the above questions or ignores answers he does not like, he may find himself dealing with a nightmare scenario. This will certainly happen when a financier:

●   Thinks the client's business is viable

●   Bases his finance on the continuing viability of the client

●   Thinks the collateral secures the funds in use

●   But the collateral does not secure the advance

●   Does not think the business will fail

●   And the business fails

●   Or he totally misjudges the abilities and integrity of the client.

We need to re-emphasize that asset-based financiers require key staff supported by systems and procedures that give early identification of clients with potential difficulties and which can assist in the successful management of crises. Client failures can wipe out years of previous profitable trading for a financier.

Recoveries

Debtor Litigation

A factor or invoice discounter may need to take legal action against overdue debtors of a terminated client to recover his funds in use. Specialist lawyers can play a significant part in the recovery process. If the client is insolvent there is every incentive for debtors to raise spurious defences or set-offs to avoid payment. There is little motivation for a debtor to pay when they are no longer reliant upon the client for the future provisions of goods or services. In addition customers resent disruptions to the supplies. This can be mitigated through the continuing cooperation of the client's directors and employees even though the client may have ceased to trade. The threat of enforcing their personal guarantees can act as a powerful incentive.

It is vital that the financier can provide information relevant to the sales ledger, such as copy invoices, delivery notes, purchase orders, copy correspondence, remittance advices, and collection letters. Collection through the courts can fail if the financier cannot prove that goods or services were actually delivered.

Indemnity and Guarantee Actions

Directors of a company often give the financier personal guarantees and indemnities in support of the facility. Should a financier be unable to recover its funds from the collateral, legal action taken against the guarantors and indemnifiers may be instigated as a means of recovering the shortfall.

However, a guarantee has value only if the guarantor has sufficient assets. If the directors of a failed client have personal financial difficulties, the financier will have an actionable guarantee of no value. If he issues proceedings he may well obtain a bankruptcy order against a director. Whatever feelings of revenge it may satisfy, obtaining the bankruptcy of a penniless former director will not recover the funds in use.

However, guarantees can be useful as a lever to convince a guarantor to assist with the collection/recovery process. The directors' input can often be useful in resolving queries and disputes that would otherwise be used by debtors to avoid payment.

Corporate guarantees, a guarantee given by a second company in support of the first company's facility, are often provided where a client is part of a group or has strong associations with other entities that may influence or control the viability or prosperity of a client. Such guarantees can provide a useful back up, subject again to the solvency and ability of the corporate guarantor to meet the demands of the financier if the client fails.

7

MANAGING THE FINANCIER'S BUSINESS

7.1   Pricing

In this section we shall be looking at how factoring/discounting services are priced to generate sufficient income to balance the risk/reward equation.

At its simplest a costing is calculated by using a simple formula:-

Cost + Profit = Ideal Selling Price

If we know how much it costs to produce the product and how much profit we want to make on each product, we can calculate the price we need to sell it for, but for many products we have an additional requirement – that of matching the reward to the potential risks.

Relating Risk to Reward in Costing Products

We can follow a simple three-stage model linking reward to risk:

1. If you have £1,000 savings you can deposit it in a bank at no risk whatsoever, but you will only obtain a 'reward' in terms of interest at the rate of, say, 5% p.a.

2. As a shareholder in the bank you are looking for a higher return because there is a risk that some of the customers your bank lends money to might default on the repayment. In return for this higher risk you would seek say a 7% return on your invested money.

3. As the bank itself you now need to generate sufficient money to pay your shareholders their 7% and your customers their 5%. So you decide to undertake a number of business activities, some of which are more risky than others. At the 'safest' end of the 'scale' you lend on mortgages at low interest rates and at the riskiest end you lend at high interest rates on unsecured overdraft.

4. Within this package of products you offer are factoring and discounting and you calculate that any investment you make in these products is fairly risky, so want at least a 30% return on the money you invest.

The figures above are obviously artificial but they do illustrate the basis of all costing: getting a level of return that is in line with the risk of the product.

So our first issue to consider in a costing is the return required for the investment. The second issue concerns recovering all the costs involved in the activity itself.

Types of Costs

There are two broad categories of costs, variable costs and fixed costs. This categorization while not exact does assist in the analysis of costs.

Typical Costs of Factor and Discounter

Variable costs	Fixed costs
These are the costs that vary in direct proportion to the volumes being handled. Examples in a factoring/discounting company could include: staff and staff-related costs of all the processing departments. e.g. post-room, cash processing, filing, data control and preparation – credit assessment – collections and bad debts – client relations – stationery – communications – loan interest – litigation – new client set-up costs.	These are the costs that do not vary within quite wide bands of volume. Examples in a factoring company could include: establishment costs – rent, rates, power, heat, light, insurance etc. – general administration – personnel, canteen, purchasing, accounts, audit, O & M, directors, computer department and staff, sales, marketing and advertising – depreciation on furniture, fittings and equipment – computer hardware and software.

Relating Costs to Product Pricing

We have seen how the overall cost of a financier's company is made up and the total profits required. We must now relate this to the individual client in order that we can arrive at a costing formula for calculating factoring fee rates. Before doing that we should review the main charges levied by a factor to a client.

1. The Factoring or Service Fee
    This is the basic fee used to recover the bulk of the costs incurred by a factoring company. It is a straight percentage of the value of debts assigned (including VAT on debtor invoices) and compensates the factor for the cost of administering the sales ledger and collection functions.

2. The Re-Factoring Charge
    This is an additional fee more common with recourse arrangements. If a debt exceeds the terms and becomes age disapproved (often at 90 days), extra work is involved in the collection.

3. Set-Up Charge (Retrospective Charge)
    This is an additional fee designed to recoup the initial extra expenses involved in taking on a new client's ledger, running initial credit checks, setting credit limits and generally

straightening out the clients ledger maintenance and control procedures and updating the *financier's* computer systems. This is a separate fee paid only by new clients.

4. Rechargeable Costs

   Charge made where additional work is requested by the client, for example litigation work, telegraphic payments and other activities specifically requested by the client.

5. Discount Fee

   The purchase of a debt payable in the future in consideration for an immediate payment in full or in part gives rise to a discount fee. This is the compensation for the purchaser of the debt (the factor) for the amount of finance provided for the period until the debt is recovered. The courts have distinguished discounts of this nature from the payment of interest, which helps to remove any suggestion of money lending and also dissuades the Inspector of Taxes from demanding that clients withhold basic rate tax from the interest payments to the factor. (See section 349 of the Income and Corporation Taxes Act 1988 (as amended).)

For our purpose we shall assume that the income generated from re-factoring, retrospective income and recharged costs is matched by the costs involved in supplying these services. The two remaining areas then to consider are factoring fees and discount fees, which can then be considered as contributing directly to profits.

Discount Fees

Discount has only one 'cost' attached to it, i.e. the interest the financier has to pay to its supplier of finance. The discount rate charged to clients is generally set at around bank base + 3% or +2½% throughout the industry. The profits from discounting (income less cost of money) are therefore easily assessable and, when deducted from the total profits required, determine the profit needed to be recovered from the factoring fee alone.

In fact it is incorrect to say that discount has only one cost.

You have only to think of a strong solid client compared to a weak client. If you lent each of them £10,000 would you charge them both the same rates? The answer, hopefully, is no because the majority of your time and expense would go to maintaining your security behind the money advanced to the weakest client in order to guarantee repayment. Normally this extra effort and cost would be recharged to the client by means of a higher discount rate. However, because factoring companies in general do not vary the money cost very much client to client, this extra cost is built in to the service fee through the elements of its charges that cover security.

The Pricing Calculation

There are, therefore, three elements of recovery that need to be applied to each client in order to arrive at their factoring/service fee:

1. Variable costs, which can be directly related to the workload of the client. These costs

are usually split into four sections:

1) the cost of handling each invoice or credit note.

2) the cost of maintaining each debtor account.

3) the cost of client liaison.

4) the cost of safeguarding the security of advances.

2. Fixed costs, which cannot be directly related to workload. These can be recovered in a variety of ways, but for the purposes of this example we shall recover them:

    a) 50% by way of 'ability to pay', i.e. the larger the client the more it contributes. This is achieved by levying a percentage of turnover.

    b) 50% by work load, i.e. the more work we have to do for the client the more they contribute to overheads. This is achieved by applying a mark-up to the variable cost recovery.

    (Note – the split of 50/50 is being used to simply illustrate the approach; in practice each financier company will have its own split to reflect the real costs of running its own business.)

3. Profit after allowing for the contribution from discount. Like fixed costs this can be recovered in a variety of ways, but for the purposes of this example we shall recover it as in 2. a) and b) above.

Worked Costing Example

The Welsh Finance Group plc own a factoring/discounting subsidy named TOP FACTORS LIMITED and have advanced them £ 1,000,000 for financing clients. It requires a return on this investment of 30% p.a.

Information

All costing/pricing calculations are based on assumptions and projections of business levels/activity, and the accuracy or otherwise of this information can make a considerable difference in the final accuracy of the pricing calculation. For our example, we have the following information:

● clients of TOP FACTORS LIMITED are expected to assign £ 50,000,000 worth of invoices in the year.

● the total current accounts (the amount advanced to and outstanding to clients) are estimated to be constant at £5,000,000 throughout the year.

● TOP FACTORS LIMITED, in addition to the £1,000,000 from its parent company, will also need to borrow £4,000,000 at 8% p.a. for the year, which will meet the client's demand for money

- it will be charged at an average discount rate of 2.5% over base (assume base rate remains at 8% p.a.)

- TOP FACTORS LIMITED's costs for the year will be:

Variable costs	£	%
Invoice-related	20,000	10
Debtor-related	100,000	50
Client-related	30,000	15
Security-related	50,000	25
	£ 200,000	100%
Fixed-costs	£ 150,000	

Client statistics for the year will be:

Invoices assigned	80,000
Debtor accounts	10,000
Clients	60

Calculation

The Welsh Finance Group will require TOP FACTORS LIMITED to make a profit of:

$$£ 1,000,000 \times 30\% = £ 300,000$$

TOP FACTORS LIMITED will generate profit from discount fees of:

Income £5,000,000 at 10.5% (2.5% over 8% base)	£ 525,000
Cost £ 4,000,000 at 8%	£ 320,000
	£ 205,000

The profit requirement from factoring will therefore be:

£ 300,000 – £ 205,000   £ 95,000

To complete our costing calculation we now split all the variable costs, fixed costs and required profit figure into the costing categories. As shown in the following table.

Factoring Cost Calculation

	Total	Invoices (10%)	Debtors (50%)	Clients (15%)	Security (25%)	F
Variable costs	200,000	20,000	100,000	30,000	50,000	
Fixed costs						
(1)	75,000	7,500	37,500	11,200	18,800	
(2)	75,000					75
Profit						
(1)	47,500	4,750	23,750	7,125	11,875	
(2)	47,500					47
Total to be recovered	445,000	32,250	161,250	48,325	80,675	122
Volumes expected		80,000	10,000	60	£ 5m	£
Costing (rounded up)		41p	£16.13	£ 806	0.016p	0.

So if TOP FACTORS LIMITED charge each client:

- 41p   for each invoice sent to them
- £ 16.13   for each debtor account handled
- £ 806   for each client
- .016p   for every £1 advanced per annum
- .003p   for every £1 of turnover

... and if all their sales projections are met, they would in total receive £445,000 f revenue which, after deducting £350,00 fixed and variable , would produce a £95,000 to be added to the profit made on discount of £205,000, a total of £300

The Welsh Finance Group plc would therefore get the return it desired and would to invest in TOP FACTORS LIMITED.

This would of course be an extremely clumsy way of charging clients and s FACTORS LIMITED would follow the accepted practice in the financier indu work out the amount to be recovered from a client (by looking at the estimated vol the first year of factoring and multiplying these by the various elements of the costi dividing this by expected turnover to produce a factoring fee expressed as a perce invoice value.

Costing Application Examples

A prospect company Newstart Limited approaches TOP FACTORS LIN requesting a quote for a full factoring service. Its estimated statistics for the next 12 are as follows:

Number of Invoices	950
Number of Credit Notes	50
Number of Debtor account	125
Advance required	£100,000
Turnover	£1 million

Using our previously calculated costing we have all of the information we require and can cost out quite easily all the following items:

			£
Invoices	(950 x 41p)	=	389
Credit Notes	(50 x 41p)	=	20
Debtors	(125 x £16.13)	=	2,016
Client Liaison	(£ 806)	=	806
Security	(£ 100,000 x £0.016)	=	1,600
Turnover	(£1m x .003p)	=	3,000
Recovery from client		=	7,831

It remains only to divide the recovery required (£ 7,831) by the expected turnover (£ 1,000,000) to arrive at the factoring fee of .78% The prospect would also pay the factors standard 2.5 % over bank base as the discount rate.

Factoring Fee	=	0.78%
Discount Rate	=	2.5% over bank

Adjusting the Formula

Up to now we have taken only the most straight forward of prospect situations. Let us now examine some of the more common variations and how we can adjust our product pricing to cope with these..

1. Newstart Ltd request a lower discount rate than normally quoted.
   The normal discount rate is 3% over bank base rate. The prospect maintains they can get 2% overbase from their bank or a competitor and want the financier to match it. We however need to retain our same level of profitability so we must alter our costing to reflect this lower discount rate and still make the same income during the year.

   Using the same statistics and costing calculation that we calculated for Newstart Ltd we must adjust our calculation to take into account the loss of discount income.

		£
Normal recovery required	=	10,000
Income lost with lower discount		
Rate (1 % x £ 100,000)	=	1,000
Recovery now required	=	11,000

Factoring fee is now the 'new' recovery figure (£11,000) divided by t
(£1,000,000)

Factoring fee	=	1.10%
Discount rate	=	2.00% over bank

2. This second variation looks at the prospect who requires only a small advance. Newstart Limited have just been in touch with the new business manager to s following their discussions about factoring, it has recalculated its requirements next year. As a result it will only be requiring a facility of £50,000 and not £10(initially requested. They also confirm that they will want to be offered 2% ov base for the money charge.

The changes, from the original calculation, are in bold print.

			£
Invoices	(950 x 41p)	=	389
Credit notes	(50 x 41p)	=	20
Debtors	(125 x £16.13)	=	2,016
Client liaison	(£ 806)	=	806
Security	(**£ 50,000** x £0.016)	=	**800**
Turnover	(£1m x .003p)	=	3,000
Normal recovery from client		=	7,031
Recover loss on discount		=	**500**
New recovery required		=	7,531
Factoring quotation			
Factoring fee	=		0.75%
Discount rate	=		2.00% over bank

3. Once again, Newstart phones. This time it says that the bank has promised i money it needs. But it has been so impressed with the professional way the enq been handled that it would like to go ahead with a 'collection only service'. (Tl will run the sales ledger but not advance any monies to the client and when th

pays, all the money collected will be passed to the client.) This type of facility is often called Service Only.

Invoices	(950 x 41p)	=	389
Credit notes	(50 x 41p)	=	20
Debtors	(125 x £16.13)	=	2,016
Client liaison	(£ 806)	=	806
Turnover	(£1m x .003p)	=	3,000
Recovery from client		=	6,231

The factoring fee to quote is recovery (£6,231) divided by turnover (£1,000,000), which equals a factoring fee of 0.62%. There is no discount charge because the client is using none of the factor's money.

Calculating Investment

Up to now we have based our calculation on a 'fixed' investment in the client. It is more normal for this investment level to be calculated based on the debt turn of the prospect. There must, however, be some care exercised in this calculation when looking at a prospect with large seasonal or exceptional peak/trough in trade at the time the figures are extracted.

The aim is to calculate the average investment by a simple calculation using debt turn and the prepayment percentage. The following steps are followed:

1. Obtain current debtor figure, and establish if this is representative of the average level of trade (remove seasonal variations or one-off situations by studying past trends). If it is artificially high or low adjust the figure to give an average figure for debts outstanding over the past 12 months.

2. Obtain turnover for past year.

3. Calculate debt turn by dividing annual turnover by debtor figure.

4. Take the projected turnover figure for the next 12 months and divide it by the debt turn. This will give you the average debtor figure for the next year.

5. Multiply this debtor figure by the prepayment percentage and you will have the investment level. This calculation presupposes that all invoices will be assigned to the factor and all will be approved.

To put some figures into this calculation:

Current debtors	=	£ 100,000
Turnover last 12 months	=	£ 560,000
Debt turn	=	x 5.6
Estimated turnover next 12 months	=	£ 1,000,000

Estimated average debtors	=	£ 178,571
Investment at 80% prepayment	=	£ 142,857

Having produced a set of pricing formulas and looked at how they can be applied to different circumstances, we must also consider the question as to when the factor should consider breaking the pricing formula. For most situations the pricing formula is a guide, not a rule, and there are many reasons why the formula may be overridden.

The 'Exceptional' Prospect

Listening to a new business manager sell the virtues of his or her prospective client you could be persuaded that the exceptional prospect is 'every prospect,' but there are some sound reasons for ignoring the costing calculation for truly exceptional situations.

- One of the most common reasons is competition from another factor or discounter. Or indeed from a competitor outside the industry. The marketplace is very competitive, and while factors/discounters should never underprice their product, the market pressures are very fierce with regarding to pricing.

- A prestige prospect that offers the factor marketing spin-offs.

- The parent company of the factor may request factoring services as part of a package of financial facilities for one of its large debtors. Some bank-owned factors/discounters have special schemes that are used more to secure the bank's lending position than to enter a normal commercial arrangement.

- In the examples given the assumption has been that the prospect represents an average risk. High-risk prospects may well attract higher fees than this 'artificial' standard, and conversely those prospects with low risks may be suitable for a lower fee.

- Subsidiary companies of already factored/discounted clients may obtain a lower rate based on the figures of the whole group. The lower rate may also be offered as an inducement to large groups to factor further subsidiaries.

- Prospects with high growth potential. This situation is often met with a table of pricing – as the turnover level increases, the costs drop.

- The first prospect in a particular industry in which the factor or discounter would like to be involved or with a particular group, e.g. a franchising operation, which may bring many more potential clients.

- A prospect whose debtors may also be suitable as factoring or discounting prospects.

When the costing is overridden it is normally replaced by a 'marginal costing ' approach. This approach argues that as long as the factoring fee recovers the variable costs arising from servicing a particular prospect plus £1, the factoring company is better off by accepting that prospect because there is a £1 contribution towards paying for the fixed costs – which would be incurred anyway.

There would need to be an exceptionally good reason to accept as little as £1 because costings are only estimates and assume that all variable costs are truly variable and all fixed costs are truly fixed. Shaving down rates is, however, not an uncommon practice. It carries with it only one danger in that the factor may not hit its profit targets unless other clients subsidise the ones paying on a marginal basis. If all clients were on marginal costings the factor would run at a loss.

Managing Costs

Following on from constructing our pricing model we need to look at how the cost elements incorporated within our pricing structure can best be managed. In this section we shall therefore be considering how the costs of running a factoring/discounting facility can be managed to ensure, firstly, full cost recovery and, secondly, maximizing profit. There are a number of areas that we shall consider.

- Cost/value information
- Client acquisition costs linked to client retention issues
- Client service management costs
- Collateral management costs
- Client termination costs

Cost/Value Information

As a starting point we should revisit the sales activity and in particular the gathering of information that was used within the pricing calculation. The initial assessment of the prospective client included the gathering of certain cost-based information but it would also have included a number of projections and assumptions about the progress of the prospect's business over the next year or so. It is these projections and assumptions that need to be carefully monitored as the client's life as a factored/discounted company rolls forward. In particular the financier would watch for:

Changes in turnover

Either

- lower than projected, which will result in an under-recovery of costs. Within the costing formula the total recovery needed was divided by the projected turnover to calculate the service fee, so a 50% fall in projected turnover would result in a 50% fall in the costed recovery needed.

- higher than projected turnover results in some excess recovery (over the costing). While this sounds good it can result in the client paying a much larger service fee than the costing would have calculated with the increased turnover level. If the client knows this, and it may well be aware that the original pricing structure was based on its turnover level, it could consider that the *financier* was overcharging. In the highly competitive marketplace for factoring/discounting it is also likely that clients are regularly sent mailings by other factors/discounters advertising their services. If these competitors have the opportunity to re-cost the business, the gap between a costing based on current levels of turnover and the lower levels of turnover predicted may well cause a renegotiation of the whole facility. This is a particularly sensitive area and the question of when you go back to a client and offer a reduction in fees, because of changed circumstances, versus when you do nothing but enjoy the extra profit being generated is a constant one for the factor's/discounter's account managers.

Changes in Workload

Caused by changes in how the client conducts its business can also effect the costing. For example:

- a change to weekly invoices from invoicing monthly could greatly increase the number of invoices handled in a year
- a change of customer base, either increasing or decreasing
- a change in customer pricing by the client resulting in many more smaller or far fewer larger invoices

Factors and discounters manage these changes in costing through the use of the regular statistics produced from their computer systems (see sections on Information Technology for more information on this topic) and the interaction of their account management staff with the client.

Unfortunately what this type of statistical information does not fully reflect is the amount of work that goes into running a client; rather it simply presents today's situation, as calculated by current volumes (invoices, debtors, investment etc.), the latest pricing/costing formula, against the fees currently being charged, which are based on either the original costing or which have been renegotiated at some time.

It is not common in the factoring/discounting industry to constantly change client costing/ pricing. The problems of costing systems are that they are rather 'blunt instruments', ignoring many 'intangible' cost elements such as time spent on client, problems with debtor base or with client, and perhaps travel times/distance for visits and the highly competitive nature of the market mitigate towards making as few changes as possible. However costings are reviewed regularly at client review meetings (at least annually) and while action may not often be taken, a client who is either proving very expensive to maintain, or represents an increased security risk, or one when we are under competitive pressure, will almost certainly have its fees renegotiated.

7.2 Managing Client Acquisition Costs and Client Retention

We have seen in earlier sections that client life is a critical factor in the industry. This can also reflect on the pricing of the product. Although definitive industry figures are not available it is generally taken that the average life of a client, across the industry, is between three and four years. In the early years, little if any profit is made from a client because the income being earned after paying the variable costs of running the client and of making a contribution towards fixed costs is largely paying the acquisition costs of the client.

These acquisition costs include all the sales and marketing and related costs that the *financier* has incurred in gaining the client. A simple illustration is to take two factors, Factor A and Factor B. Factor A retains clients for only around 4 years whereas factor B retains them for 6 years.

Factor A

Total cost of sales team (salary, cars, overheads etc.)	£ 500,000
Total cost of marketing activity during the year	£ 150,000
Total acquisition costs	£ 650,000
Total 'net' increase in new clients during the year	
Client numbers at start of year	1,000
New clients taken on during the year	450
	1,450
Lost clients during the year (*)	250
Clients at end of year	1,200
Net new clients during the year	200
Acquisition cost of each client (£650,000/200)	£ 3,250

(*) Lost clients calculated by assuming a 4-year average life of a client, so the financier would lose 25% of the clients it has at the start of the year.

This calculation demonstrates that to obtain a single client it costs 'Factor A' £3,250, which must be recovered within the pricing formula before any profit can be made.

Factor B

Factor B, however, through excellent relationship management, high levels of service and involvement of the whole factor's/discounter's team in delivering exceptional service levels (all issues discussed elsewhere), manages to extend client life to 6 years.

Total cost of sales team (salary, cars, overheads etc.)	£ 500,000
Total cost of marketing activity during the year	£ 150,000
Total acquisition costs	£ 650,000

Total 'net' increase in new clients during the year

Client numbers at start of year	1,000
New clients taken on during the year	450
	1,450
Lost client during the year (*)	170
Clients at end of year	1,280
Net new clients during the year	280
Acquisition cost of each client (£650,000/280)	£ 2,321

(*) Lost client calculated by assuming a 6-year average life of a client, so the financier would lose 17% of the clients it has at the start of the year

Factor B has to recover only £2,321 to achieve the same return as Factor A. This gives it scope either to take increased profits or to reduce the price of the product to prospective new clients, giving it a major pricing advantage.

If the profit (after recovering all operating costs and making a contribution to fixed costs) earned from the client is £1,000 per annum, Factor A will take 3.25 years to recover the acquisition costs whereas Factor B will do so in only 2.32 years.

If both factors charged exactly the same fees to each client, Factor B would make an extra profit of £929 per client, multiplied by the extra 80 clients they gained during the year to give an extra income = (£929 x 80) of £74,320.

In addition Factor B has ended the year with an extra 80 clients than Factor A. These extra 80 clients will almost certainly grow and produce additional income for Factor B, which again may be taken as profit, because the costing has already recovered all the fixed costs, or again used to make Factor B's pricing even more competitive in the marketplace.

It cannot be emphasized enough how important the retention of clients is to financiers.

So let us take a final look at Factor A and Factor B and make some assumptions about how their businesses will develop over the next 5 year period.

● Both companies achieve identical sales targets for obtaining new clients each year as follows:

●

Year 1	600 new clients
Year 2	700 new clients
Year 3	800 new clients
Year 4	900 new clients
Year 5	1,000 new clients

Asset-Based Working Capital Finance

Details	Factor A	Factor B
	Average client life 4 years	Average client life 6 years
Client no's at start of year 1	1,000	1,000
New clients during year	600	600
Lost clients during year	(250)	(170)
Clients at end of year	1,350	1,430
Client growth	350	430
Acquisition cost of each client	£700,000/350 =£ 2,000	£700,000/430 =£ 1,628
Client no's at start of year 2	1,350	1,430
New clients during year	700	700
Lost clients during year	(338)	(243)
Clients at end of year 2	1,712	1,887
Client growth	362	457
Acquisition cost of each client	£770,000/362 = £2,127	£770,000/457 = £ 1,685
Client no's at start of year 3	1,712	1,887
New clients during year	800	800
Lost clients during year	(428)	(320)
Clients at end of year 3	2,084	2,367
Client growth	372	480
Acquisition cost of each client	£847,000/372 = £2,277	£ 847,000/480 = £ 1,645
Client no's at start of year 4	2,084	2,367
New clients during year	900	900
Lost clients during year	(521)	(402)
Clients at end of year 4	2,463	2,865
Client growth	379	498
Acquisition cost of each client	£931,000/379 = £2,456	£931,000/498 = £1,869
Client no's at start of year 5	2,463	2,865
New clients during year	1,000	1,000
Lost clients during year	(615)	(487)
Clients at end of year 5	2,848	3,378
Client growth	385	513
Acquisition cost of each client	£1,024,870/385= £ 2,662	£1,024,870/513 = £ 1,998

- And they both manage to maintain their sales and marketing costs at an annual increase of 10% per annum.

Year 1 costs being £700,000

Year 2 costs being £770,000

Year 3 costs being £847,000

Year 4 costs being £931,700

Year 5 costs being £1,024,870

During this 5-year period certain interesting information can be observed, illustrating the effect of client retention on product pricing and profitability.

1. Factor A has grown by 1,848 (2,848 – 1,000) clients. To achieve this growth has cost it acquisition costs of £ 4,272,870 or an average of £ 2,312 per client.

2. Factor B has grown by 2,378 (3,378 – 1,000) clients. To achieve this growth has also cost it acquisition costs of £ 4,272,870 or an average of £ 1,848 per client.

3. If both factors had charged exactly the same fees, Factor B would have made additional profits of (client growth x saving of acquisition costs)

Year 1	430 x (£ 2,000 – £ 1,628) =	£ 159,960
Year 2	457 x (£ 2,127 – £ 1,685) =	£ 201,994
Year 3	480 x (£ 2,277 – £ 1,765) =	£ 245,760
Year 4	498 x (£ 2,456 – £ 1,869) =	£ 292,326
Year 5	513 x (£ 2,662 – £ 1,998) =	£ 340,632
		£ 1,240,672

This extra 'profit' figure represents for Factor B more than year 5's total spend on acquiring new clients or, if used to reduce pricing, could have been used to gain a larger number of new clients and increase profitability through that route.

And all this extra profit/increased flexibility is based on reducing the attrition rate of client losses from 25% per annum to 17% per annum. This is a vitally important area to factors and discounters and crucial to the whole costing/pricing exercise.

Client Service Management Costs

We have just considered the importance of retaining clients and it must be said that the key mechanism for managing client costs is to retain the clients as long as possible. Exceptional levels of service, coupled to strong client/financier relationships, are the cheapest and most efficient way of managing costs. A good relationship – as we have seen elsewhere in this course – also reduces security risks, which in turn reduces security costs. The delivery of the financier's service therefore becomes a cost control activity in itself.

The role of the financier's account manager in renegotiating fees is also critical in this area where the balance between fee income levels in the short term versus client retention in the long term are so important. An attempt to increase a fee may result in the client seeking funding elsewhere and lead to the loss of a client, even before the financier has fully recovered its acquisition costs.

One good way of managing the loss of income when having to reduce fees is to tie the offer of a lower fees into a longer agreements (increased client retention), although it must be said that competition has, over a number of years, been driving minimum agreement periods down, and again this may be difficult.

In managing costs we must not overlook the potential to improve our income stream, and there are a number of ways that this can be done.

Many financiers also make additional charges for extra elements of service or extra facilities requested by a client; these can contribute substantial income streams. The most common 'additional' fees are:

Clearance days   The financier may make a payment by a method that will take a few days for the cash actually to reach the client's account, e.g. a payment to a client by cheque may well take 1 day in the mail and perhaps 3 days to clear. But the financier has already charged the payment to the client's current account on day 1. So it is charging discount on monies that it has not yet had debited to its bank account. This ability to earn income without actually advancing cash is normally called 'free income'. Newer methods of payment, such as BACS and CHAPS, reduce this opportunity.

Factors can also gain income on the collection of cash direct to itself. A payment received today will, for client payment purposes, almost certainly be set against a client's current account on day of receipt. However the discount fee will continue to be charged for a number of days to allow for clearance of the payment through the banking system. It is not uncommon to allow 3 days for UK payments and longer for overseas payments. Factors will, however, use their more sophisticated cash processing systems to speed the payment through the clearance process (particularly bank-owned factors) and will try if possible to receive cleared funds before they stop charging discount.

Additional fees   The financier may charge additional fees for certain types of payments made to a client. For example, a payment against a schedule of invoices received today against which the client requires payment today may attract a 'non-processed' payment charge. Or if a client requires a payment in excess of the agreed prepayment level, again an additional charge may be levied.

Managing costs by means of these additional fees, while easy to impose, is however not always commercially acceptable. Factors/discounters differentiate their service on such issues and a financier who as part of its normal processes pays out on the day of receipt of schedule will have a sales advantage against a company that charges for the privilege. Once again we are back to the balance between short-term income and long-term client retention.

Financiers may also supply extra services for clients, which may bring in additional income. The most common are:

- Charging for CHAPS/telegraphic payments, the income coming from the difference paid by the client and what the financier pays its bank for the transfer.
- Charging for using the financier's credit insurance policy/facility.
- Charging for additional visits or management time spent on the client.

Managing income is in many ways the easiest way for financier to manage costs because it is entirely within the financier's own control. Direct cost control, however, is much more difficult because the costs incurred will vary directly according to the effort needed to manage the overall client relationship and maintain the financier's security – and this is an unknown. The main mechanisms available for controlling client service costs are:

- Structure of the client service functions (account management and audit)
  A major cost for factors/discounters is their client management team, and there are many ways of structuring these departments/functions which attempt to balance the need to deliver service to the client with the need to protect security – and all at a reasonable cost.

  Lots of regular visits to clients may well enhance customer service, lead to increased client retention levels, add to the security of the financier through better knowledge of a client's current situation but it is expensive, very expensive. All factors and discounters structure their 'client service' function differently.

  - From those who rarely visit clients but have permanent in-house teams that speak on a daily basis to clients and build excellent rapport. The is cheaper to operate but more potential security risks and far less face-to-face client contact. This approach is more common in smaller factors.

  - To those who have specialist managers who do nothing but visit clients, ensuring that both the client is happy with the financier and that the financier is happy with the client. Much more expensive, but can cause problems with communication between 'the office' and the manager in the field, plus it may be difficult for the field manager to build relationships when only in contact, say, three times a year., the bulk of contacts taking place on the telephone to other service personnel in the financier's operations department. This approach is more common in larger factors and in discounters, who also normally have a regular audit function that visits clients on a regular basis.

- Between these two extremes there is a range of structures combining elements of both approaches.

All the approaches are designed to balance the costs of delivering the service and maintaining the security against income. (In the section on current developments we shall look at some new approaches in this area of service delivery that are starting to come into the marketplace based on improved technology)

- Automation of security risk review processes
  Managing security is expensive. The financier could at one extreme have a permanent member of staff placed in each client's premises on a daily basis to closely watch the clients activities. Or at the other extreme it could take a gamble and assume everything will be OK. Neither is acceptable as a way of monitoring security or from a cost point of view. So factors/discounters establish account management functions to manage this potentially extremely costly (in case of fraud) element of their business.

The problem facing the account manager is how to identify what is and is not a risk. With so much information available on computer systems it is often extremely difficult to try to differentiate between data that is important and data that is not important. The automation of risk identification is one way of both managing the risk and also controlling the costs. We shall be looking at the latest developments in this area in the Information Technology section.

Collateral Management Costs

In addition to controlling the client service costs, we need to look at the management of costs concerned with managing the collateral. In this area we need to consider the nature of the collateral that needs to be managed because some types are easier to manage than others. For example, collateral that by its nature does not change or that moves/alters very little during the life of the financial arrangement needs little management after initial assessment, e.g. a facility under a transactional or trade finance scheme for the purchase of a block of goods would require little in the way of daily management because the flow is very straightforward one – transaction via well defined route – the security issues being taken care of within the acceptance and original checking of the goods. However, with a factored sales ledger or a stock finance facility, the management task becomes considerably greater because the nature of the collateral is constantly changing.

The costs in managing this more volatile collateral are extremely difficult to calculate, although obviously the financier includes an element of collateral management costs in its overall product costing. The difficulty is that the normal approach to costing that we have already seen assumes a fair distribution of costs/income and more importantly effort across the whole client base, and this is equally obviously not true.

The main costing problems occur in the daily management of these collateral groups and the relationship between the financier and its clients. For example, we could tell a story of two companies, each factoring their debts with the same financier.

- Both client companies have a similar turnover.

- Both client companies have a similar sized debtor base who are all good credit risks.

- Both client companies have a similar cash requirement.

- So both companies have had a fee rate calculated on the standard costing, which are again very similar.

- At this point we could be looking at two identical companies, but it is not until we start operating our agreement and managing the debtor collateral that the differences start to emerge.

- One client company is run by a managing director who requires copious amounts of information on a daily basis and telephones the operations department of the factoring company many times each day.

- The factor then has problems with the same client's debtors who are reluctant to accept factoring, will not verify debts when telephoned and generally take a lot of extra effort to manage.

- This client then takes on a large order, which creates a concentration limit. The financier is reluctant, for security reasons, to finance the full invoicing on the concentration account; this produces even more contact with the client, who is now short of funding.

- The shortage of funding, perhaps assisted by poor client/financier relationship, results in the client pre-invoicing. Although not a serious attempt to defraud the financier, when this is discovered the financier starts to conduct even more security checks and spends even more time on managing the collateral, including extra client visits.

- The other client continues as planned, well within the original costing framework of activity, causing the factor no extra work – or costs – to run the account.

You can see that very quickly this financier was starting to experience very heavy extra costs in managing one of these two 'identical' clients. The difficultly is that it is often not possible to anticipate the actual costs of managing the collateral, debtors, stock etc. before the financier has 'hands-on' experience of the business.

But all financiers anticipate these 'unexpected' costs and make efforts to make some provision for them within their costings, which means that good well-run clients effectively subsidise the poorer more difficult clients. Again this is a situation that the financier does not want because commercially it wishes to offer the most attractive pricing structure possible to its existing and potential clients. It is against this background that we can look more specifically at collateral management costs.

We can break these down into two key areas:

- Managing client-related costs
- Managing the direct costs of the collateral management

Managing Client-Related Costs

A good relationship between the financier and the client lies at the heart of managing client-related costs, and is key to managing the overall collateral costs. The good relationship will:

- enable client and financier to feel comfortable with each other's activities and reduce the necessity for 'checking up' contacts, which are time consuming, expensive and often exacerbate problems rather than resolve them. The client will feel that the financier is doing its job and the financier will feel that it has a trustworthy client.

- reduce security costs in that the relationship will often mean that the client will talk to the financier before issues become problems. A good and very common example is a client who needs additional funds from the facility.

    - with a good relationship the client speaks to the financier, who more often than not will agree additional funding to address the current increased need. This has strengthened the relationship, with the client seeing the financier as helpful and co-operative while the financier has been kept fully in touch with the client's needs, and has been able to assist (and make more money through the increased funding) at no extra costs to itself.

    - with a poor relationship the client does not feel that the financier will listen nor assist with the increased funding. It therefore commits a fraud (pre-invoicing, banking cheques, altering reconciliations or stock figure) to provide the extra funding it requires. When the financier learns of this fraud (through audit, verifications etc.) it tightens up security, makes more frequent visits, further alienates the client and costs itself a lot of money in the process – ultimately this can lead to a loss of the client and the related non-recovery of acquisition costs.

With client-related costs the simplest way to mange them is for the financier to direct its main activities towards forging excellent open relationships with all the clients.

Managing the Direct Costs of Collateral Management

Here we are looking at the activities financiers undertake to control their prime security – the collateral.

A rather simplistic view would be to use the word 'professional' and link this word to all activities related to collateral management – audit, credit control, stock taking/checking, reconciliation, cash allocation and processing etc. – because professionally conducted activities will result in cost control, i.e:

- professional credit control would mean that no telephone collection call would be made that did not move the collection of the debt nearer.

- professional audit would mean that problems and potential security risks would be spotted at the earliest stage before damage had been done to the overall collateral value.

- professional stock audit would identify the true value of the stock.

However, professional activity at this level applied to all situations – while ideal – would demand huge efforts and that in itself would produce massive costs. So the financier manages collateral costs on what is termed an 'exception basis'.

The financier, in whatever area of funding it operates, identifies those situations that can most commonly lead to risk, fraud and loss – we have already seen these situations earlier in the course in the sections on risk and fraud. It then manages these areas by selecting activities that will give sufficient information to make security decisions without the need to manage everything. This approach means that it can be extremely cost effective in managing security while maintaining good overall risk management. For example:

- auditors carry out random checks rather than checking everything – i.e. sampling 100 invoices with 50 taken as a block (invoice numbers 100 to 150) and 50 at random (invoice numbers 234, 4556, 256 etc.) – and following the audit trail though production of the goods on those invoices on to their delivery.

- stock auditors carry out selective inspection of goods.

- credit controllers identify key customers and ensure that their balances are always confirmed with the debtors.

- those undertaking verification do not verify all invoices but only those that could have an impact on overall security, i.e. large balances or high concentration limits.

In addition financiers are more and more often using information technology to provide exception information and collateral management tools that deliver improved controls at less cost. This will be considered further in a later section.

Client Termination Costs

Once again it is really difficult to clearly simplify the costs of termination because they can fall into as many different categories as there are reasons for terminating an agreement. If we therefore look at the reasons why agreements are terminated and trace the related costs, we shall be able to more clearly identify the potential costs involved.

Reasons for termination fall into two main groups – terminations by the client and terminations by the financier.

Terminations by the Client (and Mutual Consent, i.e. Non-Hostile)

Factoring/discounting or other product no longer needed by the client because it

- is now profitable enough to replace the funding provided by retaining profits in the business

- has perhaps been taken over by another company which does not need the funding or services of the financier

- has gone to a competitor

In these cases the direct costs are straightforward to identify because they are almost certainly covered by the agreement, which is likely have a minimum termination period coupled to

---

[1] *Minium charges are normally set out in standard factoring/discounting agreements*

penalty clauses for those that wish to terminate immediately. Common clauses set a minimum three or six months' notice or a similar period of 'minimum charge[1]'. Some agreements go further by charging the greater of three or six months minimum charges or 5% of outstanding debts at the date of termination.

Although either of these methods brings in a sum of money to (sometimes a substantial figure), the financier has still lost a client and the potential income from that client over an extended period. The opportunity cost of losing clients who terminate their agreements in a relatively short period of time can be calculated by a simple formula:

Average life of all factors/discounter clients

less	Time client has been with financier
=	Lost income years
x	Average annual income from client (or minimum annual charge)
=	Lost potential revenue

Once again we must also compare the life of the client with the acquisition costs of gaining the client in the first place. A client leaving within 12 or 18 months of take-on will almost certainly not have repaid its acquisition costs.

Client Unhappy with Service or in Dispute with the Financier

Some factors/discounters offer clients 'Service Level Agreements' which give a client an option, if unhappy with the service being received, to opt immediately out of the agreement without the usual notice periods.

While conceived as a marketing tool for the financier, it does give a route out for a small number of clients. The costs involved with this type of termination are again generally covered in the agreement. However if the client has invoked a 'Service Level Agreement' within a few weeks or months of starting the agreement, the acquisition costs will not have been recovered by financier and it is likely that taking the client on will have given the financier a loss.

Termination by the Financier

Financiers only terminate agreements if they really have no other option. It is not in their interests to terminate an agreement that has cost them many thousand of pounds to set up. However, there are circumstances when factors and discounters do terminate agreements.

In such cases there is often a degree of hostility between the financier and the client – and perhaps the indemnifiers to the financing agreement. This hostility is a consequence of actions taken by the financier to protect its own position, or of the client's reaction to having its needs not met within the facility.

It is, however, in the financier's best interests to ensure that good working relationships are maintained with its clients even when a termination is taking place. This relationship is needed to assist the financier to collect monies and recover advances. Without client cooperation this task becomes more complex and difficult, and can result in vastly increased costs.

The reasons the financier may terminate the agreement are:

- in cases of fraud or serious security problems
  - discounter's disclosure
  - legal actions v. client and debtor
  - recovery from indemnifiers
- in cases of client liquidation
- in cases of clauses within the agreement being invoked
  - changes in ownership or control
  - changes in nature of client's business
- when it is unable to assist the client because of an inability to meet the funding levels required by the client or because of incompatible service issues between the financier and client.

7.3   The Role of Information Technology

One of the most rapidly growing activities within the financier industry is the use of information technology (IT) to manage and control all of the many operational areas that financiers have to manage and also to monitor the service delivery to its clients. While it must be said the use of IT varies considerably across the wide range of different financier companies, its use has in recent years become more and more important.

In this section we shall take a broad overview and examine various uses of IT that are being used in the industry both in the UK and overseas. We shall also revisit this topic when we take a view into the future of the industry and its operation.

In view of the massive variation in IT approaches within the financier industry, the following areas are not in any form of ranking or priority ordering. However before we start our review of IT, we should consider both a general problem of all companies who wish to maximize the use of IT in their businesses and the way in which the latest approaches to IT overcome it.

Data Warehousing and Data Mining

Computers are a part of everyone's life, and the development of computer technology, while providing immense benefits, has also brought with it its own problems. For the business, computers deliver almost instant access to vast stores of information, data and information on the business itself, its customers/clients, its suppliers, its stocks, its financial records etc., etc.

The scope of information is always available but that itself gives rise to the basic problem.

Imagine the financier thinking about its computer systems and databases.

> *We have access to literally millions of facts and pieces of information on our clients and their customers. We can use our computers to generate reports and information telling us almost everything; we may wish to know. The problem we have is that we don't actually want to know everything; we only want to be told about a tiny piece of information that tells us something of value in protecting our security, minimizing risk or perhaps how we can identify potential service or security problems before they happen. We know the information is in there somewhere, but where?*

The latest approaches to this fundamental problem are data warehousing and data mining. These techniques take the idea of 'exception reporting' (reporting only on things that are out of the ordinary) to new levels of sophistication and practical applications.

Data warehousing is the approach that effectively records where in your database (the warehouse of information) every piece of information is stored. Data mining programs now have a 'location map', which enables it to mine through all the unimportant data to discover the valuable and useful information needed by the financier.

The development of these techniques is of immense value to the financier because we have seen that it is often information taken from very different sources that indicates risk/fraud or other problems. The practical application of these techniques is already appearing in the financier industry in products and IT solutions covering risk management and audit control.

Rather than an account manager trying to read and analyse masses of statistical information, an IT solution based on these new approaches can provide a single screen of information that simply highlights areas for more attention. This information will, however, be based on a very complex and detailed analysis of multiple factors. The information screen can then be interrogated by the account manager to establish which trends, movements, events etc. triggered of the highlighting of the current situation for his or her attention. So rather than spend time firstly trying to spot problems hiding in a mass of data and information and then secondly trying to interpret exactly what the information is telling them, their attention has been immediately focused directly on a specific problem area and the reasons identified as to why this is a problem.

Both commercially available and programs developed by financiers themselves are actively being used in today's industry. The uses of IT in this risk management area are already showing considerable benefits in the industry.

This use of data management is vital in all areas of the financier's business and underlies all aspects of its activities.

The following sections cover the main uses of Information Technology in the financier industry today.

Client Access Systems

One of the most rapidly growing uses of IT is to provide the financier's clients with direct access to the financier's computer systems, thus giving them both additional information and services. The growth in client access is driven by two compelling reasons:

● client service – enhancing service perceptions, easing client workload and providing commercial advantage in the marketplace.

● time saving by the financier in processing activities and in certain security areas.

These services include:

● Direct access by the clients for statistical and financial information held on the financier's computer system. This information could include:

   ● up-to-date information on value of the collateral held

   ● what is and is not financed, with reasons for non-financed

   ● statistical data on volumes and related trends

   ● up-to-date financial information, availability of cash, last cash receipts, last payments etc. as well as latest financial statements of transactions between the client and the financier

   ● in a factoring facility latest aged debtor list, access to file information on debtor contacts etc.

● Access to additional services such as the ability to automatically transfer cash from the financier to client's own bank account without reference to the financier.

   The use of IT as in these types of service raises a key issue in the use of IT in the financier company, that of the changed relationship between client and financier. As more and more technology is introduced and the benefits in terms of process are experienced by both clients and financiers, the drive towards even more computerization of the processes will continue to gain speed. However, many of these new uses of technology reduce the need for human interaction and that points towards a danger that relationships will become more distant. We have already throughout this course continually stressed the importance of the relationship between client and financier, particularly in areas such as service delivery, client retention and security. The challenge of technology in the industry of tomorrow will be to maintain the considerable benefits of a close personal relationship while at the same time reaping the benefits of technology. We will revisit this issue.

● Ability to automatically transmit transactions directly to the client's account from its own computer, e.g. assignment schedules of invoices as well as copies of the invoices themselves. This replaces the need to print and then mail hard copies to the financier; all paperwork can flow via a modem-linked computer system. This saves considerable costs and effort at both the client's and the financier's end of the transaction to the extent that financiers have been know to offer free PCs to clients to enable these systems to be set up.

From the financier's viewpoint these client access systems also offer considerable benefits in that they do offer two-way access – client to financier and financier to client. Although the second route, financier to client, is less developed in the industry, the gateway that can be provided by IT links offer considerable benefits. At present financiers are seeing the following types of benefits.

Client to Financier Access Benefits

- reduction in workload in processing data and transactions because these are sent direct from client to financier.

- automation of verification and security routines – rather than depending on someone spotting a potential problem the computer can identify such issues (using complex analysis tools) and highlight them before decisions about financing are taken.

- in straightforward non-problem situations (again identified by analysis tools) automatic financing without the need to involve people.

- time saving in contact with clients who simply want information that they can access themselves.

Financier to Client Access Benefits

- access to a client's own financial accounting package, enabling management accounts to be drawn off for review without the need to involve the client.

- access to asset information that, while not part of the normal collateral taken by the financier, may be covered by a charge, e.g. the non-vesting debts in a factoring or discounting arrangement covered by a book-debt charge.

- access on a daily basis to sales ledger information in a confidential discounting facility – for monitoring purposes.

- automatic extract from a client's database for discounting month-end reconciliations.

- automatic access to the client's own financial accounts, to enable the financier to directly obtain up-to-the-minute financial information such as creditors lists, bank reconciliations, debtors list (important for discounters), stock lists, as well management accounts

Other Information, Access Issues

Besides having access to a client's computer system and the information it contains, some financiers have additional access opportunities. In particular those financiers owned by banks may have access to the banking account of their clients who bank with their parent bank. This is tricky area into which financier companies have been cautious in entering because the confidentiality agreements between banks and their customers are strong and the banks do not wish to be seen to break them. However, with the changes within the financier industry towards bank-owned financiers becoming trading divisions of their parent bank and the use of carefully worded legal agreements allowing this type of information to be passed, the use of this type of access is likely to become far more common in the future. A financier with this access enjoys a considerable benefit in being able to cross-reference information it has obtained via the client to information held by the bank. This is extremely valuable in protecting the financier's security when cash movements can be tracked

IT Inside the Financier

We have already seen the growth in IT systems to handle and analyse information and have reviewed using IT for access. The other huge growth in IT is within the financier's own computer and IT systems. In reviewing this area we shall select certain IT issues that are having a major impact on how financiers run their businesses under the following three headings.

- Automation processes
- Collateral management process
- Client and customer process

Automation Processes

We have already seen the use of IT in direct client access with such activities as sending data on transactions (invoicing, stock movements etc.) directly to the financier, and how the financier can use IT systems to monitor and internally process such data. In addition there are many other process carried out by financier that have and are being converted by IT solutions. For example, the processing, allocation and reconciliation of cash payments is a major task for many financiers and this is an area in which IT can play a considerable role. We can now follow a process from receipt of cash to demonstrate IT solutions.

Cash Receipts

Although much cash is still sent by cheque, the number of companies using automatic cash transfer facilities such as BACS and CHAPS is growing rapidly. So we shall look at both types of receipt process.

- BACS and CHAPS are receipts that have been electronically sent from one company direct to either the financier's or the client's bank account. IT solutions enable the information on who sent the payment and the reference numbers to be automatically passed on to the financier – in effect an electronic bank statement. The financier can then link this data file directly to its own data and automatically allocate cash to the account/client for whom it was intended. The benefits are a massive time saving, no manual activities and the 100% correct allocation of cash as intended by the payer – and all virtually immediately it is received.

- With cheque receipts the process can still be speeded up radically by the use of encode machines. These machines allow the processing department to automatically read the magnetic strips (or encode, which contains bank sort code and account number details) from the bottom of cheques and simply enter the amount of the cheque before electronically passing this information directly into the bank clearing system. Remember we looked earlier at the issues surrounding 'free capital' money which has been received from debtors but against which clients are still paying discounting charges. This process of getting cheques into the clearing system as soon as possible plays a big role in the amount of free-capital available to the financier.

Having received the payments, the next task is to correctly allocate it to the right account/debtor and then ensure that it is correctly reconciled. Again IT can play a major role here.

Allocation and Reconciliation

Once again there are many possible ways that these processes can be automated to bring benefits to the financier. Let us take one example, that of the use of the encode machine technology that we have just been looking at and link it to data handling. The financier is already reading the debtor's encode – its bank sort code and account number – this information is unique to that debtor. The financier files the encode information on each debtors and then whenever future payments are received these can automatically be allocated directly to that debtor's account.

To handle the reconciliation this process can then be linked to other IT solutions.

To enable reconciliation to take place the debtor account has to be linked to individual client accounts. Once this link is made the computer systems can rapidly carry out a search of amounts that equal the amount that has been received and automatically reconcile the cash received against debts outstanding. Once again IT plays a role in carrying out checks to identify which cash receipts can be automatically allocated and reconciled and which cannot, e.g. if the cash received was £1,234.00 and there were two debts of the same amount due by the same debtor to two different clients, this cash should not be automatically allocated.

Likewise if there are two or three different combinations of invoice values that would make up the same value as the cash receipt, again automatic reconciliation will not take place.

Within the financier industry, with the use of sophisticated cash processing and reconciliation software and hardware, levels of up to 80% of volume received have been correctly automatically allocated and reconciled.

Alternative Cash Collection Routes

Financiers can also take advantage of the other routes of automatically collecting payments – namely direct debits and utilizing credit cards, in particular the specialist 'corporate or supplier' credit cards that are starting to be offered by the main credit card companies. Both these routes of 'cash' collection can be linked into the automatic allocation and reconciliation systems. The use of these payment routes is still in its infancy in the industry but it is likely that there will be considerable growth in the use of all new ways of automating cash/payment transfers across the whole spectrum of financier activities.

Collateral Management Processes

Computer systems to manage collateral have been available for many years. The aged debt analysis, the stock control record, the creditors listing etc. can all be computer-generated reports that are very useful to the financier. But IT is moving rapidly forward from producing simple reports and is now used to assist with the overall management of the collateral. Let us take one use of IT as an example in the area of debt management in a full service factoring facility – predictive dialling.

Predictive dialling is a process which has the computer select debtors for credit control activity, make the contact with the debtor and manage the workflow of the collections department. The process would run as follows:

- The computer is programmed with instructions of how to prioritize debtor accounts. The priority program might select debtors by a combination of any or all the following criteria:
  - i.   value of debt
  - ii. concentration of debtor within client's ledger
  - iii. age of debt
  - iv. risk factor of debtor
  - v.   or any other criteria thought by the financier to be significant

- In its data banks would be the sales ledgers of all the financier's clients. From this data it would use its priority program and establish which debtors should be contacted first.

- The computer is networked across the collections department and would know how many collectors were logged on to its network. It would also know how long an average call took. Using this information (which it constantly reassesses and adjusts as the day goes on) it would automatically dial the first debtor account, placing the debtor information on the screen of an available collector. It would then do the second, third etc. until all collectors were handling calls. It would then continue to calculate average phone call times as well as recognizing free collectors and automatically dial and place the next priority call to the next available collector.

This use of predictive dialling massively increases the number of collection calls possible each day, maximizing the use of the collectors. Its weakness is that it prevents relationships being established between debtors and collectors and moves away from what many clients feel is a benefit of factoring – a recognized collector who is in effect an extension of their own company. To balance this view if the money is collected and no debtors are unhappy the clients are not likely to object to this type of technology being used on their accounts.

But this does illustrate another issue about the use of IT in the financier industry – that is, how the smaller companies who are less able to install such sophisticated IT solutions are competing. They will compete on the basis of personal service versus the faceless IT-driven team. It is an interesting argument in that it demonstrates very well the flexibility and commercial diversity of companies within the financier industry – we shall return to this topic later.

Electronic Shipping Tests

We have already seen that one of the basic security checks carried out by financiers is the process of verification – confirming the delivery and acceptance of goods by a debtor. For those financiers offering confidential facilities, this can prove difficult as they try to verify deliveries while at the same time maintaining confidentiality.

Some financiers are starting to use IT approaches to assist in the verification process by linking with major courier/transport companies and taking advantage of their computerized distribution control and tracking systems. The concept is simple if we explore the nature of the courier/transport industry of today.

The massive demand growth in courier and transport services has meant that over the last 10 years the development of new ways of managing the movement of goods from supplier to customer. One problem they have is how to cost-effectively manage small deliveries over long distances, because it is seldom cost-effective to have a truck carry only a part-load the length of the country. Their solution to this problem was to establish the process of using 'Hubs' and 'Groupage' where goods are dropped at central points (hubs) and then 'grouped' with other goods that are going to the same part of the country. As a consequence of this approach, the delivery of goods is seldom direct from point A to point Z.

For example, a delivery from the Exeter area to Glasgow may be taken to a hub outside Bristol, where it is grouped with other goods going to a Birmingham hub, where it is grouped with goods going to a Manchester hub. From the Manchester hub there may well be a direct delivery to the Glasgow hub, from which the transport company would complete the local delivery.

This approach has managed the costs of transport very effectively by maximizing loads. However, the logistics of moving goods in this way are very complex and has been managed by introducing sophisticated IT solutions using the 'bar-coding' of packages and the tracking of goods by scanning the goods in and out of hubs and of their collection and delivery from supplier to customer. Even the delivery drivers have portable computer terminals to record collection and delivery information. These highly sophisticated logistics tracking systems can tell the transport company exactly where in the process the delivery is, and when it has been delivered to and accepted by the customer. Commercially large companies who delivery their goods across the UK already have access to the computer tracking facilities of their transport companies.

It is this access to the tracking systems of the transport companies that can give the financier the ability, without contacting the client, the debtor or the transport company, and without the need for paper-based delivery notes and 'proofs of delivery', to verify the delivery of goods from client to customer. The information contained can be very useful for:

- confirming that the client has actually sent goods to a customer, i.e. prevent false invoicing when there has been no delivery of goods.

- confirming delivery prior to financing.

- confirming delivered quantities against despatched/invoiced quantities – pre-empting disputes and claims on short delivery, damaged goods or wrongly delivered goods that are not going to be accepted by customer.

- confirming acceptance by customer – some systems allow copies of the customer's acceptance signature (including its name).

  Note – this does not of course mean that the customer will pay for the goods – that may need a more traditional direct contact approach.

- enabling the financier to trace deliveries to small depots of very large companies that are often difficult if not impossible to verify by telephone contact. (We saw this problem when examining risk and fraud.)

- confirming overseas deliveries.

Also from a financier's viewpoint the information obtained is independent of both client and debtor (who may be influenced by the client to confirm non-existent deliveries in fraud situations) and as such can be depended upon for its reliability.

Compliance with Data Protection Legislation

This is an important issue that while not strictly a topic of information technology does flow from it. The Data Protection Act 1998 (DPA) controls how information is held by anyone on a computer system can be kept, and used. The 1998 Act extends considerably the requirements under the earlier 1984 Act and it now covers all processes from obtaining to destroying data. In particular it controls the accuracy of such information and the rights of the individual to have access to and to demand corrections. The DPA now extends to manual records in a 'relevant filing system' which is:

Structured either by reference to individuals or by reference to criteria relating to individuals in such a way that specific information relating to a particular individual is readily accessible.

Although a financier has always been subject to DPA 1984, the changes in the 1998 Act mean much stricter compliance. Those companies involved in factoring and invoice discounting have until 24 October 2001 to bring themselves fully in line with the DPA 1998.

Client and Customer Processes

The relationship between the financier's clients and the clients's customers is also effected by information technology and new ways of working. Among the areas that are rapidly developing and are of particular interest to the financier are:

- Just in time (JIT) management systems are growing strongly in many businesses sectors. From the customer's view they carry minimum stock levels reducing their need for storage space and their working capital requirements. To do this they need very detailed information on usage of stock and a means to transmit this information to the supplier.

From the client's (supplier's) view they have a 'tied' customer who depends on them for a regular supply of raw materials, components or finished goods. Linked to customer by e-mail, a stock control system or simply visiting on a very regular basis the client replenishes the stock to pre-determined levels. JIT can be seen as a mechanism based on a long-term relationship between seller and buyer. From a general business perspective this is good news; however, the financier may well see this differently.

- The JIT arrangement between client and customer may well be in the form of a written (or perhaps unwritten) contract. Besides specifying the goods and their quality criteria, the JIT contract calls for ongoing guaranteed delivery over an extended time period.

- Failure to fulfill the deliveries over the full contract period may well result in 'liquidated damages claims' (a claim covering the extra costs or damages caused by the failure of the supplier to meet their contractual liabilities). Legally the financier could be caught by substantial set-offs against collateral in cases when their client, say, goes into liquidation during the contract period.

- This is an increasing problem, particularly for factors and discounters who may not always be fully aware of the nature of the contractual terms under which the client is supplying the customer. The invoices will not of course show any indication of this problem because each separate delivery will stand as a unique order, but – and it is the 'but' that causes the problems – subject to the overall supply contract.

- A variation on the JIT approach is the automatic ordering systems that companies are using. This is the processes where the sale of a product triggers of an automatic re-ordering message to be electronically sent to the supplier to re-stock the sold item.

- Technological growth is likely to force more and more clients towards the JIT-type supply systems with the consequence of increased risk for the financier. Financiers have to explore the supply chain in more depth than ever before and, through regular visits and audit, maintain a vigilance on the supply contracts entered into by their clients.

7.4 Current Developments

The UK industry continues to see excellent growth patterns and potential. The newsletter of the FDA covering the half year to end June 1999 presented the following information:

- FDA members' business grew by 10% to £ 29.9bn compared with the first half of 1998.

- Funds provided for clients rose at the same rate to £ 4.4bn.

- At the end of June there where 24,925 clients of FDA member companies – a 9% growth over the previous June figures.

So the market of today, for the wide range of financier products, is strong, growing and developing rapidly, and as we will see when looking at the future, moving into a future of much change. Before we can start to look towards this future we must first look at the current market and then we can perhaps more accurately project the industry into the future.

Today's Marketplace

Banks Absorbing Subsidiarys and the 'Take-over' of Banks

The financial press almost daily speculates on the likely take-over or merger deals concerning the UK's leading banks. The almost daily changing of the names of UK-based financiers reflects this pattern of changing ownership. It has even affected some of the oldest established financiers in the UK – Griffin Credit Services Ltd becoming HSBC Invoice Finance (UK) Ltd and International Factors changing ownership twice in a few years to become GMAC Commercial Finance Ltd.

As the industry has grown in respectability the banks, which once held their financier subsidiaries at arm's length, are today recognizing the role they can play in developing and promoting their business interests and drawing them into the main banking operation. Barclays Commercial Services Ltd has become a division of the bank operating as Barclays Bank plc (Sales Finance). Other banks are also making similar moves.

New Entrants – Small and Large Parents

We are also seeing new entrants into the market, both small new-start companies (City Factors Ltd, Argent Factors Ltd), as well as companies being established by larger organizations (GE Capital, Credit Lyonnais).

The appearance of Bank of New York in their purchase of International Factors a few years ago demonstrated a very different business culture and approach to business development in the UK industry. The ripple effect of a large 'outsider' with different ways of working was met with considerable interest from established industry players.

Specialised New Entrants – Transactional Finance, Trade Finance and Large Balances

We have seen in recent years the development of new products being offered in the UK market and although these may be seen as some as the latest 'flavour' of the month, they are having an impact in the same way that stock finance had when the first UK financiers started to offer it a few years ago. The learning curve for these new products is steep and those companies who are today exploring them will set the standards for others to follow in the future. They also, of course, run considerable risks because they are moving into largely unchartered waters.

Innovative Combined Products/Services

The emergence of 'linked' products is another recent development, either from existing financiers or being offered by new entrants into the market. A typical example would be the factoring company who in addition to offering finance against invoice purchase is also offering payroll services or other financial services. This appears to be an area for future opportunities for the niche players.

Growth in the Export Sector

International factoring is continuing to develop and grow with the gradual growth in UK exports. The current market has a number of companies that are parts of European or international companies and are targeting the export market between their parent and sister company countries. Also the international factoring groups (International Factors and Factors Chain International) are reporting increased volumes being handles by their members as well as a growth in membership numbers.

Market Restructuring

Another sign of the times is the partial restructuring of the FDA's sub-committee base away from large and small members into factors and other products. This reflects the way the various companies are starting to split – larger companies towards more 'packaged products' and the smaller companies focusing the more traditional factoring and discounting products in the small- and medium-company marketplace.

Internet and EDI Systems

Both these areas are seeing rapid developments (see IT section for more comment and information), with new products being tried in the market based around the technology. For example, Alex Lawrie is offering a small company package comprising of an Internet link to process invoices to themselves coupled to automatic acceptance and payment systems at their offices. Designed for the smaller companies, it offers a high-tech approach to factoring.

Increasing Fraud

On the negative side the industry is experiencing increasing attempts of fraud, and for the first time in recent years criminal fraud rather than the more normal 'commercial fraud'. This worrying trend is being resisted by the development of sophisticated detection systems and much vigilance by the operations staff of all financiers.

7.5   Future Direction

Although it is always difficult to make accurate predictions about the future shape of the industry, we can make a number of predictions if we follow the current situation and project them forward. The following issues are not presented in any form of priority order.

Industry Structure

Linked so closely as it is with banking, the industry will be caught up in the trend towards bank mergers. At the time of writing this material there is a battle between the Bank of Scotland and the Royal Bank of Scotland for ownership of National Westminster Bank. All three of these banks own companies offering financing services.

It is thought that there will be continued consolidation of the UK banks, impacting on the larger asset-based financiers. It is likely therefore that the larger financiers will reduce in number but grow substantially in size as a consequence of these mergers/takeovers.

We are already seeing banks altering their strategic approach to lending, and starting to direct all working capital financing to their financing subsidiary. This will almost certainly accelerate the process already taking place of the disappearance of traditional bank overdraft financing. This may result in related problems for the non-bank owned financiers as the market opportunities reduce for independent products as the banks tighten their grip on their customer base by offering wider-based and more flexible products than in the past.

Following this trend within the UK to a worldwide perspective we are likely to see the first really international financing group – there are already a number of trans-European groups operating in a small way. Extending these across the world might push the industry towards the same status as the large accountancy practices have created a very few huge organizations. There is already evidence of such moves (Heller Group and HSBC being two organizations following a path of globalization)

Product and Service Development

This development of banking will also see a change in delivery of the financiers service. The banks will be, and already are in certain cases (Barclays and Bank of Scotland), offering the range of the financier's products via their bank branch network. Although this connection has been used in the past this was normally only as a sales/lead-generation point. The new approaches have the branch working closely with the financier on issues such as funding levels and service delivery etc.

New products and variations on existing products will continue to be developed to provide even more comprehensive packages of working capital finance – linking all the present financier products and services with traditional banking and additional services – possibly including insurance. Increasing export services etc. will continue to be developed to satisfy the changing needs of clients and potential clients.

Economic and Business World Influences on Industry

Although the general impact of e-commerce on business is still a largely unknown quantity, it can be anticipated that it will impact on the working capital of companies and hence on the financier industry. The ability to search for and review products from your desk before placing orders via the Internet will give companies considerable opportunities to present their products to a far wider market. In this way e-commerce is likely to impact on traditional buying patterns of companies. The results of these changes is very difficult to predict but could include:

● changes in payments methods, removing the need to grant trade credit (impacting on factoring and discounting)

- changes in company stocking levels – quicker ordering processes and expectations of quicker delivery times (impact on all financier products)

- increases in export trade (an Internet 'seller' can be anywhere in the world) (impact on all financier products)

The last ten years have also seen a steady growth in just-in-time (JIT) supply chains; again this is likely to continue. These schemes have an impact on the financier's security.

- ownership of stock

- increasing retention of title (ROT) issues

- potential ban on assignments

- improvements in supply chain may also reduce debt (less stock held requires less working capital) and hence directly affect asset-lending in both debtors and stock.

Some writers even project a picture of an almost Utopian business society with no trade credit being offered to purchasers because business is run in closed business transaction chains (supplier/client/debtor).

Moving on to the less developed parts of the world, it is likely that the products that have seen such rapid growth in the West we will also start to see similar patterns of growth in other parts of the world. We are already seeing signs of interest in the financier's products and services in the new emerging markets, in particular in eastern Europe as well as the re-emerging Far-East markets and longer-term financiers' business development in China and India.

Impacts of Europe on the UK economy – whether we are in or out of the Euro and the difference this might make to business (either massive growth with needs to provide working capital – or recession and survival finance) with all its related problems and risks – will also affect UK Limited and the related products offered by UK-based financiers.

Issues that Impact Directly on the Financier Companies

Over the last few years there has been a considerable growth in more complex contractual arrangements between seller and buyer. For example 'blanket contracts' covering supply of goods or services over extended periods, often in excess of one or even two years, are now not uncommon and likely to grow in the future. The financier is faced with increasing risks and must consider extra question when assessing business:

- do these extended supply contracts hide potential liquidated damages claims if the supplier is unable to maintain supply over the extend contact period. This is critical in the area of debt finance. For example:

  - a factor receives invoices and has the agreement of the debtor that each debt is a separate supply, individually delivered and to be invoiced separately and paid separately. However, unknown to the factor, the supply of these goods is also covered by a master supply contract (perhaps dated some time ago) which specifies that continuous maintenance of supply is required over the whole contract period. The factor's client goes into liquidation and the factor attempts to collect the outstanding debt. The debtor responds with a claim in damages claiming that the master supply contract has been broken.

- Although the factor can protect itself by examining every contract in detail, this adds cost, and perhaps more importantly in such a highly competitive market, time to the acceptance process. It is not inconceivable that such complex contractual arrangements may well be missed, leaving the factor exposed to increased, though not fully understood, potential security risks.

Increased competition in the market, when set against the other 'predictions' in this section, is easy to predict. The last 20 years has seen ever-increasing levels of competition both from within and without the UK. In the main this competition has been from banks and other financiers. While this will almost certainly continue in the future, we will also see competitors from outside these traditional competitor areas. In particular the huge growth in commercial debt insurance has created a small number of very large insurers. These insurers are already running collection services for their insured debts and are likely to move into financing debt directly in the very near future, thus becoming direct competitors to the receivables financing industry and in the medium term extending their financing to other areas that they also currently only offer insurance on.

Another area that will demand increasing attention is how to manage client expectations. As knowledge and acceptance of the financiers grow so too will the expectations of the clients for those services change. Already we are seeing service level agreements, which offer client's service terms that go beyond simply the supply of the base service. The financiers will have to be even more conscious in the future of balancing their product developments with the clients expectations. This is likely to lead to even more tailored and sophisticated packages of asset-based lending.

As the larger financiers manage their increasing business volumes with ever more sophisticated IT solutions, the smaller financiers will likely identify niche markets and exploit these by offering 'personal' delivery of service at a higher level that the large financiers can offer via their automated services. This is likely to fragment the market, with a fairly clear split emerging between smaller niche plays and larger possibly bank-owned financiers.

However, the need for more IT to support even these smaller companies will become much more commonplace in the future. The gap between the large wealthy financiers installing and using the most up-to-date IT and computer-driven service systems and the smaller financiers using simpler less expensive IT solutions further widens, although providing at the same time opportunities for the smaller 'personal' service-driven financiers.

A more negative development across the industry has already been seen. This is the growth in fraud – particularly criminal fraud. The future will almost certain reveal more and more complex frauds being attempted, and some successfully committed, against the industry. We are also more likely to see the emergence of money laundering, particularly exposure to the 'layering stages' of money laundering which involves laundered money passing through semi-legitimate business ventures.

With the increase in export/international trade and the lowering of trade barriers across Europe and perhaps across the rest of the world, there is considerable potential for international cross-border frauds involving multiple clients in different jurisdictions with cross-transactions to an international debtor base. One such fraud has already been discovered in Europe.

- Fraudulent companies established in three European Countries

- Each invoiced goods and services to fictitious debtors in each other's countries

- Only through luck was the attempt discovered and only a small sum lost

- The complications caused by the cross-border nature of the transactions coupled with the free trade between these areas made it relatively easy for the attempted fraudsters to hide their fraudulent activities.

Conclusion

Some 40 years ago the first factoring companies were set up in the UK. Now we have a well-established and respected industry arranging the financing of working capital via debtors and stock and other assets. The next 40 years will certainly continue this growth, see new players, new products, innovative services and new competitors.

Appendix 1
WORKING PAPERS FOR SURVEY OF PROSPECTIVE CLIENT

The content and type of working papers will vary between financier's dependant upon their own requirements and criteria. However, the tables on the following pages look at the reports and information, which will usually be required.

Working Paper 1 - Spread and Profile of Debts

Table A – Aged Profile of Debtors
Top 5 balances. This highlights the biggest debtor balances in order to identify any concentrations and the performance of those debtors by examining the ageing profile.

Table B – Analytical Review
This review compares the current ageing profile with the previous months. This review is conducted to identify any trends, which may indicate an improvement or deterioration of the debts.

Table C
Debt Composition - this looks at the composition of the sales ledger in terms of the spread of debtors, volume of transactions, terms of trade and other features of the debts such as credit insurance and export involvement.

Table A

Aged Profile of Debtors							
£K **Top 5 Balances**	**£K** **%**	**£K** **Total**	**£K** **01-30**	**£K** **31-60**	**£K** **61-90**	**£K** **91-120**	**£K** **121+**
1. Ameom Group	10%	2,534	1,100	700	350	154	230
2. BRA	6%	1,402	645	350	210	190	2
3. Foster Freeman	3%	805	560	300	121	(9)	(2)
4. GRC plc	3%	717	420	240	2	60	43
5. Middlesex RHA	2%	600	321	190	155	18	35
Balancing Figure	74%	17,837	7,269	6,716	1,655	673	1,524
	100%	24,222	10,315	8,496	2,493	1,086	1,832

Table B

Analytical Review

Last Month End	100%		43%	35%	10%	4%	8%
Prior Month	100%		58%	27%	5%	4%	6%
Previous Month	100%		34%	34%	10%	16%	6%

Table C

Debt Composition

1. Number of Live Accounts — 1500
2. Average Receivable Balance — £16K
3. Number of Invoices Per Month — 3750
4. Average Invoice Value — £2.75K
5. Terms of Trade — 30 Days from Date of Invoice
6. Extended Terms — 60 Day Terms at discretion of Directors
7. Debtor Insurance — Yes (copy of policy held)
8. Exports — <1% Not Material
9. Discount Schemes — NO

Working Paper 2 - Overdue Debtor Accounts

Table D – Overdue Debts

This is an analysis of the overdue section of the Sales ledger. This task is usually performed by the surveyor discussing overdue debtors with the prospects credit control department to identify any debt related issues that affect the existing and future value and the collectability of the debts.

For example this analysis will identify such issues as:

● Product problems

● Customer quality problems

● Credit control weakness

● Client practices, such as selling goods on sale or return

Table E – Bad and Doubtful Debts

This is used to compare the prospect's accounting of bad debts against the test carried out above to establish if appropriate provisions for bad debts are being maintained.

Table D

Overdue Debts

Debtors	£K Balance	£K 90+ Days	Credit Control Notes
Accol Group	84	52	A/C in query
Accol Group	300	59	Rec. in progress cash not reconciled
Accol Group	210	20	Payment promised
Rosten Technology	52	26	Ongoing discussions with customer
Bradway	20	10	Payment in transit
Comnet UK	300	22	Due and Payable, expected on next chq. Run
Reardon Smith UK Ltd	68	34	Old queries now resolved, a/c clear by end month
Kerrin (Banbury)	215	17	Due and Payable, expected on next chq. Run
Kerrin (Brighton)	30	14	Due and Payable, expected on next chq. Run
Magnus William UK Ltd	13	13	Meeting with customer arranged
Regency Services (UK) Ltd	23	19	Due and Payable, expected on next chq. Run
Gower Hammond UK Ltd	300	(11)	Duplicate payment, will await customer query
R.B. Partis Plc	178	(12)	Currently being reconciled
Parity Computers Ltd	200	23	Due and Payable, expected on next chq. Run
Microchip Ltd	200	49	Due and Payable, expected on next chq. Run
Digitec UK Ltd	200	19	Meeting with customer arranged
RBV UK Ltd	22	14	Dispute
Middlesex RHA	54	17	Disputed, meeting arranged with customer
Middlesex RHA	290	10	Special project delayed settlement
Broadway Assurance plc	200	35	Sales meeting with cust. Arranged to resolve
Arron Software	180	74	Balance will probably be written off.
Foster Freeman	28	9	Goods returned
Apex Harvey	60	18	Now clear credit issues
National Shipping	260	37	Meeting with customer arranged
Palmer Mitre	100	24	Meeting with customer arranged
Tyrrel Consulting	77	43	Due and Payable, expected on next chq. Run
Total	3,664	635	

Percentage Coverage of Overdues   21%

Table E

Bad & Doubtful Debts in the Clients' Books
Profit & Loss

	£K
Bad Debt Write Off in Current Financial Year	11
Prior Year Comparative	745
Balance Sheet Provision	1039

Working Paper 3 – Sales Ledger Control Account

Table F

This table extracts the totals from prior month end sales ledger figures to provide a historic 12-month analysis.

F1 Invoices

The monthly invoice table will identify invoicing trends with regards to sales volumes increasing or reducing and also seasonal trends.

F2 Credit Notes

Details month end total credit note activity. A high level of credit notes would require further investigation, see also table G.

F3 Cash

Details customer collection levels to assess against sales levels.

F4 and F5

Identifies sales ledger adjustments through journals. If journals are significant they will require further investigation and analysis.

F6 Closing Balance

Lists the closing sales ledger balance at each month end, which can be used to calculate debt turn.

F7 Debt Turn

This is a rolling debt turn, identifying positive or adverse trends in the debt performance.

F8 Credit Note %

This tells us the percentage value of invoices credited each month and the overall collectability of the ledger. See credit note analysis.

Table F   Debt Turn

Period: Jun-98 to May-99

Month	Invoices	Credit Notes	Cash	Dr. Jnls	Cr. Jnls	Closing Balance	Debt Turn	Credit Note %
	F1	F2	F3	F4	F5	F6	F7	F8
Jun-98	22,100	(1,034)	(19,399)	4	0	24,466	50	4.7%
Jul-98	21,000	(1,504)	(20,288)	0	(9)	23,665	51	7.2%
Aug-98	19,300	(915)	(17,331)	0	(47)	24,672	39	4.7%
Sep-98	18,500	(947)	(17,476)	52	0	24,801	40	5.1%
Oct-98	21,000	(1,130)	(19,672)	0	(23)	24,976	42	5.4%
Nov-98	22,000	(1,237)	(15,806)	0	(51)	29,882	46	5.6%
Dec-98	21,100	(1,674)	(16,650)	0	(22)	32,636	51	7.9%
Jan-99	17,200	(1,731)	(21,067)	0	(82)	26,956	51	10.1%
Feb-99	19,573	(962)	(15,934)	4	0	29,637	51	4.9%
Mar-99	26,000	(1,169)	(20,354)	2	0	34,116	48	4.5%
Apr-99	17,000	(932)	(21,678)	179	0	28,685	49	5.5%
May-99	16,000	(669)	(15,533)	0	(3)	28,480	48	4.2%
	240,773	(13,904)	(221,188)	241	(237)		48	5.8%

Working Paper 4 – Credit Note Analysis

Table G – Credit Note Turn

By taking a sample of Credit Notes issued during the last 4 months we are able to establish:

1. The reason for issue.

2. The time taken to issue or the CR Note turn

The value and turn of credit notes is fundamental to determining a financier's level of funding against the purchased debts. The percentage of the ledger that is credited off is referred to as dilution. Table F shows us that 6% of invoices are credited which equates to 6% dilution.

Most financiers look for a margin between their prepayment percentage and the dilution level of 15%. Therefore a business showing a credit note dilution of 10% would not expect to exceed a prepayment rate above 75%.

$$100\% - 10\% = 90 - 15\% = 75\%$$

Table H – Credit Note Reason Composition

From the table G reason code we can understand the reasons for the issue of credit notes. This analysis gives further insight into the performance of the debts.

Table I – Credit Note Dilution

This takes the credit note percentage and from the credit note turn calculates the value of credit notes yet to be credited. Credit notes issued more than 30 days from invoice date (+1 month) suggest that there is a lag and therefore the following calculation is used in order to establish dilution levels including this lag.

$$\text{Credit Note \%} / 30 \times \text{CR Note turn} = \%$$

This exercise enables the examiner to identify potential hidden dilution resulting from a lag or slowness of the prospect raising credit notes.

Table G – Credit Note Turn

Credit Note Number	CRN Date	Amount £	Customer A/C	Reason Code	Invoice Number	Invoice Date	Turn Days
88888	21.06.99	22700	Apex	2	999902	21.05.99	30
88879	21.06.99	6200	Vega	2	999900	19.05.99	32
88878	20.06.99	5555	Nortech	3	999899	14.05.99	36
88877	18.06.99	29100	Saturn	5	999892	02.06.99	16
88875	16.06.99	6444	Infomax	5	999890	16.05.99	30
88873	15.06.99	2298	Netco	1	999884	15.05.99	30
88867	14.06.99	5100	Compulex	1	999887	30.04.99	44
88863	30.05.99	8900	Miromart	1	999878	26.04.99	34
88861	21.05.99	7698	Bluview	1	999870	20.03.99	61
88859	21.05.99	9900	Broadbean	5	999868	18.03.99	63
88854	29.04.99	67098	HRP	3	999865	11.04.99	18
88852	22.04.99	7300	Cirus	4	999858	09.03.99	43
		178293					28

Table H – Credit Note Reason Composition

Reason Composition

		£	%
1	Goods Returned	23996	14%
2	Price Error	28900	16%
3	Faulty Goods	72653	41%
4	Wrongly Ordered	7300	4%
5	Invoice Error	45444	25%
		178293	100%

Table I

Credit Note Dilution

Credit Note Level	x	Credit Note Turn	Credit Note Dilution
6%		28	5.7%

Working Paper 5 – Contra Trading

Table J

This table identifies all suppliers on the purchase ledger that also appear as debtors on the sales ledger. This enables the level of any potential reduction in the value of the sales ledger to be determined and the requirement and value of any contra reserve.

The surveyor needs to consider the timeliness of the purchase ledger postings. If there are delays in the posting of the supplier invoices then any contra reserve could be understated.

Likewise, if cheques or payments are posted to the sales ledger prior to their release, the potential contra reserve could be understated (see cash book).

Table J – Contra Trading

Receivable/Payable	£K Sales Ledge Balance	£K Purchase Ledger Balance	£K Reserve Required
Adavance	48.2	58.0	48.2
Comcore	107.6	3091.2	107.6
Comber Ltd	2.0	25.3	2.0
Compex 2000	10.6	490.9	10.6
DRF	75.6	2050.9	75.6
GBH Services Plc	18.1	104.8	18.1
IJ Graham	0.0	284.3	0.0
Infomax	1.0	7.9	1.0
Softex	600.7	650.0	600.7
RG Data Ltd	16.4	32.1	16.4
Simplex	2.2	1.6	1.6
Singer Lucas	1.6	63.2	1.6
Tamplin Int	19.0	3370.0	19.0
			902.4

Working Paper 6 – Unapproved Debts

Table K – Calculation of Unapproved Debts

The unapproved debts report is completed following the identification of debtors that should not be funded. These will include:

1. Inter-company or associate company balances

2. Goods sold on sale or return

3. Non-trade sales (to employees or members of the public)

4. Certain export markets may be deemed ineligible for funding

5. Government departments because of the Crown's right of set off

Table K

	Calculation of Unapproved Debts					
	£K	£K	£K	£K	£K	£K
	Total	01-30	31-60	61-90	91-120	1201+
Accounts Receivable	30,544	12,415	9,216	2,995	1,936	3,982
	30,544					
Less Ineligibles:						
Inter Co	4,220	1,900	420	370	680	760
S.O.R	150	10	15	35	60	30
HM Gov	1,952	190	285	97	110	1,360
Exports	0					
Non Trade	0					
Other	0					
	6,322	2,100	720	502	850	2,150
Total Approved Ledger	24,869	10,224	9,000	2,578	1,500	1,567

Working Paper 7 – Shipping Test
Table L

This test is designed to make sure that the prospect:

- Ships goods against purchase orders
- That proof of shipment exists
- That invoices are generated close to the delivery date

The level of testing varies between financiers but a minimum of 10% of the total sale is normally tested.

This test helps to identify operational or system problems.

The test is conducted by taking a sample list from the sales ledger and then pl checking against them to delivery documents and customer purchase orders.

L1 – identifies the lag between the invoice being raised and the actual shipment

L2 – this is the total value tested

L3 – this is the total value as a percentage of the sales ledger

Table L – Shipping Test

L1

Inv'g No.	Inv. No	Customer Name	Date	Amount £K	Order	POD Date	POD Signed	Pre Inv'g.	C
1	7221	Kerrinert	10/06/99	12001	100	12/06/99	y	2	
2	8336	Kerrinert	09/06/99	45890	98	11/06/99	y	2	
3	6276	Magnus William	01/06/99	304518	102	01/06/99	y	0	
4	3887	Regency Services	20/05/99	145908	105	21/05/99	y	1	
5	4980	Gower Hammond	20/05/99	1254609	110	21/05/99	y	1	
6	5009	R.B. Partis	20/05/99	1266263	187	11/06/99	y	21	
7	6870	Parity	20/05/99	898732	167	21/06/99	y	1	
8	7777	Microchip	22/05/99	16534	155	30/05/99	y	8	
9	8878	Digitec	22/05/99	66667	143	30/05/99	y	8	
10	9786	RBVCW	20/05/99	243434	132	20/05/99	y	0	
11	1011	Middlesex RHA	20/05/99	27407	199	20/05/99	y	0	
12	1189	Middlesex RHA	20/05/99	64546	156	30/05/99	y	10	
13	1276	BRP Assurance	20/05/99	89272	188	21/05/99	y	1	
14	6677	Arrons Software	20/05/99	90202	177	30/05/99	y	10	
15	1489	Foster Freemant	16/05/99	190990	166	30/05/99	y	14	
16	1590	Apexen Harvey	14/05/99	2676543	103	22/05/99	y		
17	1698	National Shipping	10/05/99	212232	101	22/05/99	y	12	
18	7768	Palmer Mitren	03/05/99	31223	196	03/05/99	y	0	
	L2			7636971					

L3 - % of GSL Tested = 31.5%

Working Paper 8 – Purchase Ledger

Table M – Purchase Ledger Spread and Profile

The top 5 breaks out the biggest creditor balances in decreasing order. This helps the surveyor to identify any concentrations and supplier dependencies.

Table N – Analytical Review of Creditors

This enables the surveyor to contrast current ageing of creditors with previous months to see if there is any improvement or deterioration in the management of their accounts.

Table O – Taxes and Government Liabilities

PAYE

From investigating the PAYE returns the surveyor seeks to identify any Inland Revenue arrears and to check that monthly declarations of PAYE and NI are being completed and paid.

VAT

Examination of Customs and Excise declarations enable the examiner to identify any arrears.

Corporation Tax

Identified through year-end declarations based on previous financial year-end.

The tax and Government liability analysis is seen as critical to the overall examination as businesses which are behind with payment and/or declaration of liabilities can be closed down very quickly by these bodies.

Appendix 1 – Working Papers for Survey of Prospective Client

Table M

Purchase Ledger Date

Top 5 balances	%	£K Total	£K 01-30	£K 31-60	£K 61-90	£K 91-120	£K 121+
1. Able & Dexter	36%	5800	1600	160	40	3	2
2. ARG Services	20%	3240	3000	40	150	50	0
3. Omex UK Sales	12%	1894	600	850	100	244	0
4. Whitt Bros Ltd	9%	1400	450	250	442	210	48
5. Wylan Ltd	6%	929	475	106	310	38	0
Other Creditors	17%	2881	605	973	520	428	455
	100%	16,144	10,725	2379	1562	973	505

Table N

Analytical Review of Creditors

Last Month End	100%	66%	15%	10%	6%	3%
Prior Month	100%	68%	17%	4%	4%	7%
Previous Month	101%	74%	16%	14%	3%	3%

Table O

Taxes and Liabilities to Government

	Period	Due Date	Amount £	Cleared Bank
PAYE	April	19/04/99	750,890.98	21 April
	May	19/05/99	700,300.76	20 May
	Jun	19/06/99	450,134.87	18 June
VAT	Mar	30/04/99	190,056.98	30 April
	Dec	31/01/99	856,873.56	5 Feb

Corporation Tax Due £Nil

Working Paper 9 – Liquidity

Table P – Bank Profile

Table P simply states the current position of all bank accounts held by the business. This is to check that at the time of the survey that these accounts are operating within the agreed facilities.

Table Q – Bank Usage

Based on the trading accounts of the business the purpose of each column is as follows:

1. Takes the best position (i.e. most in credit) in each of the last six months

2. Takes the worst position (i.e. least in credit or biggest debit) in each of the last six months

3. Takes the end balances at the end of the last six months

4. Takes the cash book position at each month end for the last six months from prospect's cash book reconciliation. The cash book position is determined by:

   (a) Taking the closing position of the preceding month

   (b) Adding all debits (cheques or payments issued) in the current month

   (c) Less all payments received in the current month

The cash book position is critical. It shows what the bank position would be if all payments made and received hit the account at that time.

A comparison of the month end cash position to the actual facility will identify potential cash flow difficulties and cash management competency.

This table is used to identify bank account swings and the 6-month trend, it may identify an improving or deteriorating cash position.

A deteriorating cash position is not necessarily viewed negatively by a financier as this creates an opportunity to provide facilities in line with the prospect's working capital needs.

Appendix 1 – Working Papers for Survey of Prospective Client

Table P

Liquidity

Bank & Cash

Current A/C

Bankers	A/C No.	Statement Date	Balance £K	Facility £K	Security	Review Date
A Bank	324667	31/5	3575o/d	4000	All Assets	1/10

Loan A/C

Bankers	A/C No.	Statement Date	Balance £K	Repayment	Terms	Security
A Bank	324669	31/5	2365	9 yr mortgage quarterly	Fixed Charge	1/10

Table Q

Bank Usage

	Best Position £K	Worst Position £K	Bank bal. Month End £K	Cash Book bal. £K
Dec	1311	3807	3576	4231
Jan	903cr	3992	3756	3967
Feb	287	2975	2577	4371
Mar	567	3978	3861	4111
Apr	2356	3787	3543	3977
May	977cr	3988	3766	4569

Audit trail

Part of the examination process will involve a walk-through test or audit trail in association with the shipping test detailed in table L above.

This process is designed to test the sales accounting process from the generation of a sale through to the delivery of goods or services and production of the invoice. This test is then extended through credit control to the eventual cash collection and allocation.

This process is quite often assisted by a control sheet, which provides prompts to the surveyor and enables an understanding of the prospect's systems and controls to be evaluated and recorded. A sample control sheet now follows.

Prospect Examination Control Sheet

Accounting and Administration

1. Describe the sales ledger, open item, ageing method.

2. How and when is cash allocated?

3. Describe sales accounting function.

4. Can ageing be run at any time?

Credit Control

1. Describe procedures for extending credit to new customers.

2. Are credit limits set and adhered to?

3. Describe dunning/chasing routines. (including stop lists).

4. Are solicitors or debt collectors used? If so, who?

5. Detail credit insurance held.

6. Describe the organisation of the credit control department.

Accounting Systems

1. Check that general ledger and supporting records are up-to- date.

2. Confirm that regular and timely management accounts are produced.

3. Describe the frequency and timing of bank reconciliations.

Creditors

1. Confirm there are regular purchase ledger reconciliations.

2. Confirm supplier statements are reconciled to the purchase ledger.

3. Note suppliers who sell with reservation of title.

4. Note special terms.

5. Are there any major disputes.

6. Detail legal proceedings received or outstanding.

Tax and Preferential Creditors

1. Note Corporation Tax or Income Tax unpaid.

2. Check last VAT, PAYE and Corporation Tax payments.

Borrowings

1. Detail long term borrowings.

2. Analyse directors loan accounts.

3. Detail other borrowings.

Associated Companies

1. List all associated or group companies

2. Examine the extent of any inter-company trading.

Stock Levels

1. Raw Material.

2. Work In Progress.

3. Finished Goods.

4. Basis of valuation.

5. Frequency of stock take.

6. Figure used in accounts.

7. Provision for obsolescence.

Plant and Premises
Check:

1. Adequacy for business needs.

2. Tidiness and security.

Insurance
Check:

1. Asset values are fully covered.

2. Adequacy of fire and burglary cover.

3. Premiums are paid to-date

4. Recent claims:

Survey Report

At the end of the process the surveyor will complete a survey report for submission to the credit committee with the working papers.

Survey Report for Credit Committee

There now follows a guide to the matters to be included in the survey report.

Introduction and Scope

- Confirm purpose of the examination and any specific requirements the business development manager requested before the survey took place

- State how long the survey took and at which locations

Business

- Comment on the history of the business and the management

- Explain business activity, product process, market and customers

- Detail number of employees

- Remark on the premises – leasehold, freehold, location and state of repair

Debts and Collateral

This part of the report should explain the working papers and test results in the same sequenc:

- Concentration and spread, customer quality and type

- Ageing

- Debt turn, credit and payment terms

- Analysis of overdues and disputes

- Bad debt levels

- Contra trading and exclusions

- Sales ledger control and account trends

- Dilution and credit notes

- Shipping test and purchase order quality

- Systems procedures and control

The surveyor will give an overall assessment of the debts and the systems that support it.

Appendix 1 – Working Papers for Survey of Prospective Client

Liquidity

● Spread and profile of creditors' accounts

● Pressure from trade creditors

● Purchase ledger accounting functions and process

● PAYE and VAT position

● Bank accounts and cash position

● Overall assessment of the cash position of the prospect at the time of survey

● May comment on cash flow forecasts if provided within the scope of the survey

Financial Condition

● Comment on financial performance

● Speed of production of management accounts

● Analysis of audited financial statements

● Reliability of management accounts and financial forecasts and budgets

Conclusion

The conclusion will provide an overview of the survey, identify any issues relating to the debts, liquidity, business or systems and make recommendation either for or against doing business with the prospect.

Sometimes a qualified recommendation is made e.g. supporting the proposal subject to:

1. Further information

2. Changes to the prospect's systems and/or services

3. Confirmation of matters or facts

Appendix 2
UNDERWRITING PROCESS

Information

The quality, depth and effectiveness of credit analysis is only as good as the level of information available. Credit/underwriting decisions cannot be reached in a vacuum. As well as relying on the information provided by the on site survey the underwriting process will require an assessment of the prospect companies structure and financial position.

The following details the issues surrounding this element of the underwriting process and the approach and considerations necessary when assessing the financial information received from a prospect.

Sources

- Financial statements
- Public/Government records
- Credit reporting agency
- Trade suppliers and creditors
- Customers
- Management
- Company site visits

Financial and Non-financial Information

Non-financial Information:

Legal status of subject company:

- Sole proprietorship
- Partnership (review partnership limited agreement)
- Subsidiaries

- Corporation

Business history

Market/industry characteristics

Product mix

Production process

Sales - mix, volume, concentrations

Distribution network

Major competitors, suppliers, and customers

Banking relationships

Management Review

Ownership

Key managers

Succession

Principal managers:

- Responsibilities

- Experience

- Education

- Commitment to success of the business

Information systems (refer to survey)

Competitive strategy - review business plan

Strategic plan:

Strategic analysis must not be overlooked. The overall performance of company and repayment risks is tied to strategic decisions of the company. Is company's strategic plan sound?

Company's life cycle stage has impact on funding need and ability to repay.

Financial Information

- Target minimum of three years of financial statements

- Sales and Purchases ageing

- Stock summary/ageing

- Management Accounts

The Issues, which will affect the quality of financial information, provided:

Are the Management Accounts:

- Internal - company prepared
- External by
  - § Management accountants
  - § Auditors

    Are they

    - v Local/Small/Unknown
    - v Big 5

Basis on which the financial statements were prepared

- For Internal use
- For External Purposes

Are the Financial Statements being provided the same as those being used internally or shown to others?

Financial statements do not present 'real life'/'truth in accounting'

Financial statements are a report card on business activity based on how the various accounting rules are applied.

Accounting rules can be open to judgement in terms of their application.

Accounting methods may change from period to period, making comparisons from period to period difficult and trends misleading. For example a change in accounting methods could make the following trends unreliable or meaningless.

- Revenue recognition
- Bad debt recognition
- Depreciation methods
- Stock valuation methods

Questions to be asked to assess the relevance of the information provided.

- Statements are prepared on a historical basis and therefore may not reflect realistic current values or serve as a predictor of future values.

- Prepared in an environment of constant change.
- Represent one period in time.
- Present only what "has" happened.
- Changing value of money is overlooked.
- Distortion due to abstraction level.

For example, total sales may show modest growth though certain products may be suffering significant losses.

Key Factors to Address Before an in-depth Analysis
Purpose
- Is the proposed advance/use of funds legal?
- Is the proposed advance in compliance with internal goals/credit policy?

Company/Industry

Does the prospects industry and company match with internal marketing goals and/or credit policy?

Strategies for Analysing Financial Statements

Newspaper analogy - read financial statements as you would a newspaper
- Look for headlines/major swings, trends
- Read the entire report

  NB: Footnotes may provide valuable information
- Make a point sheet highlighting key areas
- Rank apparent trends in order of impact
- Address the issues

Understand terminology
- Source
- Meaning
- Implications thereof

Concept of standards
- Be careful of 'value' judgements.

- What are standards for the particular industry?

Conduct 'what if thinking'

- If expenses had remained at the historical % what would be the impact on earnings?

- If A/R turnover remained at previous years' base what would be impact on cash flow?

Questions/questions

- Seek underlying cause of any relevant trend or increase in assets, liabilities, equity, sales expenses, and earnings.

Primary Focus of Financial Analysis

Profit and Loss

- Reflects management's ability to conduct business

- Reflects impact of cyclical, economic and competitive factors on stability and viability of earnings

- Level of earnings is an important determinant of the level of debt the business can maintain.

- Specific questions to be addressed on Income Statement (See attached list)

Balance Sheet

- Prepared on a historical costs basis

- Book and liquidation values are rarely the same

- Equity does not repay loans but offers lenders a cushion

  - Concept of equity cushion

    - The value of a company's assets is theoretically available for loan repayment in the event of liquidation after all liabilities other than the loan have been paid. The actual value of equity cushion depends on liquidation value of company's assets.

- Reflects distribution of assets, financing of assets, capitalisation, liquidity, source of debt repayment, collateral.

- Specific questions to be addressed on Balance Sheet (See attached list).

The focus should be on the pattern, and underlying issues behind the movements within the P & L and B/S accounts. Such as:

- Sales - mix, volume, growth rate.

- Gross profit and operating profit margins.

- Sales, general and administrative expenses.

- Dividends.

- Fixed/variable expenses

- Accounts Receivable - mix, turnover, quality.

- Stock - mix age, turnover.

- Accounts Payable - mix, turnover.

- Fixed assets - mix, age, utilisation, acquisition.

- Non-productive assets.

- Leverage

- Debt structure

- Cash flow

Analytical Tools/Methods

To identify and assess a comparative analysis is used to:

- Highlight trends in primary P & L and B/S accounts.

- Compare to prior accounting periods.

- Compare to industry norm or peer group analysis

Ratio Analysis

- Provides a means of quantifying and measuring company/management performance and decisions.

- Provides a medium for comparison and trend analysis.

- Ratios are sterile, based on financial statements set at one point in time.

- Can provide guidance for questions.

- Cannot be analysed in a vacuum.

- Basic Ratios (Refer to the attached detailed listing)

- Liquidity ratios - provide a measure of quality and adequacy of current assets to meet current obligations as due

  - Indicators of company's ability to meet current obligations

  - Current ratio

  - Quick ratio

- Composition and quality of current assets is a critical factor. A high numerical value alone does not reflect necessarily good liquidity. Movement in current ratio from 2.0 to 3.0 for example may be due to growth in A/R. That growth may simply reflect past due receivables, and thus liquidity may not be improved.

- Turnover ratios - provide measure of quality and management of current assets and trade cycle patterns

  - Sales/receivables

  - Days Receivable

  - Cost of sales/Stock

  - Days stock

  - Cost of sales/payables

  - Days payable

  - Sales/working capital

- Leverage ratios - address risks of financial structure by reflecting relative investments by 'creditor' and 'owners'. Reflect degree of financial flexibility.

  - Net fixed assets/tangible net worth

  - Debt/worth

Summary

A Systematic Approach to Credit Analysis

- Read latest financial statements carefully with attention to the accountant's footnotes.

- Understand what the company does.

- Spreadsheet the financial statements.

- Determine the extent of the bank's relationship with the company.

- Determine why the company needs to borrow.

- Continually ask two questions throughout the analytical process.

  1. Where are the risks associated with the credit? Once identified, what steps can be taken to minimise the risks?

  2. Why? Why do certain positive and negative conditions exist within the company?

- Consider major external factors, which may influence the company.

- Conduct ratio analysis focusing on liquidity, leverage, and profitability.

- Conduct cash flow analysis.

- Conduct sensitivity (what if) analysis.
- Review collateral position.
- Get in-depth answers to any questions you have regarding the company and its financial position and performance.

Appendix 3

MODEL LEGAL AGREEMENT TO BE READ IN ASSOCIATION WITH CHAPTER 2

AGREEMENT FOR THE FACTORING OF DEBTS   A

1. **PARTIES:**   (1)   TOP FACTORS LIMITED (a company registered in England and Wales with the number 1000000) of Percentage House, Discount Street, Moneytown, Bankshire FAC1 ID 1 ('the Financier', which expression shall include the Financier's assigns except where the context otherwise requires).

          (2)   The person ('the Client') described as Client in paragraph 1 of the Schedule ('the Schedule') annexed to and forming part of this Agreement.

2. **DATE:**   This Agreement shall be deemed to be made on the date on which it is executed by or on behalf of the Financier.

3. **DEFINITIONS:**

      (1)   In this Agreement, except where the context otherwise requires, the singular shall include the plural and vice versa, any gender shall include any other gender and the following expressions shall have the meanings assigned to them below:

'Approval Limit'   A limit established by the Financier at its absolute discretion on application to it by the Client in relation to any Debtor for the purpose of determining the extent to which the aggregate indebtedness of any Debtor at any one time comprises Approved Debts.

'Approved Debt'   Any Notified Debt (i) which (when aggregated with all other Debts owing by the same Debtor) falls within any Approval Limit (and where there are two or more Debts owing by the same Debtor the Debts shall be treated for this purpose in the order in which they have been Notified to the Financier) and (ii) in relation to which the Client is not in breach of any warranty or undertaking contained in this Agreement otherwise than as provided in clause 9(3) and (iii) which is not a Debt or within a class of Debts specified in paragraph 2(a) of the Schedule.

'Associate of the Client'
A director, shareholder or employee of the Client or a person whose relationship to the Client is within the meaning of associate as defined by Section 184 of the Consumer Credit Act 1974.

'Associated Rights'
All instruments and securities taken or held by the Client in connection with a Debt, the benefits of any policy of credit and/or export insurance, the title to any ledger and any computer data in which a Debt is recorded and any document evidencing the Debt and all the Client's rights under or in relation to the relevant Supply Contract (including the right to rescind or terminate such contract and/or accept a return of the Goods comprised therein) and Transferred Goods.

'Collection Date'
(i) As regards a Debt paid in cash, the date of receipt from the Debtor and, as regards a Debt paid by cheque or other instrument, the date on which the amount of the same is collected from the drawer or acceptor as determined by the Financier at its absolute discretion; or

(ii) such other date as may be specified in paragraph 2(b) of the Schedule.

'Commencement Date'
The date specified in paragraph 12 of the Schedule.

'Current Account'
An account maintained by the Financier to which shall be debited all sums of money paid and all amounts charged to the Client by the Financier and to which shall be credited amounts equal to the monies received by the Financier in respect of Debts.

'Date of Insolvency'
(i) In the case of bankruptcy, sequestration or winding up by the Court - the date of the bankruptcy order, sequestration award or winding up order respectively by the Court having jurisdiction;

(ii) In the case of a voluntary winding up - the date of the effective resolution for voluntary winding up by the members of the insolvent person;

(iii) In the case of the appointment of a receiver or administrative receiver - the date of the appointment;

(iv) In the case of any arrangement or an administration order - the date when the same is made.

'Debt'	The amount (or where the context so requires, a part of the amount) of any obligation incurred or to be incurred by the Debtor under a Supply Contract including any tax or duty payable by the Debtor.
'Debtor'	Any person who is or may become indebted in respect of any Debt or prospective Debt.
'Debts Purchased Account'	An account maintained by the Financier for recording the value of outstanding Debts notified to the Financier

'Delivered'

(i) In the case of Goods - despatch in the United Kingdom to the Debtor or his agent or collection of Goods from the premises of the Client; and

(ii) In the case of services - completion of their performance.

'Event of Default'	Any giving the Financier the right of immediate termination of this agreement (whether or not such right is exercised) including any of those listed in clause 20(2) .
'Goods'	Any merchandise and, where the context so admits, any services (and 'sale of goods' shall include the provision of services).

'Insolvency' (i) Bankruptcy.

(ii) Sequestration.

(iii) Winding up by reason of inability to pay debts.

(iv) The appointment of an administrative receiver of substantially the whole of the assets; or the making of an arrangement, whether in accordance with the Insolvency Act or otherwise, with or for the benefit of the general body of creditors.

(v) A voluntary arrangement in accordance with the Insolvency Act.

(vi) The making of an administration order pursuant to the Insolvency Act.

'Insolvency Act'	The Insolvency Act 1986 or any re-enactment thereof or of any part thereof.
'Legal Representative'	The Debtor's executor, administrator, trustee in bankruptcy, liquidator, administrative receiver or other person for the time being entrusted by law with the management of the Debtor's assets or affairs.
'Notified'	In relation to a Debt included in an Offer or in respect of which the Client has carried out its obligation to Notify the Financier.

'Notified Debt'	A Debt Notified to the Financier under paragraph (ii) of clause 8(2) or included in an Offer under clause 4(4) which has been accepted.
'Notify'	The delivery by the Client to the Financier of notification of the existence of a Debt in such form as the Financier may stipulate and 'Notified' shall be construed accordingly.
'Offer'	An unconditional Offer delivered by the Client to the Financier in such form as the Financier may stipulate, to sell a Debt to the Financier. Where more than one Debt is at the same time so offered for sale, then each Debt included on the form shall be treated as being subject to an independent Offer to sell, which the Financier shall be free to accept or reject in its absolute discretion.
'Purchase Price'	The price payable by the Financier under Clause 5 in respect of a Debt.
'Recourse'	The right of the Financier to require the Client to repurchase a Notified Debt at a price equal to the Notified amount.
'Supply Contract'	A contract for the sale of Goods by the Client.

'Transferred Goods' (i)   Any Goods the subject of a Supply Contract which shall not have been Delivered before the Debt relating to such Goods shall have been Notified to the Financier in breach of this Agreement; or

                     (ii)   Goods which any Debtor shall reject or shall return or attempt to return to the Financier or the Client or indicate a wish so to do; or

                     (iii)   Goods which the Client or the Financier recovers from the Debtor.

'Unapproved Debt' A Debt that is not an Approved Debt.

'VAT Bad Debt Scheme'   The procedures established by H M Customs and Excise to enable suppliers of Goods to reclaim the Value Added Tax ('VAT') element of bad and doubtful Debts.

(2)   Expressions which, in or for the purpose of any proceedings outside England, have no precise counterpart in the jurisdiction in which those proceedings take place, shall be construed as if bearing the meaning of the closest equivalent thereto in the jurisdiction concerned.

(3)   The meaning of the word 'otherwise' or of general words introduced by the word 'other' shall not be limited by reference to any preceding word indicating a particular class of acts matters or things.

4. TRANSFER OF DEBTS

(1) The Client agrees to sell and the Financier to purchase all Debts, arising after the Commencement Date during the currency of this Agreement, in relation to any Debtor of the class or description specified in paragraph 3 of the Schedule. The ownership of such future Debts shall vest in the Financier automatically upon the same coming into existence.

(2) Upon any Debt vesting in the Financier under sub-clauses 4(1) or 4(4) there shall also automatically vest in the Financier all the Associated Rights in relation to such Debt and the Financier shall have the right to require the transfer to it of the title to any other Goods comprised in the relevant Supply Contract.

(3) The Client shall at the request of the Financier and at the Client's expense execute a formal written assignment to the Financier of each Notified Debt and its Associated Rights referred to in sub-clauses 4(1) and 4(2) or a Debt of which the Offer is accepted pursuant to sub-clause 4(4) and deliver to the Financier any instrument or security included therein with any necessary endorsement or other signature.

(4) The Client agrees to Offer on or as soon as possible after the Commencement Date all Debts existing at that Date in relation to any Debtor of the class or description specified in Paragraph 3 of the Schedule. The ownership of each such Debt so offered shall vest in the Financier upon acceptance of the Offer. Acceptance shall take place upon the Financier crediting its Notified Value to the Debts Purchased Account. The Financier shall not be obliged to accept an Offer.

(5) If any Debt shall fail to vest effectively in the Financier in equity, the Client shall hold such Debt and any Associated Rights relating thereto on trust for the Financier.

(6) In the event of any stamp duty being payable in respect of the transfer of Debts to the Financier, the Client hereby indemnifies the Financier against all such duty and any penalties and interest arising whether under this Agreement or pursuant to any counter-guarantee or counter-indemnity or by reason of law or otherwise.

5. PURCHASE PRICE AND ACCOUNTING

(1) The Purchase Price of each Debt vesting in the Financier under clause 4(1) or 4(4) together with its Associated Rights and any Goods of which title is transferred under clause 4(2) shall be the amount (including any tax or duty) payable by the Debtor in respect of such Debt less any discount or other deduction allowed or allowable by the Client to the Debtor in relation thereto.

(2) The Client's right to payment in respect of the Purchase Price of a Debt is exercisable only by withdrawal from the Current Account as provided hereunder

and within the limits and subject to the restrictions imposed by this Agreement. The Purchase Price of a Debt and its Associated Rights shall be credited to the Current Account and (except as provided by sub-clauses (3) - (5) of this clause) shall be paid by the Financier to or for the account of the Client on the Collection Date or, as regards an Approved Debt, on the date of any earlier Date of Insolvency of the Debtor.

(3)   At any time (except as provided in sub-clauses (4) and (5) of this clause) after the expiry of 24 hours of receipt by the Financier of Notification under paragraph (ii) of clause 8(2) or an Offer relating to an Approved Debt, the Financier shall at the request of the Client prepay in whole or in part such percentage of the Purchase Price of the Debt and its Associated Rights as is set out in paragraph 5 of the Schedule or such other percentage as shall have been agreed between the parties in writing. Any such prepayment shall be debited to the Current Account. If the Client is in breach of any warranty or undertaking relating to a Debt then any

(4)   At any time (i) whilst any petition for the winding up or bankruptcy of the Client or for an administration order or whilst a proposal for a voluntary arrangement, in each case pursuant to the Insolvency Act, in relation to the Client is pending or (ii) when the Financier is entitled to terminate this Agreement under clause 20(2), whether or not exercising its right to terminate, the Financier may at its absolute discretion withhold all prepayments, and be repaid by the Client on demand any prepayment which shall have been made in respect of any Debt then unpaid and all the Client's present and future liabilities to the Financier. Where the amount of such liabilities is not immediately available, the Financier may make a reasonable estimate of the same. Such liabilities shall be debited to the Current Account. If the Client is or has been in breach of any warranty or undertaking relating to an outstanding Debt then any prepayment made in respect of that Debt must forthwith be repaid to the Financier on demand.

(5)   The Financier shall not be obliged to make any prepayment on account of the Purchase Price of a Debt if such payment would result in (i) the total amount of all such prepayments in respect of Debts then outstanding exceeding the funding limit as set out in paragraph 14 of the Schedule; or (ii) the prepayments in respect of outstanding Debts owing by any one Debtor being in excess of the concentration percentage (as set out in paragraph 15 of the Schedule) of the total amount of prepayments in respect of all Debts then outstanding.

(6)   The Financier shall at any time be entitled to debit to the Current Account any amount payable or prospectively payable by the Client to the Financier whether under this Agreement or pursuant to any counter-guarantee or counter-indemnity or by reason of law or otherwise.

(7)   Unless otherwise agreed by the Financier at the request of the Client, the Purchase Price of all Debts and the Associated Rights relating thereto shall be payable in sterling.

(8)   Where a Debt is payable otherwise than in sterling in the United Kingdom, (i) bank charges for collection and/or conversion into sterling shall be deducted in calculating the Purchase Price of the Debt and its Associated Rights and (ii) the Purchase Price which shall be payable in sterling shall be computed by reference to the rate of exchange ruling in London on the Collection Date, or any earlier Date of Insolvency of the relevant Debtor, but for administrative convenience and for the purpose of computing the administration charge in accordance with Clause 6, the Financier may provisionally apply the rate ruling in London on the date of receipt by the Financier of the notification relating to the Debt, making such adjustments as may thereafter be necessary. Similar provisions shall apply to payment of the repurchase price where the Financier has Recourse in relation to a Debt to which this clause applies and such repurchase price shall be computed at the same rate as that applied to the Purchase Price of the Debt to which it relates.

(9)   The Client will pay to the Financier a discounting charge which will be the percentage specified in paragraph 4(a) of the Schedule per annum over the Base Rate of Barclays Bank PLC for the time being in force subject to the minimum specified in paragraph 4(b) of the Schedule or such other rate as shall have been agreed between the parties in writing. The discounting charge shall be calculated daily on the balance standing to the debit of the Current Account as at the close of business on each day and the aggregate amount of such discounting charge shall be debited to the Current Account at the end of each month. For the purposes of establishing the balance on the Current Account, a Debt shall be deemed to be outstanding until the Collection Date thereof or, in respect of an Approved Debt, any Earlier Date of Insolvency of the relevant Debtor.

(10)   Upon the occurrence of any Event of Default or upon the ending of this Agreement the Financier shall have the right to net-off the Client's liability, to the extent not already debited to the Current Account, against the sums due by the Financier to the Client. Such liability and sums, together with the outstanding items in the Current Account, shall be treated as being consolidated into a single Current Account. Any debit balance arising from such treatment shall become immediately payable to the Financier and any credit balance shall become immediately payable to the Client. Any part of the Client's liability to the Financier expressed in a foreign currency may be converted by the Financier to sterling at the rate of exchange prevailing at the time of any set-off or combination of accounts hereunder.

(11)   The Parties' rights hereunder are subject to a running account and are such

that there is only one debt between them, being the debit or credit balance on the Current Account.

6. ADMINISTRATION CHARGES

(1) Upon a Debt being Notified to the Financier the Client shall immediately pay to the Financier an administration charge which shall be such percentage as is specified in paragraph 6 of the Schedule (or such other percentage as shall have been agreed by the parties in writing) of the value of each Notified Debt to the Financier, such value to be computed before deduction of any discounts or other deductions allowed or allowable by the Client to the Debtor.

(2) The Client shall pay to the Financier in respect of each Notified Debt an Additional Administration Charge at the rate shown in paragraph 7 of the Schedule, or such other percentage as agreed by the parties in writing, in respect of each month or part of a month falling more than three months after the end of the month during which the relative Notified Debt was dated calculated on the amount payable by the customer in respect thereof outstanding at the beginning of such month such Additional Administration Charge to be paid on the first day of the month to which the same relates.

(3) The Client shall pay to the Financier a charge for each payment or prepayment made by the Financier to the Client otherwise than by cheque at the request of the Client. Such charge will be made at the standard rate of the Financier in force from time to time as advised to the Client and shall be debited to the Current Account.

(4) The Client shall pay to the Financier the amount of any costs incurred by the Financier relating to cheques or other instruments which are not met upon first presentation, insofar as such cheques or other instruments are appropriated to Unapproved Debts in accordance with clause 12. Such charge will be debited to the Current Account.

(5) In addition to the administration charge referred to in paragraph 6(1), the Financier shall be entitled to charge such fee as the Financier in its absolute discretion considers appropriate in respect of additional services provided and/ or variations to this Agreement.

7. STATEMENTS OF ACCOUNT

The Financier shall send a statement of account to the Client at least once in every month and such statement shall be deemed to be correct and shall be binding on the Client (save for manifest error) unless the Client notifies the Financier of an error therein within thirty days of the date of its despatch.

8. WARRANTIES AND UNDERTAKINGS BY CLIENT

(1) The Client warrants:

(i)   that the Client's business is as stated in paragraph 8 of the Scheule;

(ii)   that, save as disclosed to the Financier in writing, the Client is the legal and beneficial owner of the Debts the subject of this Agreement and the Client has not granted any disposition or any charge or other encumbrance which affects or may affect any of the Debts the subject of this Agreement or any Associated Rights;

(iii)   that the Goods have been respectively Delivered to the Debtor and/or completely performed, on or before the Offer or notification of the Debt to the Financier;

(iv)   that prior to the making of this Agreement the Client has disclosed to the Financier every fact or matter known to the Client which the Client knew or ought to have known might influence the Financier in its decision whether or not to enter into this Agreement and, if so, as to the terms of the Agreement, including any term as to Recourse, prepayment, establishment of any Approval Limit or funds in use limit or designation of any Debt or class of Debts as unapproved;

(v)   that every Debtor has an established place of business and is not an Associate of the Client;

(vi)   that on the date on which the Client executes this Agreement that the value of the Client's assets exceeds the amount of its liabilities, taking into account its contingent and prospective liabilities;

(vii)   that no reservation of title in favour of any third party will apply to all or any part of any Goods sold by the Client nor will there be any right in favour of any third party to trace into the proceeds of sale of such Goods.

(2) The Client undertakes in addition to and without prejudice to any other undertaking given by it elsewhere in this Agreement:

(i)   to ensure that the warranties given in sub-clause (1) in relation to the making of this Agreement shall remain fulfilled during the continuance of the Agreement, and to perform any outstanding or continuing obligations of the Client to every Debtor including payment of all carriage or shipping charges under the relevant Supply Contract or any related contract;

(ii)   in respect of Debts coming into existence after the Commencement Date promptly to Notify the Financier, in such manner and with such particulars and documents evidencing the Debt as the Financier may from time to time require, of every Debt vesting in the Financier, within 10 days of the relevant Goods having been Delivered or, if so required by the Financier, at any other time;

(iii) to ensure that except as otherwise approved by the Financier in writing every Supply Contract (a) shall be made in the ordinary course of the Client's business, (b) shall provide for terms of payment not more liberal than those set out in paragraph 9(a) of the Schedule, (c) shall be subject to the law of the country or one of the countries specified in paragraph 9(b) of the Schedule, (d) shall provide for the relevant invoice to be expressed and payment to be made by the Debtor in the currency or one of the currencies specified in paragraph 9(c) of the Schedule, and (e) shall not include any prohibition of its assignment;

(iv) to ensure that every Notified Debt shall be payable by the Debtor as a legally binding obligation without dispute or claim, defence, cross claim or set-off (whether or not justified);

(v) as regards every Notified Debt, to give to the Debtor such written notice of transfer of the Debt to the Financier as may be required by paragraph 10 of the Schedule;

(vi) promptly to deliver direct to the Financier (or, if so required by the Financier, direct to a bank account specified by the Financier) the identical remittance received by the Client in payment of or on account of a Debt or its Associated Rights, and pending such delivery to hold such remittance in trust for the Financier and separate from the Client's own monies and to provide the Financier's bankers with such indemnity as may be required in respect of non transferable remittances;

(vii) to co-operate fully with the Financier in the collection of any Debt and the enforcement of payment thereof, whether by proceedings or otherwise, including the provision of evidence and witnesses, and the execution of any further documents required to perfect title to the debt, and to indemnify the Financier against all legal and other costs and expenses incurred in connection with such enforcement so far as it relates to an Unapproved Debt;

(viii) not in any way to rescind, terminate or vary any Supply Contract including terms as to payment without the prior written consent of the Financier;

(ix) not to assign, charge or otherwise encumber any Debt the subject of this Agreement or any Associated Rights, nor to enter into any other agreement for the Financiering or discounting of any Debts (whether or not the subject of this Agreement) without the prior written consent of the Financier;

(x) that no other party shall have any right to or any interest in any Debt including any tracing right;

(xi) to maintain such records as the Financier requires in connection with the Debts separate from all other records of the Client and to ensure that in all such records there are conspicuous notations that the Debts belong to the Financier;

(xii) to maintain such insurance as the Financier may require with the interest of the Financier noted thereon as loss-payee against the loss of all records referred to in Clause 8(2)(xi) in connection with the Debts;

(xiii) if any Supply Contract reserves title to goods sold by the Client until payment in full for those or any other Goods, where a Notified Debt relates to such Goods, to exercise in accordance with the Financier's instruction all rights arising from the reservation of title.

9. DISPUTES WITH DEBTORS AND CREDIT NOTES

(1) The Client shall advise the Financier promptly in writing of any dispute between the Client and any Debtor relating to any Debt.

(2) The Client will use its best endeavours to resolve any dispute as directed by the Financier. The Client hereby authorises the Financier at the Client's expense to resolve if so required by the Financier any dispute not resolved by the Client and agrees to be bound by anything done by the Financier including any consequent reduction in the Purchase Price of a Debt.

(3) A Debt, the subject of any such dispute which is resolved in favour of the Client within 60 days of the first advice of the dispute to the Financier or 90 days of the due date for payment of the Debt (whichever is the earlier), shall not be the subject of Recourse in accordance with clause 10 solely by reason of the said dispute.

(4) In respect of any credit notes relating to Debts, (i) the Client acknowledges that at any time the Financier may by written notice require that credit notes will be issued only with the prior consent of the Financier, (ii) on receipt of such notice the Client undertakes to carry out the said requirement in every particular and (iii) whether before or after such notice the Client shall promptly supply to the Financier a copy of every credit note issued by the Client.

10. RECOURSE AND SET-OFF

(1) As regards (i) each Unapproved Debt, (ii) each Debt which comprises solely discount wrongly claimed or deducted by the Debtor, (iii) each Debt which the Debtor is or claims to be unable to pay by reason of legal constraints (other than those created by the Debtor's Insolvency) or acts or orders of government and (iv) each Debt in respect of which the Debtor or his Legal Representative has disputed liability (otherwise than where the provisions of clause 9(3) apply) the Financier shall have Recourse to the Client as follows:

(a)   on the expiry of notice to the Client of the length specified in paragraph 11(a) of the Schedule; or

(b)   on the expiry of the period specified in paragraph 11(b) of the Schedule; or

(c)   on the Insolvency of the Debtor;

whichever is the earliest. After the exercise of Recourse by the Financier in respect of any such Debt and its revesting in the Client the Financier will credit the Client with all sums subsequently recovered by the Financier in respect of it as the result of enforcement or realisation of any Associated Rights. The said Debt and any Associated Rights relating thereto shall, unless otherwise determined by the Financier, remain vested in the Financier until the repurchase price has been fully discharged, whether by payment to the Financier or by set-off of an amount credited to the Client under the provisions of this Agreement.

(2)   The Financier may at any time set off against any sum payable to the Client the amount of any liability of the Client to the Financier, whether under this Agreement or otherwise, whether existing, future or contingent and whether by way of debt, damages or restitution. We may at any time also combine any accounts recording transactions between you and us.

(3)   The Client may not, under any circumstance, set off against any sum payable by the Client to the Financier any sum owing by the Financier.

11. VALUE ADDED TAX

When the terms of the VAT Bad Debt Scheme would apply to an Approved Debt but for its assignment to the Financier then:

(1)   the Financier shall be at liberty to:

(i)   reassign to the Client all its interest in such Approved Debt; and/or

(ii)   lodge in the Client's name a proof of debt in the Insolvency of the Debtor

(2)   the Client undertakes to:

(i)   accept reassignment of such Approved Debt; and

(ii)   pay to the Financier forthwith a sum equivalent to the VAT included in such Approved Debt that the Client may be able to reclaim under the VAT Bad Debt Scheme; and

(iii)   use its best endeavours to recover all VAT that it is entitled to reclaim; and

(iv)   hold in trust for the Financier any dividend or other sum (other than VAT) included in such Approved Debt recovered by the Client in proportion to the amount of such Approved Debt.

12. APPROPRIATION AND DIVISION OF RECEIPTS

(1)   In any case in which Approved and Unapproved Debts may be owing by the same Debtor then (subject to the provisions of sub-clause (2) of this clause), the Financier shall be entitled (notwithstanding any contrary appropriation by the Debtor) to appropriate any payment or other benefit received in discharge of or on account of Debts owing by such Debtor, and any credit or allowance granted by the Client to the Debtor, in discharge of or on account of any Approved Debt in priority to any Unapproved Debt.

(2)   Any dividend or other benefit received from the estate of a Debtor following the Date of Insolvency shall be divided between the Financier and the Client pro-rata to the aggregate amount of Approved and Unapproved Debts owing by the Debtor at the Date of Insolvency.

13. CREDIT BALANCES

The Client shall have no entitlement to any credit balance which may arise on any Debtor's account in the Financier's records and the Client hereby irrevocably authorises the Financier to make payment to the Debtor in settlement of any such credit balance whether such credit balance arises from the issue of a credit note by the Client or otherwise.

14. COLLECTION OF DEBTS

(1)   Where notice of transfer of a Debt to the Financier has been given to the Debtor, then until a Debt has become revested in the Client in accordance with Clause 10, the Financier shall have the sole right to collect the Debt and to enforce payment thereof in such manner and to such extent as it shall in its absolute discretion decide, and to institute, defend or compromise in the name of the Financier or the Client and on such terms as the Financier thinks fit any proceedings by or against the Financier in relation to the Debt.

(2)   Upon the occurrence of any Event of Default the administration charge, for which provision is made in Clause 6 and in paragraph 6 of the Schedule, shall be increased by 5% of the gross value of all Debts outstanding on the date that the Financier has such right and all Debts Notified to the Financier thereafter.

(2)   Upon the occurrence of any Event of Default the Financier may at its sole discretion increase the discounting charge for which provision is made in Clause 5 (9) and in paragraph 4 of the Schedule, by 1% per annum over the base rate of Barclays Bank PLC for the time being in force or such other rate as shall have been agreed between the parties in writing.

(3)   The Financier may at any time exercise its rights as the owner or beneficiary of the Associated Rights (including the right to sell Goods or Transferred Goods at such prices and in such manner as it sees fit)and will credit the net proceeds thereof to the Current Account.

15. CLIENT'S ACCOUNTS AND RECORDS

(1) The Client shall permit the Financier and its authorised agents at all reasonable times at the Client's expense (i) to inspect, verify, check, remove and take copies of all or any of the Client's records and documents relating to any transaction giving rise to a Debt or relating to the financial position of the Client, (ii) to collect any of the Goods, records and documents included in the Associated Rights and (iii) for any of these purposes to have access to the place or places where the Goods, records and documents are stored.

(2) The Client shall furnish to the Financier (i) within 6 months of each accounting reference date during the period of this Agreement the audited accounts of the Client for the accounting reference period ended on such accounting reference date and (ii) within one month of the end of each month end during the period of this Agreement a statement showing its financial position and the results of its operations for that period.

(3) The Client authorises the Financier, with effect from the date of this Agreement at any time until the termination thereof and the discharge of all the Client's obligations to the Financier, (i) to disclose to any Bank, to which payments of amounts payable to the Client by the Financier under this Agreement are to be made in accordance with the Client's instructions, any information concerning this Agreement and/or the state of the Current Account, and (ii) to obtain from such Bank any information regarding the state of the Client's account with such Bank and/or any facilities granted to or under consideration for the Client by such Bank. The Client warrants that it has authorised such Bank to pass such information to the Financier.

16. POWER OF ATTORNEY

The Client hereby irrevocably appoints the Financier and the Directors and the General Manager and the Company Secretary or any officer for the time being of the Financier jointly and each of them severally to be the attorneys or the attorney of the Client to execute or sign in the Client's name such deeds and documents, to complete or endorse such cheques and other instruments, to institute or defend such proceedings and to perform such other acts, as the Financier may consider necessary in order to perfect the Financier's title to any Debt or any Associated Rights or to secure performance of any of the Client's obligations under this Agreement or any Supply Contract. The Financier and any attorney appointed above may appoint and remove any substitute attorney for the Client in respect of the above matters. The Client will ratify whatever any attorney shall lawfully do.

17. APPROVAL LIMITS

(1) Any Approval Limit may be cancelled or varied by the Financier in its absolute discretion by written or oral notice to the Client and such cancellation or variation shall take effect forthwith except that no cancellation or reduction of any

Approval Limit shall affect any Debt which:

(i)   shall have arisen from Goods sold and Delivered before the time of the receipt by the Client of notice of such reduction or cancellation; and

(ii)   before such time shall have been an Approved Debt.

(2)   The Financier shall not be obliged to disclose to the Client any reason for the establishment, failure to establish, cancellation or withdrawal of any Approval Limit.

(3)   The amount of or absence of any Approval Limit shall not be disclosed by the Client to any third party (unless required so to do by express statutory provision or by due process of law) and the Client undertakes to indemnify the Financier against all loss, costs and expenses suffered or incurred by the Financier as a result of any breach of this provision.

18.   CHANGE IN CONSTITUTION OF CLIENT

This Agreement shall remain effective notwithstanding any change in the constitution, composition or legal personality of the Client, whether by death, retirement, addition or otherwise.

19.   PARTNERSHIPS AND SOLE TRADERS

(1)   Where the Client constitutes a partnership the following provisions shall apply:

(i)   The undertakings and warranties contained in this Agreement shall be deemed to be given by each of the partners both as individuals and as partners and trustees of the Client and the liability hereunder of each of the partners in the Client shall be joint and several and reference to the Client in clauses 5(4) and 20(2) shall be deemed to include any one or more of them. The Financier shall be at liberty (a) to release or conclude a compromise with any one or more of them without affecting its rights against the others; and (b) to treat a notice or demand, by the Financier to any one or more of them or to the Financier by any one or more of them, as a notice or demand given to or by all the others (but the Financier shall not be obliged to treat such notice or demand in such manner); and (c) to treat this Agreement as binding upon any executor, administrator or personal representative of any of them and upon any committee, receiver, judicial Financier, trustee in sequestration or other persons lawfully acting on behalf of any of them.

(ii)   If at any time a partner in the Client ceases for any reason to be a member of the partnership (a 'Retiring Partner') then the Client will forthwith advise the Financier in writing of such fact.

(iii)   Provided that the notice required in clause 19(1)(ii) has been given at least four months prior to any anniversary of the Commencement Date then a Retiring Partner shall have no obligation to the Financier in respect of Debts vesting in the Financier after whichever is the later of the date of such retirement or the next anniversary of the Commencement Date. However, a Retiring Partner shall remain fully liable to the Financier in respect of all matters occurring prior to the later of the date of such retirement or the next anniversary of the Commencement Date.

(iv)   The Client warrants that the persons executing this Agreement on behalf of the Client comprise all the partners in the Client and undertakes that upon such partners taking any other person into partnership (a 'New Partner') they shall advise the Financier in writing of such fact and shall procure that such New Partner executes such documents as may be required to ensure that the New Partner is bound by the terms of this Agreement and is placed under the same obligations and liabilities to the Financier as the other partners.

(v)   Notwithstanding any change in the membership of the Client the Financier shall be entitled to account to the Client or to exercise all rights of set off as if there had been no such change.

(vi)   At any time within three months of a new partner being admitted to the Partnership the Financier shall be at liberty to terminate this Agreement forthwith by written notice.

(2)   Where the Client constitutes either a partnership or an unincorporated sole trader the following shall apply:

(i)   By the execution of this Agreement the Client signifies its concurrence in the Financier's opinion that section 10(3) (b) (iii) of the Consumer Credit Act 1974 does not apply to this Agreement.

(ii)   If the Client changes its domicile to a jurisdiction outside England and Wales it shall forthwith advise the Financier in writing thereof and execute such further documentation as may be required by the Financier.

(iii)   The Client shall fully cooperate with the Financier to enable this Agreement to be registered at the Bills of Sale Registry.

(iv)   The undersigned will inform the Financier of the existence of all businesses in relation to which any of them have an interest and will procure that each such business if engaged in business similar to or connected with the business of the Client will also enter into separate agreements in like terms to the Financiering Agreement for the sale of its invoices to the Financier, should the Financier so require.

(v)   The Client warrants that the residential address of each of the undersigned is correctly stated in the Schedule and undertakes promptly to advise the Financier in writing of any change.

20. COMMENCEMENT AND TERMINATION

(1)   This Agreement shall remain in force for twelve months from the Commencement Date specified in paragraph 12 of the schedule and, subject to the provisions of the sub-clauses below, shall continue until:

    (i)   either party shall give to the other at least six month's written notice; or

    (ii)   it is determined in accordance with the terms hereof.

(2)   The Financier shall be at liberty to terminate this Agreement forthwith by notice upon the occurrence of any of the following events or at any time thereafter:

    (i)   if at any time the Client shall become insolvent or a petition for the bankruptcy or winding up of the Client be presented or a petition for an administration order in respect of the Client be issued; or

    (ii)   if the Client shall call a meeting to pass any resolution to wind up the Client whether by its members or creditors or, being a partnership, be dissolved; or

    (iii)   following the appointment of a receiver or administrative receiver of any part of the income or assets of the Client; or a proposal for an informal or voluntary arrangement between the Client and the general body of its creditors; or

    (iv)   if the Client's obligations to third parties for the repayment of borrowings shall become repayable prior to maturity by reason of default or shall not be paid when due; or

    (v)   if there is any change, whether direct or indirect, in the ownership or control or operation of the Client or there is any adverse change in the Client's condition or operating performance which the Financier in its absolute discretion considers significant or material; or

    (vi)   if at any time the Client shall cease to carry on or suspend its business; or

    (vii)   if at any time the Client shall commit any breach of this Agreement or any agreement with any Associate of the Financier as defined in section 184 Consumer Credit Act 1974;

    (viii)   if a garnishee order nisi obtained by any judgement creditor of the Client shall be served on the Financier or if the Client suffers distress for rent; or

    (ix)   if any final judgement award or decree against the Client is unsatisfied after 7 days; or

    (x)   if any person who has given to the Financier a guarantee, indemnity or warranty in respect of the Client's liabilities to the Financier shall give notice terminating the guarantee, indemnity or warranty or shall become insolvent or die; or

(xi)   if any person who has given to the Financier a covenant or undertaking in consideration of which the Financier entered into this Agreement shall be in breach of such covenant or undertaking;

(xii) if any party who has given a waiver consent or priority in consideration of which the Financier has entered into this Agreement shall withdraw or shall attempt to withdraw the same.

(3)   Either upon termination under clauses 20 (1) and (2) or following notice at any time after the an Event of Default (whether or not the Financier terminates this Agreement):

(i)   All outstanding Approved Debts shall forthwith become Unapproved Debts; and/or

(ii)   The Client shall become liable forthwith to repurchase at the value Notified to the Financier all Debts then outstanding together with their Associated Rights but so that none of the said Debts and Associated Rights shall revest in the Client until the repurchase price of all such Debts and Associated Rights shall have been paid; and/or

(iii) The Client shall be liable to repay immediately to the Financier any debit balance on the Current Account as certified by the Company Secretary or a Director of the Financier.

(4)   Except as provided in sub-clause 20(3) and 5(4), such termination shall not affect the rights and obligations of the parties hereto in relation to such Debts and any Associated Rights as came into existence prior to termination, which shall remain in full force and effect until duly extinguished.

(5)   In the event of any dispute between the Financier and the Client, a statement of account, certified as true and correct by the Company Secretary or a Director of the Financier, shall be treated as adequate proof of indebtedness and in any proceedings shall be conclusive evidence of the amount so certified.

21. EXCLUSION OF OTHER TERMS; PRESERVATION OF FINANCIER'S RIGHTS

(1)   This Agreement, including the contents of the Schedule and any Annexe hereto, contains all the terms agreed between the Financier and the Client to the exclusion of any representations or statements made by or on behalf of the Financier, whether orally or in writing, prior to the making of this Agreement. No variation of any of the terms in this Agreement shall be valid unless it is in writing and is signed on behalf of the Financier by a director, secretary or manager and on behalf of the Client, being a corporate body, by a director or,

not being a corporate body, by every person named as Client in this Agreement. All references to the Financiering Agreement shall be deemed to include all variations thereto or agreements in substitution thereof.

(2)   The Financier's rights under this Agreement shall not in any way be affected by any delay or failure to exercise any right or option, whether under this Agreement or otherwise, nor by the grant of time or indulgence to the Client or to any Debtor, guarantor or indemnifier.

22. ASSIGNABILITY OF THIS AGREEMENT

The Financier shall be at liberty without the consent of the Client to assign to any other party all its rights, benefits, and remedies in this Agreement and the provisions hereof shall apply to such other party. The Client will not assign or charge any of its rights or delegate or subcontract any of its duties hereunder. The Financier shall be entitled to novate this Agreement to any other party and the Client hereby consents to the same.

23. NOTICES

(1)   Any notice by the Client to the Financier (including notice to terminate this Agreement) must be in writing and may only be given by recorded delivery or registered post to the registered office of the Financier or such other office as the Financier may designate in writing and shall only be effective upon receipt.

(2)   Any notice given by the Financier to the Client and required to be in writing (including notice to terminate this Agreement) may be given by delivering the same at or sending the same through the post addressed to the Client at the address shown in the particulars or such other place of business of the Client as the Financier may select and shall take effect on posting. Any other notice may be given by telex, telephone, cable or facsimile transmission and shall take effect upon transmission.

24. APPLICABLE LAW AND JURISDICTION

This Agreement shall be governed and construed in accordance with English Law and the Client hereby accepts the jurisdiction of the English Courts, but without prejudice to the right of the Financier to bring proceedings in the Courts of any State in which the Client carries on business.

Appendix 3 – Model Legal Agreement

THE SCHEDULE (forming part of an Agreement for the Financiering of Debts between Top Financiers Limited and the person named in paragraph 1)

1. Name and Address of Client (Clause 1(2)):

    (a) Name:

    (b) Place of registration   England and Wales
         and registered number:

    (c) Principal place of business:

2. (a) Debts within Approval Limit
         which are not Approved Debts   All save for the purposes of
         (Clause 3(1)):   Clause 5(3).

    (b) Collection Date other than as
         defined (Clause 3(1)):   Not applicable.

3. Debtors for inclusion (Clause 4(1)):   All debtors in the United
                                                      Kingdom.

4. Discounting charge (Clause 5(9)): (a)   % above Barclays Bank Base Rate.

                                       (b)   Minimum .. % per annum.
                                                   up to ___%

5. Prepayment percentage (Clause 5(3)):   %

6. Administration charge (Clause 6(1)):   % (with a minimum of £.. per calendar
                                                   month)

7. Additional administration charges
    (Clause 6(2)):

8. Nature of Client's business
    (Clause 8(1)(i)):

9. Client's Supply Contract with Debtor (Clause
    8(2)(iii)):

    (a) Terms of Payment:

    (b) Governing Law: England

    (c) Currency of Invoices: Sterling

10. Notices to Debtors (Clause 8(2)(v)):   On each invoice and copies representing a
                                                   Debt sold to the Financier in a form
                                                   prescribed by the Financier from time to time.

11. Recourse for Unapproved Debts
    (Clause 10):

(a)   Period of notice: 60 days

(b)   Period after invoice date: At the end of the third month after the month
                                             in which the invoice was dated

12. Date of commencement of Agreement   The day following the date of
    (Clause 20(1)):   this Agreement
                                           (Clause 2)

13. Period of Agreement (Clause 20(1)):   One year (minimum period) and
                                           thereafter as determined under
                                           the provisions of Clause 20.

14. Funding limit (Clause 5(5)(i)):   £

15. Concentration percentage (Clause 5(5)(ii)):   %

16. Special Conditions: (i)   The following assignment notice is to be pre-
                                            printed on all invoices within 3 months of
                                            the Commencement Date:

                                            *This account has been purchased by and
                                            assigned to Top Financiers Limited to whom
                                            payment is to be made direct at Percentage
                                            House, Discount Street Moneytown,
                                            Bankshire FAC 1 ID 1or by credit transfer
                                            for the credit of their account number
                                            10776971; at Barclays Bank PLC (00-11-
                                            22) 1 Financiering Alley , Moneytown,
                                            Bankshire, REC 0 URSE*

                                            *Only payment to or for the credit of Top
                                            Financiers Limited as above will discharge
                                            your obligations in respect of this account and
                                            they should be advised directly of any claim
                                            or dispute.*

                                     (ii)   The client shall furnish to the Financier ...
                                            Management Accounts showing balance
                                            sheet and profit and loss accounts. These
                                            Management Accounts shall be delivered to
                                            the Financier within 30 days of the month/
                                            period end.

IN WITNESS whereof the parties have executed this document as a deed

THE COMMON SEAL OF

TOP FINANCIERS LIMITED

was affixed to this Agreement on the   day

of   20   in the presence of:

_____   _____

a Director   Signature of Director

and

_____   _____

Authorised Signatory   Signature of Authorised Signatory

SIGNED AS A DEED BY

acting by Mr _____   _____

a Director   Signature of Director

and

Mr _____   _____

its * Company Secretary (or a Director)   Signature of * Company Secretary (or a
                                             Director)

on the   day of   20

* Delete as applicable

Appendix 4

MODEL DOCUMENT B – WAIVER TO BE READ IN ASSOCIATION WITH CHAPTER 2

WAIVER

To: Top Factors Ltd

Percentage House

Discount Street

Moneytown

Bankshire FAC1 IDI

From: Excel Bank plc

Base Rate Plus House

Importville

Lombardshire

MON IES

Dear Sirs

Re: Best Client Ltd ('the Company')

1. We have been informed by the Company that it has entered into or proposes to enter into an agreement for the factoring of debts ('the Agreement') with you, whereby all amounts of indebtedness incurred or to be incurred during the currency thereof by the Company's debtors in respect of supplies of goods and services by the Company ("the Debts") and 'Associated Rights' as defined in the Agreement are to be purchased by you free from any charge or lien.

2. We write to confirm that:

   (a) we consent to the Company's entering into the Agreement with you;

   (b) all Debts and the said Associated Rights so purchased by you from the Company shall be free from any trust, charge or other security held or to be held by us over the assets of the Company; and

   (c) this consent shall extend to any Agreement which is supplemental to the Agreement or is made by way of variation or replacement thereof so long as a copy of such Agreement is given by you to us.

3. For avoidance of doubt it is hereby confirmed that any amount owing or which shall become due by you to the Company shall be and remain subject to any assignment or charge in our favour over money due from you to the Company but any such assignment or charge shall be subject to:

    (i) all defences or rights of set off you may have against the Company whether arising before or after your receipt of notice of such assignment or charge.

    (ii) any other charge having priority over such amounts.

Yours faithfully

Appendix 5

MODEL DOCUMENT C – GUARANTEE AND INDEMNITY TO BE READ IN ASSOCIATION WITH CHAPTER 2

GUARANTEE AND INDEMNITY

TO: Top Factors Ltd

      Percentage House

      Discount Street

      Moneytown

      Bankshire

      FAC1 1D

THE PARTICULARS

A.   **My Details**:

      Dell Bouy   (Full Names)

      Mon Repos   (Address)

      Hopetown

      Debtshire

B.   **Details of the Client:**

Best Client Ltd   (Name)

Dreamland Works   (Address)

Hopetown

Debtshire

England and Wales   (Country of Registration)

2000000   (Companies Registry Number)

C.   Date of this Deed: 1 January 2000

1. I hereby:

    1.1 guarantee the due performance of all the obligations to you of the Client under the Agreement or any other agreement with you or any other form of obligation to you; and

    1.2 undertake immediately upon demand to pay to you all amounts now payable or which may at any time hereafter become payable to you by the Client, whether they arise under the Agreement or otherwise so that my obligations to you under this provision may be enforced against me at any time, without any prior demand on the Client; and

    1.3 undertake to pay you all costs and expenses (including legal costs on the basis of a full indemnity) incurred in enforcing or attempting to enforce either the terms hereof against me or the terms of any other guarantee and indemnity given by any other party in respect of the obligations of the Client to you.

2. Without affecting Clause 1 above I will also indemnify you and hold you harmless against all Losses you may suffer or incur by reason of any failure of the Client to comply with any term or condition of the Agreement or of any other agreement with you or any other form of obligation to you.

3. The guarantees and indemnities given herein shall be continuing obligations which shall apply to the ultimate amount payable by the Client. They shall not be discharged by any intermediate payment or satisfaction by the Client or the occurrence of a nil balance on any account.

4. My liability under this guarantee and indemnity shall not be affected by:

    4.1 any indulgence granted or made by you to or with the Client, or any Customer; or

    4.2 any variation in the Agreement or in any other agreement between the Client and you (even if my liability to you is increased as a result) or by any defect therein or in their execution; or

    4.3 any failure by you to take or perfect any security from the Client or any other person or keep it unencumbered; or

    4.4 any change in the constitution of the Client;

    4.5 the absence of any intended guarantor or indemnifier for the Client's obligations to you

5. I shall be liable to you in every respect as a principal debtor.

6. If at any time there is a Co-Surety then my liability to you shall be joint and several. and shall not be affected by: :

    6.1 any Indulgence granted or made by you to or with any Co-Surety;

6.2 any defect in the execution of any deed or document by any Co-Surety; or

6.3 any defect in any other guarantee or indemnity or other security held by you in respect of the Client's obligations to you or in the execution thereof; or

6.4 any notice of termination or the termination of any guarantee and/or indemnity given to you by any Co-Surety; or

6.5 any limitation (whether or not I am aware of it) attached to the liability of any Co-Surety.

7. I shall be liable to pay you interest on all sums demanded by you hereunder from me. Such interest shall accrue from day to day and be calculated at same rate as the discounting charge referred to in the Agreement. It shall run, from the date of your demand to the date when payment is received by you, both before and after any judgment. Interest will be compounded on the last day of each month.

8. As security for the due performance of my obligations hereunder:

8.1 I hereby assign to you the Client's present and future indebtedness to me;

8.2 I irrevocably appoint you, your directors, Company Secretary and officers for the time being jointly and each of them severally to be my attorneys to execute in my name such documents and to do such other things as you or they may consider requisite in order to perfect your ownership of and to collect any such indebtedness or to collect any dividend or to vote in respect of such right of proof.

9. In the event of the winding up or other form of insolvency of the Client, any monies received by you by virtue of or in connection with this guarantee and indemnity may be placed by you to the credit of a suspense account with a view to your preserving your right to prove or vote for the whole of your claim against the Client.

10. For the purpose of determining my liability under this guarantee and indemnity (which shall be additional to and not in substitution for any other security taken or to be taken by you in respect of the Client's obligations to you) I shall be bound by any acknowledgement or admission by the Client and by any judgment in your favour against the Client. For such purpose and for determining either the amount payable to you by the Client or the amount of any Losses I shall accept and be bound by a certificate signed by any of your directors. In any proceedings such certificate shall be treated as conclusive evidence (except for manifest error) of the amounts so payable or of any Losses. In arriving at the amount payable to you by the Client or of any Losses you shall be entitled to take into account all liabilities (whether actual or contingent) and to make a reasonable estimate of any liability where its amount cannot immediately be ascertained.

11. Any discharge given by you to me in respect of my obligations under this guarantee and indemnity shall be treated as being void and of no effect if any security taken from or payment made by the Client or any other person, which had been taken into account by you in giving the discharge, is subsequently avoided or reduced by or in pursuance of

any provision of law or legal process. This deed shall remain your property even though my obligations to you are discharged.

12. This guarantee and indemnity shall remain in full force and effect until the expiry of not less than three months written notice, from me to you of its termination delivered to your registered office (and acknowledged by you) no earlier than the ending of the Agreement (and if the Agreement comprises more than one agreement the last such ending). However the termination of this guarantee and indemnity shall not affect my liability for any obligation of the Client arising out of any transaction having its inception before the expiry of my notice.

13. Any notice or demand on me shall be validly given or made if handed to me or, if delivered to or sent by post, to the address stated in section A of the Particulars or my address last known to you. If sent by post it can be treated as being received by me within seventy-two hours of posting.

14. I shall not be entitled to be subrogated to any securities held by you for the performance of the Client's obligations to you until I have discharged my obligations to you nor will you be obliged to enforce such securities for my benefit.

15. You may disclose this and other information supplied by me to any member or associated company of the Excell Bank plc's group of companies ('Group') or to any person acting on my behalf for any purpose connected with the Group's business. You and the Group may also use my name and address to mail me about services which may be of interest to me. I may advise you that I do not wish to be included in such mailings.

16. This guarantee and indemnity is governed by English law. I accept the non-exclusive jurisdiction of the English Courts. If any provision hereof shall be invalid or unenforceable no other provisions hereof shall be affected. All such other provisions shall remain in full force and effect. This document contains all terms agreed as to my liability to you as a guarantor and indemnifier of the Client's obligations to you. All prior negotiations, warranties, offers and representations shall be of no effect unless set out in this document.

17. In this deed except where the context otherwise requires:

   (1) the singular includes the plural and vice versa and any gender includes any other; and

   (2) any words or phrases which are defined in the Agreement have the same meaning assigned to them herein and any form of construction used in the Agreement is to be used herein; and

   (3) the following words and expressions have the meanings given to them below:

'Agreement'

   any agreement between the Client and you for the sale and purchase of debts or other financial accommodation as amended, varied, replaced or added from time to time and whether before or after the date of this deed;

'Client'

    the company whose name and address appears in section B of the above particulars;

'Co-Surety'

    any person (other than myself) giving a guarantee and/or indemnity for any obligations of the Client to you;

'Indulgence'

    the grant of any time or indulgence or the conclusion of any agreement not to sue or of any compromise or composition or the release of any charge lien or other security or any part thereof;

'Losses'

    losses, costs, damages, claims, interest and expenses;

'Particulars'

    the particulars at paragraphs A to C above.

IN WITNESS whereof the Guarantor and Indemnifier has executed this document as a deed and delivered it on the date stated in paragraph C of the Particulars.

Declaration on behalf of Guarantor and Indemnifier

I confirm that before I signed this document and in relation to its nature, meaning, effect and risks:

(1)   I was recommended to take independent legal advice; and

(2)   I have taken or have had the opportunity to take independent legal advice.

I confirm that I fully understand the obligations placed upon me following my signature **(and in particular that my liability to you has no financial limit). I have signed this deed of my own free will without duress or undue influence.

I declare that in deciding to sign this guarantee and indemnity I have not placed any reliance upon any advice, opinion or representation of (i) any person having any interest in the Client whether by reason of directorship, shareholding or employment, or (ii) any other representative or agent of the Client, or (iii) you or any representative or agent of yours or of any company in the Excel Bank plc's group of companies.

SIGNED and DELIVERED by* **DELL A. BOUY**   )

in the presence of:

)

....(signature of witness)   )

....

....(full name of witness)   )   Signature of Guarantor

....(address of witness)   )   and Indemnifier

....   )

....   )

....(occupation of witness)   )

*   insert name of Guarantor and Indemnifier

**   N.B. delete words in brackets if there is a limit

Appendix 6

MODEL DOCUMENT D –
BILLS OF SALE AFFIDAVIT
TO BE READ IN ASSOCIATION
WITH CHAPTER 2

BILLS OF SALE AFFIDAVIT

IN THE HIGH COURT OF JUSTICE	**Deponent:** ....
QUEEN'S BENCH DIVISION	**Filed on behalf of Top Factors**
BILLS OF SALE REGISTRY	**Limited**
	First Affidavit
	Exhibit 'A'

Sworn:..**20**........

RE: [¹..   ....]

and   [¹..   ....]

and   [¹..   ....]

Together trading as [²...]

AFFIDAVIT ON REGISTRATION
OF ASSIGNMENT OF BOOK DEBTS
BY A PARTNERSHIP IN FAVOUR OF
TOP FACTORS LIMITED

I [³..............................] of [⁴...]

a Solicitor of the Supreme Court of Judicature **MAKE OATH AND SAY** as follows:

1. The documents annexed hereto marked "A" are true copies of an Invoice Discounting Agreement ("Agreement ") and all annexes therein referred to containing an Assignment ("Assignment") made by

    ¹...and by

    ¹...[**and by

    ¹..]

    together carrying on business in partnership under the style of [²..] ('Assignors') in favour of Top Factors Limited of Percentage House, Discount Street, Moneytown, Bankshire, FAC 1D1 ("Factor") and of every Schedule and annexe therein referred to or thereto annexed and of every attestation of the execution thereof.

2. The Assignment relates to the Assignors' book debts arising from sale contracts by the Assignors for the sale or hire of goods or the provision of services or work done and materials supplied to customers of the Assignors (and referred to in the Agreement as 'Debts') coming into existence at any time after the commencement date of the agreement (as set out in paragraph 12 of the Schedule) during the currency of the Agreement. The Debts to which the Assignment relates are all Debts referred to in paragraph 3 of the Schedule to the Agreement.

3. The Assignment of any Debt coming into existence after the date of the execution of the Agreement shall, pursuant to clause 4(1) of the Agreement, be complete in equity and the Debt shall belong to the Factor upon the Debt coming into existence. The Assignment is thereby deemed an assignment of existing and future book debts within the meaning of Section 344 of the Insolvency Act 1986.

4   (a) The Agreement was executed on the .... day of...............20..............
        at..........o'clock in the [*fore][*after]noon by one of the
        Assignors [¹...]
        in my presence and I saw [*him][*her] execute the same and I duly attested [*his] [*her] execution thereof.

    (b) The Agreement was executed on the.............day of.....................20..............

        at...........o'clock in the [*fore][*after]noon by one of the Assignors
        [¹...]
        in my presence and I saw [*him][*her] execute the same and I duly attested [*his][*her] execution thereof.

5   (a) The said [¹...]
        resides at [⁵..]

        and is a [⁶...]

(b) The said ['..]

resides at [⁵...]

and is a[⁶..]

[**]

6. The said Assignors ['...]

and ['..]

[**]

carry on business at [⁷...]

under the style of [² ....]

and the said business is that of [⁸...]

7. The signature of myself subscribed to the said Agreement as that of the witness attesting the execution thereof is in the proper handwriting of me

[³...]

and I reside at [⁴...]

and I am a Solicitor of the Supreme Court of Judicature.

8. Before the execution of the said Agreement by the said ['................................

.................................] and ['..]

I fully explained to them the full nature and effect of the Assignment referred to above.

SWORN at ....)

....)

this .... day of...................... .)

20.. .)

Before me:)

Signature: ....

Print Name: ....

A solicitor authorised to administer oaths.

This Affidavit is filed on behalf of **TOP FACTORS LIMITED**

Appendix 6 – Model Document D – Bills of Sale Affidavit

Key to Insertions

1 *Full names of Partner*

2 *Partnership name*

3 *Full names of Solicitor*

4 *Address of Solicitor*

5 *Residential address of Partner*

6 *Occupation of Partner*

7 *Partnership's Trading address*

8 *Nature of Partnership Business*

*   *Delete as appropriate*

**   *Continue for all Partners*

Appendix 7

MODEL DOCUMENT E – DEED OF CONSENT AND PRIORITY TO BE READ IN ASSOCIATION WITH CHAPTER 2

DEED OF CONSENT AND PRIORITY

THIS DEED is made the ....day of .... 20...

BETWEEN:

> **EXCEL BANK PLC** whose office for service is at Base Rate Plus House Importville, Lombardshire, MON 1 ES (hereinafter referred to as "the Bank");

> **TOP FACTORS LIMITED** whose registered office is at Percentage House, Discount Street, Moneytown, Bankshire, FAC1 ID1 (hereinafter referred to as "the Financier"); and

> **BEST CLIENT LIMITED** incorporated in England and Wales with official incorporation number 2000000 and whose registered office is at Dreamland Works, Hopetown, Debtshire, LOS T1T (hereinafter referred to as "the Company").

RECITALS

WHEREAS:

a. By a Debenture dated .... (hereinafter referred to as the "Bank's Charge") and made between the Bank and the Company all the undertaking and assets defined therein were charged, by way of fixed and floating charge to the Bank.

b. By an agreement dated .... between the Financier and the Company (the "Financing Agreement") the Company assigned to the Financier its Debts and their Associated Rights as each is therein defined) to vest in the Financier by way of purchase free from any assignment, charge, pledge, trust, lien or other security or encumbrance.

c. By a charge dated ....(hereinafter referred to as "the Financier's Charge") and made between the Financier and the Company the charged assets as defined therein (herein called the "Charged Assets") were charged by way of fixed and floating charge to the Financier.

d. The Bank's Charge and the Financier's Charge are hereinafter together referred to as the "Charges".

e. The parties hereto have agreed that the Financier's Charge shall rank in priority to the Bank's Charge in respect of the Charged Assets, upon terms set out herein.

NOW THIS DEED WITNESSETH as follows:-

1. Consent and Confirmations

1.1   At the request of the Company, the Bank hereby consents to the execution, performance and delivery by the Company of the Financier's Charge and any security contemplated therein.

1.2   The Bank, at the request of the Company, hereby:

1.2.1   consents to the Financing Agreement between the Company and the Financier; and

2.2.2   confirms that all the Company's Debts and their Associated Rights which are or become vested in the Financier are to be free from any assignment, charge, pledge, trust, lien or other security or encumbrance held or to be held by the Bank over the assets of the Company; and

2.2.3   this consent and confirmation shall extend to any agreement which is supplemental to the agreement or is made by way of variation or replacement thereof so long as a copy of such agreement is sent by the Financier to the Bank.

1.3   For the avoidance of doubt the parties hereto confirm that, subject to the rights of any other party having priority, any amount owing or which shall become due by the Financier to the Company shall be and remain subject to the Bank's Charge. However the amount owing or becoming due shall be subject to the ranking for which provision is made herein and to all defences or rights of set-off that the Financier may have against the Company whenever arising.

2. Ranking

2.1   The parties hereby agree and declare that, notwithstanding the terms of the Charges and the respective dates of execution and registration thereof or any provisions as to ranking contained therein, the security contained in the Financier's Charge over the Charged Assets of the Company from time to time thereby secured shall rank in priority to and take effect ahead of the security over such Charged Assets contained in the Bank's Charge.

2.2   Save as otherwise provided in sub-clause 2(a) above the security contained in the Bank's Charge shall rank in priority to and take effect ahead of the security contained in the Financier's Charge.

2.3   Such priorities as are set out in sub-clauses 2(a) and (b) above shall however extend only to the Company's liabilities to the Bank or the Financier respectively as at the Calculation Date (as defined below). Advances made, liabilities incurred or obligations entered into by the Bank or the Financier subsequent to the Calculation Date shall be deemed for the purposes of the priority arrangements recorded in this Deed to form part of the amounts due to one party in respect of which that party is to have priority over the other, only if the other shall so agree in writing.

2.4   "Calculation Date" shall mean the earlier of the first date on which the Financier or the Bank appoints a receiver or the Company is wound up voluntarily or ordered to be wound up compulsorily (save in connection with an amalgamation or reconstruction previously approved in writing by the Financier and the Bank.)

3. Bank's Undertakings

The Bank hereby agrees and undertakes with the Financier that :-

3.1   it will not take any action to enforce the security conferred upon it by the Bank's Charge over the Charged Assets without first notifying the Financier, providing that nothing contained in this paragraph shall prevent the Bank from appointing a receiver or administrative receiver for the company pursuant to its security when the Bank deems it necessary to make such appointment; and

3.2   prior to any transfer or other disposal of the Bank's Charge it will procure the agreement of the proposed transferee to a Deed of Priority with the Financier in similar terms to those set out herein in particular as to ranking of the respective Charges and the consents and confirmation in clauses 1.2.1, 1.2.2 and 1.2.3 of this Deed and it will not transfer or otherwise dispose of the Bank's Charge or agree or attempt to do so without first notifying the Financier.

4. Enforcement

The Financier may take any action to enforce any of its rights and powers under the Financier's Charge or the Financing Agreement.

5. Application of Proceeds

The proceeds of any enforcement by the Bank or the Financier of their respective Charges over the Charged Assets received by the Bank or the Financier (as the case may be) shall be applied in the following order:

5.1   in reimbursement of all outgoings, costs, charges, expenses and liabilities incurred by the Bank or the Financier or on their respective behalf in connection with such enforcement;

5.2　　in or towards the payment of all amounts due to the Financier under or in respect of the Financier's Charge;

5.3　　(subject to the amounts referred to in (ii) above being completely discharged) in or towards the payment of all amounts due to the Bank under or in respect of the Bank's Charge; and

5.4　　in or towards payment of any balance to the Company or any other person entitled hereto.

6. Indulgence, etc.

Until enforcement of the Financier's Charge, the Financier shall be entitled without reference to the Bank to grant time or indulgence, release or compound or otherwise deal with or receive monies in respect of the Debts or any security or guarantee at any time held by it or exchange, release, modify or abstain from perfecting or enforcing any of the rights which it may now or hereafter have against the Company or otherwise without prejudicing its rights under this Deed.

7. Memorandum

At the request of either party, the Bank and the Financier shall endorse a Memorandum of this Deed on their respective Charges.

8. Production of Charges

The Bank and the Financier respectively acknowledge the right of the other to the production of its respective Charge and documents comprised and referred to therein and to delivery of copies thereof.

9. Termination

This Deed shall cease to have effect when the Bank's Charge or the Financier's Charge shall have finally been discharged.

10. Company's Acknowledgement

The Company acknowledges that nothing contained in this Deed shall as between the Company on the one hand and the Financier and the Bank on the other, affect the rights and remedies of the Financier and the Bank under their respective Charges which shall remain in full force and effect as effective securities for all monies, obligations and liabilities therein mentioned without limit subject only to the ranking of the Charges thereby created as provided herein.

11. Liquidator

In the event of a liquidator or receiver being appointed of the Company, and such liquidator or receiver refusing, as agent or representative of the Company, to give effect to the terms hereof, each of the Bank and the Financier shall make arrangements with the other to give effect to the repayment schedule contained in clause 5 or any other such schedule agreed from time to time between the parties.

12. Interpretation

In this Deed, unless the context otherwise requires (a) references to any of the parties shall be construed so as to include their respective successors and permitted assigns; (b) references to a "clause" is a reference to a clause of this Deed; (c) references to this Deed shall be to this Deed as amended, varied, supplemented or novated from time to time; (d) headings are inserted for ease of reference only and shall be ignored in the construction of this Deed.

13. Enforcement of Security

13.1   The Bank and the Financier shall consult and cooperate with each other to the intent (without any requirement) that:

13.1.1 the Charges shall so far as practicable be enforced by the same method and at the same time;

13.1.2 in the case of an appointment of a receiver or receivers by either the Bank or FSL under its Security the same person(s) shall be appointed receiver(s) by the other (if the other shall also make such an appointment).

13.2   The provisions of this clause 13 shall not prevent either the Bank or the Financier from appointing a receiver under its Charge or from the exercise or enforcement of its Charge without any consultation if it considers it expedient to do so.

14. Information

Whilst this Deed subsists the Bank and the Financier shall be at liberty from time to time to disclose to the other of them information concerning the Company and its affairs in such manner and to such extent as the discloser may decide.

15. Entire Agreement

This Deed forms the entire agreement between the parties relating to the priority of the Charges and the application of the proceeds thereof and supercedes all earlier meetings, discussions, negotiations, correspondence, faxes, telexes, letters, transactions, communications, understandings and arrangements of any kind so relating.

16. Variations

Any variation of this Deed shall be binding only if it is recorded in a document signed by or on behalf of each Securityholder.

17. Severability

The provisions of this Deed shall be severable and distinct from each other. If at any time any one or more of such provisions is or becomes invalid, illegal or unenforceable, the validity, legality and enforceability of each of the remaining provisions of this Deed shall not in any way be affected, prejudiced or impaired thereby.

18. Facilities

Nothing contained in this deed shall bind either the Bank or the Financier to make any advance or payment or to grant any credit or other facilities to the Company.

19. Governing Law

This Deed shall be governed by and construed in accordance with English Law. The parties to this Deed irrevocably submit to the exclusive jurisdiction of the English courts to settle any disputes which may arise out of or in connection with this deed.

IN WITNESS whereof this Deed has been executed and delivered as a Deed on the date first above written.

BANK

Signed as a Deed by EXCEL BANK PLC

Acting by .... Director

.... Director/Secretary

FINANCIER

Signed as a Deed by TOP FACTORS LIMITED

Acting by .... Director

.... Director/Secretary

COMPANY

Signed as a Deed by BEST CLIENT LIMITED

Acting by .... Director

.... Director/Secretary

Appendix 8
CLIENT REVIEW REPORT

The client review report is written for submission to the financier's credit committee at regular intervals or in response to specific circumstances. The responsibility for preparation usually rests with the Account Manager. The issues to be included are set out below under each heading.

Background

Date business established, its history, ownership and date it became a client

Types of business and industry sector in which located, e.g. distributing, manufacturing, service

Location of premises

Details of employees

External Conditions

Financing Facility

Type of facility, e.g. factoring, invoice discounting, stock financing, plant and machinery finance

Details of prepayments, discount and fees

Security taken

Exposure formula – financial covenants

Conduct

Adherence to conditions of the facility

Credit policy exceptions

SWOT Analysis

Some financiers will complete the review process with a SWOT analysis of:

    Strengths

    Weakness

    Opportunities

    Threats

Appendix 8 – Client Review Report

Management

Who are the prime movers?

Describe their background and integrity

Describe their skills

Describe the management structure, recent or planned changes, obvious successors

Debts

Spread/concentration/debtor profile/number of customers/dilution.

Debt turn and ageing

Credit strength of customers

Contractual issues

Credit control

Overall performance

Stock

Type

Mixture

Systems

Valuation and method

Location

Plant and Machinery

Description

Last valuation

State of repair

Last Audit

Quite often a client review will follow shortly after an audit visit. Any issues identified by the audit process should be addressed in this report.

Financial Condition

Type and date of last financial information, compare and contrast with

● Peer group

● Previous performance

● Budgets

A number of formulae and ratios can be used to give further emphasis to the interpretation of financial statements. These include:

- Gearing
- Current ratio
- Quick ratio
- Gross profit
- Net Profit

Liquidity

A view should be expressed about the client's management of its working capital and its availability and usage including bank overdrafts and other facilities. An overview should be given of the creditors' position including VAT, PAYE and taxes.

A review of recent cash flow projections should be included.

Corporate Strategy

This is an opportunity for the Account Manager to state the client's corporate strategy and comment upon its past effectiveness and likely future outcome.

Conclusion and Recommendations

Here the Account Manager makes a précis of the review process, draws his conclusions and makes any recommendations regarding the future running of the facility and any changes needed.

Appendix 9

FDA LIST OF MEMBERS AND SERVICES 31/12/99

F = Factoring

E = Export Services

I = Invoice Discounting

A = Additional Services

MEMBER	SERVICES
AIB Commercial Services Ltd	E,I,A
Aston Rothbury Factors Ltd	F,I
Bank of America, NA	E,I,A
Bank of Ireland Commercial Finance Ltd, Dublin	F,E,I,A
Bank of Ireland Commercial Finance, Croydon	I,E,A
Bank of Ireland Commercial Finance, Belfast	F,I,A
Barclays Bank PLC Sales Financing	F,E,I
Bibby Group of Factors Ltd, *inc.*	F,E,I
Bibby Commercial Finance Ltd	
Bibby Factors Ltd	
Bibby Factors Bristol Ltd	
Bibby Factors Leicester Ltd	
Bibby Factors Scotland Ltd	
Bibby Factors Sunderland Ltd	
Bibby Factors Sussex Ltd	
Maddox Bibby Factors Ltd	
Burdale Financial Ltd	I,A
Capital Bank Cashflow Finance	F,E,I
Close Invoice Finance Ltd	F,E,I
Credit Lyonnais Commercial Finance Ltd	F,E,I,A
Deutsche Financial Services (UK) Ltd	E,I,A
FMN Financial Ltd	F,E,I,A

First National Invoice Finance Ltd, *inc.*	F,E,I
First National Factors Ltd	
Five Arrows Commercial Finance Ltd	F,I,A
First Trust Bank	E,I,A
Fortis Bank Commercial Finance	I
Gaelic Invoice Factors Ltd	F
GMAC Commercial Credit Ltd	F,E,I,A
HSBC Invoice Finance (UK) Ltd	F,E,I
ICC-Heller Ltd	I
Lloyds TSB Commercial Finance, *inc.*	I,A
Alex Lawrie Factors	
Lombard NatWest Commercial Services Ltd	F,E,I
Metropolitan Factors Ltd	F,I
NMB-Heller Ltd	F,E,I,A
National Australia Group Europe Ltd	F,E,I
RDM Factors Ltd	F,E
Reedham Factors Ltd, *inc.*	F,A
Argent Commercial Services Ltd	
Royal Bank Invoice Finance Ltd	F,E,I,A
Transamerica Distribution Finance Ltd	I,A
Ulster Bank Commercial Services Ltd, Dublin	E,I,A
Ulster Bank Commercial Services (NI) Ltd	I
Venture Finance PLC	F,E,I,A

For current information on the FDA visit the website at www.factors.org.uk

GLOSSARY

Words used in this book have the following meanings.

A

Account Payable: A creditor;
or **A/P.**

Accounts Receivable: Same as 'Debt';
or **A/R.**

Advance: In relation to finance for stock, plant and machinery or property it means a loan. In relation to factoring or invoice discounting it is the same as the Prepayment.

Agreement: The factoring or invoice discounting agreement between the Financier and its Client.

Approved Debt: A Debt against which a Prepayment can be made and/or is subject to Credit Protection.

Approval Limit: A financial limit against a Debtor for the purposes of Prepayments or Credit Protection.

Asset-Based Finance: Finance provided to businesses based on specific assets pledged, charged or sold to the financier and based on the financier's perceived value of those assets.

Assignment: The transfer of a debt from a Client to the Financier.

Audit: The process of review carried out on a regular basis after the Client has signed an agreement to ensure that the rules of the Agreement are being met and that there are no other risk issues that effect the Financier's security.

Auditor: A person who carries out an Audit on behalf of the Financier.

C

Charge: Security over an asset.

Client: The supplier of goods or services to a Debtor who sells the resulting Debt to the Financier.

Collateral: Strictly means an asset over which legal security, such as a mortgage or charge, is granted but in this work we often use the word not only for such secured assets but also for those assets to which the financier looks to recover its funds in use, including purchased debts under factoring or invoice discounting facilities.

Collection Date: The date on which the Purchase Price (or its balance taking into account any Prepayment made) becomes payable to the Client and/or any discounting charge for Prepayments stops.

Concentration: When the indebtedness of a single Debtor exceeds a set percentage of all the outstanding Debts, e.g. 20%.

Contra Trading: Where the Client regularly buys goods from its Debtor with the intention that their respective accounts are regularly set-off and only the balance is payable one way or the other.

Contract of Sale: A contract between a Client and its Debtor for the sale of goods or rendering of services.

Credit Protection: The purchasing of a Debt on a Non-Recourse basis.

Current Account: The account whose balance is the basis of the respective financial rights and obligations between the Financier and its Client.

D

Debenture: A legal document given by a company to its creditor (including a bank or a Financier) giving security by way of fixed or floating charges over the assets referred to in the document.

Debt: The amount (or where the context allows part of an amount) incurred or to be incurred under a Contract of Sale.

Debt Financing: Factoring or Invoice Discounting.

Debtor: The party responsible for paying the Debt under a Contract of Sale.

Dilution: Any event that reduces the value of the asset.

Discounter: The Financier purchasing a Debt under an Invoice Discounting Agreement without notice to the Debtor.

E

Event of Default: An event giving the Financier the right of immediate termination of the Agreement (whether or not such right is exercised).

F

Factor: The Financier purchasing a Debt under a Factoring Agreement with notice to the Debtor.

Factoring: The purchase of Debts by a Financier with notice of assignment to the Debtors and with the sales ledger being kept by the Factor and the collection of such Debts being made by the Factor.

Fees: The income for the Financier however known, including service fees, administration charges, refactoring charges and discounting charges.

Field Examination   See **Audit** or **Survey**.

Field Examiner   See **Auditor** or **Surveyor**.

Financier: This includes a factor, invoice discounter, stock financier and any other type of asset-based provider of working capital finance – unless the text specifically calls for the use of a more specific descriptive term.

First File: A file containing the information gathered by new business managers and Surveyors. Used for underwriters to consider acceptance of the Prospect as a Client.

Funds in Use: In the case of factoring or invoice discounting, the value of the outstanding Prepayments made against unrecovered Debts and unpaid charges and fees; in the case of finance for stock, plant and machinery and property, the outstanding Advance and all unpaid charges and fees.

H

High Involvement: Same as Concentration.

I

Industry: The entire range of companies and their products involved in asset-based working capital finance.

Insolvency/Insolvent: Inability to pay creditors as Debts become due or any formal procedure referred to in the Insolvency Act 1986 including bankruptcy, sequestration, winding up, administration, receivership or a voluntary arrangement.

Invoice Discounting: The purchase of Debts by a Financier and generally with no notice of assignment to the Debtors, with the sales ledger being kept by the Client and collection being made by the Client as the undisclosed agent of the Financier.

L

Liquidated Damages: Loss, cost, expenses, or damages that may be claimed by a Debtor by way of offset against monies owed to the Financier arising out of the non-performance of the Client in relation to a contract between a Client and a Debtor.

M

MBO or Management Buy-Out: The purchase of a company's shares from its existing owners by a management team not previously involved in the company.

MBI or Management Buy-In: The purchase of a company's shares from its existing owners by the present management team.

N

Notified: Having notified the Financier of the existence of a Debt or having offered a Debt for sale to the Financier.

Non-Recourse: Purchase of an Approved Debt on the basis that the Financier cannot require the Client to buy it back (except upon breach of warranty and sometimes on termination of the Agreement).

P

Prepayment: A sum payable by the Financier to the Client towards the Purchase Price of a Debt, earlier than its Collection Date.

Prime Debtor: A Debtor whose outstanding Debts exceed the Concentration.

Prospect A company that is a prospective user of the Financier's services. Normally those who have made an enquiry which is being followed up by the Financier's new business staff.

Purchase Price: The amount payable by a Financier for a Debt, however calculated.

R

Recourse: The purchase of a Debt on the basis that the Factor can require the Client to buy it back after certain events or after a fixed period.

Reserves: Same as ***Unapproved Debts***.

Retention of Title (or ***ROT***): Where a seller of goods, which have been delivered, still retains ownership until they are paid for.

S

Survey: The process of detailed investigation prior to taking on a Prospect as a Client under an Agreement with the information obtained being added to that obtained by the new business manager and then used by Underwriters to consider the acceptance of the Prospect.

Surveyor: Person carrying out a survey.

U

Unapproved Debt: A Debt that is not an Approved Debt. This can be because of age, dispute, contra accounting, concentration or being in excess of a credit limit.

Underwriter: The person or group of persons who decide whether to accept a Prospect as a Client and the terms upon which the facility will be offered.

Index

Index

Index

Index